The Two Milpas of Chan Kom

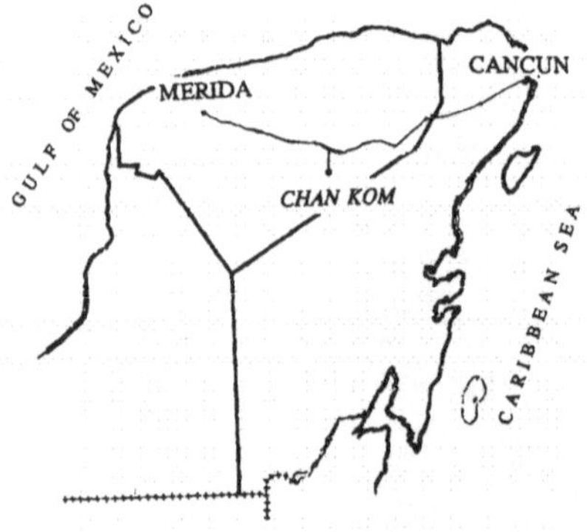

GULF OF MEXICO
MERIDA
CANCUN
CHAN KOM
CARIBBEAN SEA

The Two Milpas of Chan Kom

Scenarios of a Maya Village Life

Alicia Re Cruz

STATE UNIVERSITY OF NEW YORK PRESS

SUNY Series in "Anthropology of Work"

June Nash, Editor

Published by
State University of New York Press, Albany

For information address State University of New York Press, State University
Plaza, Albany, NY 12246

Production by Laura Starrett
Marketing by Bernadette LaManna

Library of Congress Cataloging in Publication Data

Re Cruz, Alicia, 1962–
      The two milpas of Chan Kom : scenarios of a Maya village life /
Alicia Re Cruz.
          p.   cm.—(SUNY series in anthropology of work)
      Includes bibliographical references and index.
      ISBN 0-7914-2829-X.—ISBN 0-7914-2830-3
      1. Mayas—Social conditions.   2. Mayas—Economic conditions.
   3. Mayas—Migrations.   4. Social change—Mexico—Chan-Kom.   5. Chan
   -Kom (Mexico)—Social conditions.   6. Chan-Kom (Mexico)—Economic
   conditions.   7. Cancún (Mexico)—Social conditions.   I. Series.
      F1435.3.S68R4   1996
   972'.67—dc20   95-15375
                                                                       CIP

10   9   8   7   6   5   4   3   2   1

Contents

Tables

Acknowledgments

Behind these written words, there is a wonderful and intricate plot of friendship, moral support and intellectual insights. I have been enormously fortunate to be inspired by the people who, at different times and in different places, have contributed to my intellectual journey. The seeds for the inspiration to recognize my personal and professional world through the anthropological enterprise were given to me by my parents Carlos Ré García and Rosario Cruz Santos, because of their ferrous faith in me and my work. This faith has been the constant provider of the needed strength and courage to articulate my pluralistic self and vision of the culture with my divergent selves and other's peoples identities. My family also gave me the keys to put my hands, mind, and heart at work to create. This is why they are constantly with me, regardless the world, the community, and the family I am part of.

I am grateful to those who fostered my approach to look at the world through anthropological eyes. Manuel Gutierrez Estévez of the Universidad Complutense at Madrid gave me the initial tools to read the symbols implied in the social phenomena. I would like to thank especially my professors at the University of New York at Albany. Gary H. Gossen helped me begin the 'American adventure', closely following and greatly motivating my academic career. He has taught me how to render the social reality understandable by viewing the individuals as the main characteres of their lives and histories' performances. Gary H. Gossen also taught me to bring anthropology to life in the classroom; in doing so, he nurtured my devotion to a profession that allows me to develop a dialectical relationship between conveying and spreading the message of cultural understanding, and the student's reactions and reflections upon it. Robert Carmack has opened up and monitored my political and economic understanding of the social phenomena. Gail Landsman greatly influenced my thinking on the symbolic reading of political issues. In particular, I appreciate the comments, criticisms, and the time that James Collins offered me, especially in moments of intellectual quandary. I do not have enough words to express my thanks to Brenda Rosenbaum, who, by sharing her professional and personal heart with me, has illuminated my journey through the intriguing labyrinth of accommodating to North American society.

The first version of this manuscript was my Ph.D. dissertation. Elizabeth Bronson, Geoffrey Purcell, Antonella Fabri, Quetzil Castañeda, and other graduate students in the department of Anthropology at SUNY-Albany, patiently helped me to organize my thoughts and to understand the importance of my dissertation work. The insights derived from the discussions with them strengthened my conviction that scientific knowledge advances through joint efforts. My special thanks go to Michael McCarthy, who devoted his time as well as his knowledge of computers to teach me the rudiments of statistics.

I received financial assistance from different sources, whose magnanimity I much appreciate. The DeComier Scholarship from the Institute for Mesoamerican Studies, a Research Fellowship from the Department of Anthropology, and a Benevolent Association Grant from the University of New York at Albany, funded various stages of my dissertation research (1987–89). The Spanish Ministry of Education granted me a Fulbright Fellowship (M.E.C.) that supported four years of Ph.D. studies, including the field work and the writing of the dissertation.

While in the field, formal and informal talks with colleagues and friends stimulated intellectual debates that served as models for the approach undertaken in this book. As such, I am extremely grateful to the group of anthropologists in the INAH of Yucatan, directed by Carmen Morales, Pedro Bracamonte of the Escuela de Antropología de la Universidad de Yucatán, and Sergio Quezada of the Centro de Investigaciones Regionales "Dr. Hideyo Noguchi." I also owe much to Don Domingo Dzul, Don José Ocampo López in Mérida, Marisa Góngora in Oxkutzkab, and Germán and Rocío González in Cancún, who showed me the generosity and hospitality of the Mexican people.

Over the years, many people have helped me to understand the Maya people of Yucatán. I feel priviledged to have breathed the tremendous humanism and encyclopedic knowledge of 'el Maestro', Don Alfonso Villa Rojas, an invaluable source of inspiration, ethnographic information, and an unsurpassable model for collaborative scholarship. I give sincere thanks to Mary Elmendorf, who generously made available her Chan Kom fieldwork files; Mary's knowledge and experience, interwoven with our friendship, is a consistent source of encouragement and support. Allan Burns offered valuable comments and insightful critiques during our conversational history on the Maya people; his knowledge and commitment to the indigenous population, within and across national borders, are the prototype of humanistic scholarship that characterizes my anthropological work. I am grateful as well for intellectual exchanges with experts on contemporary Maya culture: Betty Faust, Ellen Kintz, William Hanks, Peter Hervik, John Sosa.

Since the time I left Spain to pursue graduate studies in the United

States, other colleagues have undertaken the adventure of marrying the Spanish and North American anthropological tradition while living in this country. Through countless conversations, I shared with Soledad Vieitez the blessings and hardships involved in exploring the tribulations of our female, Spanish and anthropological background developed in the North American realm; Soledad's friendship, experience and advice always calmed me in times of adversity. I also thank Pilar Montreal, Mercedes Jabardo, and other members of the seminar directed by Carlos Jiménez at the Universidad Autónoma de Madrid for letting me present and share the advancements of my work at their meetings; their perspectives and knowledge is much appreciated.

Students are a special audience for this book. I thank my students who have been exposed to the developments of my work among the Maya of Yucatán. Their curiosity, atonishment, and quandaries have helped me to find answers to my questions. In particular, I thank T. D. Rogers, who was of great assistance in reading the last version of the manuscript with her student. To Marci Goodman of the department of Anthropology at the University of Florida in Gainesville, thank you for being such a sensitive audience.

My husband, José Calderón, is also part of this wonderful plot of supporters. He has offered more than patience to help me get through the frantic time of making this book readable and enjoyable. José took his time in reading the different versions of the book. His comment: "I am enthralled by the way you write, but I am more fascinated by the way you rebel against English syntax" helped me to overcome my frustation at writing in a language that is not my mother language; it was also an invitation to assist me in the time-consuming task of revising the manuscript. My appreciation extends also to June Nash; thank you for reading my manuscript and for believing that I could complete this work.

I am deeply indebted to the people of Chan Kom, who opened homes, hearts and souls to me. Their world views and ways of living are reflected in my own views and in my approach to life. This book is my *primicia* (thanksgiving) for them.

Chapter 1

A Community "In Crisis"

SATAHOL: *Good night* my friend!

CHEQUEREQUE: ¿Qué dice señor?, no le entiendo.

SATAHOL: Dije "buenas noches", huiro. ¿Ya no te acuerdas de mi?, tu gran amigo Satahol, peón del monte, médico naturista, graduado en la Universidad de hechicería de Yobain, experto de pesca-pesca y busca-busca, cantante exclusivo de Tixcocob y puntos intermedios y probable picher de refuerzo de los Leones de Yucatán.

CHEQUEREQUE: Maare, Lotería y no borren. ¿Y qué tanta cosa eh?

SATAHOL: Pues ya lo viste, Chequereque, estoy llegando directamente de los Estados Unidos y con muchos dólares en la bolsa.

CHEQUEREQUE: ¡Maare! Cuando eras chico te creías un pan de peso, pero ahora te crees un pan de a dolar. ¿Masinó?

SATAHOL: ¡Cállate!. ¡Cómo se ve que eres un ignorante!

SATAHOL: *Good evening* (in English), my friend!

CHEQUEREQUE: (in Spanish) What do you say, sir?

I do not understand you!

SATAHOL: I said "Good evening." Don't you remember me? I am your great friend Satahol, peon from the forest, naturalist doctor, graduate of the school of witchcraft at Yobain, and expert in fishing-fishing and seeking-seeking (meaning looking for survival), the chic and popular singer from Tixcocob and the auxiliary pitcher for *los Leones de Yucatan* (the Major Leage Baseball team in the region).

CHEQUEREQUE: My God, you are really something, aren't you?

SATAHOL: You see, Chequereque, I just now came from the United States with a lot of dollars in my pocket.

CHEQUEREQUE: My God, when you were little you were content to be a one-peso (the national currency) piece of bread, but now you believe that you are a one-dollar loaf of bread. Isn't that so?

SATAHOL: Shut up! You are obviously ignorant!

1

It is June 27, the end of the 1988–89 academic year for the students of *la primaria* (elementary school) and *la secundaria* (secondary school) in Chan Kom, a Maya[1] community in the Yucatán peninsula. Those who graduate face new decisions in their lives: to join the migrant group in Cancún, the tourist emporium on the eastern coast of the peninsula, or to stay in the village. A few will have the opportunity to pursue their education, particularly those whose families have enough resources to sponsor them. To celebrate the end of school, teachers and students have been engaged in the preparation of a program called *la Velada* (evening function), consisting of songs, poetry recitations, dances, and skits to show off the students' abilities as actors and performers. The preparations for the event start at 7:30 P.M., right after the celebration of the Catholic mass, which is attended by the female and male students, their families and the *padrinos* (godfathers) and *madrinas* (godmothers) that they chose. The female students, ranging from fifteen to nineteen years old, all are dressed up. Probably it is the first time they wear heels and panties; all of them wear a blue dress, tied at the waist with a ribbon that falls down the back. The style and other details contributing to the embellishment of the design depend upon the money the family could gather to invest in *el vestido de graduación* (the graduation dress). The male students wear dark suits and ties. A square has been arranged at the plaza, with chairs for the public and a big table for the authorities. The square is flanked by the Catholic church and the municipal palace. Women with children start sitting down, while the men wander around the plaza or stand a short distance away, until the event takes place. The west side is occupied by women and children. Once the seating is filled on the east side, people prefer to stand rather than to move to the vacant chairs on the west side. The graduation is celebrated on a week day; most of the migrants are working in the city, Cancún, and will not return until the weekend. That may explain the empty areas on the west side. Since it is a comunity celebration, I am wearing a colorful *huipil matizado*[2] that Raimundo finished embroidering that afternoon, with a dark *rebozo* displayed as a bandana from my waist to my shoulder. Raimundo, a dear friend, is showing me everyday the art of initiating an outsider woman into the knowledge and work in the fields. He is the only man in the village who embroiders *huipiles*. Raimundo somehow forgot that my height is considerably different from the norm among Maya women and cut the white cotton cloth too much; I am feeling very unconfortable because the skirt is very tight and short, and when I am sitting, I have to pull the *pik* down constantly. When it is almost 8:30 P.M., the authorities gather at the table; the president, treasurer and secretary, who are either temporary or permanent migrants in Cancún, extend their hands towards the president of the school board and the main professor in the *secunda-*

ria, both of them recognized as leaders of the traditional peasant group in Chan Kom. Living in the community for two months, observing the frictions between the migrant and the traditional groups, has made me aware of how cautious I need to be in building my social network in the village. This is the first event that allows me to observe the interaction between the two groups, their members and their leaders. I can see perplexed faces, as well as fixed looks at the shaking of hands among these five men. It seems that the ceremonial context encourages the cordial encounter between the two groups. As such, the president, microphone in hand, addresses the audience with a short speech, in which he exhorts the collaboration of everyone in creating a spirit of unity and cooperation for the welfare of the community. Meanwhile, I surender to the sudden need to explain why these five men in front of me, obviously the heart of the initiation of the event, strike me so much. I abandon myself with pleasure to my mental machine, which was shaped and developed during my years of apprenticeship in anthropology, which deals with symbolic malabarisms of past and present associations. Digging into my knowledge of and experience with Maya culture, I find that number five is present in those contexts that imply completion and order. Number five encapsulates the four directions plus the center, which makes five or completion. The *Popol Vuh*, the ancient account of the Maya origins, along with other sources of the Mesoamerica epistemological knowledge, narrates the four experiments of world creation previous to the current fifth, the world of corn people. Previous field experience, during the summer of 1986 and '87, allowed me to understand the Maya conceptualization of the cosmos, *milpa*, and the human body as three structural alter egos, divided into four sectors, balanced by the center (Re Cruz, in prep.). This spontaneous and unrefined symbolic digression transforms the setting for me into a scenario where the actors, taking advantage of the ceremonial and festivity aspect of the event, interact and agree to bring social order back to the community.

The various acts presented at *la Velada* include the play *No Hay Novedad* (There is No News), which attracts public attention.[3] *No Hay Novedad* is a short play performed by the senior students in secondary school. The first act introduces two characters, Satahol and Chequereque, who meet at the village. Satahol, a Maya migrant, born and raised in Chan Kom, returns to the village affecting the cultural values of the "civilized" urban world, puffed up with conceit over his new monetary wealth. Although most of the migrants in Chan Kom go to Cancún, Satahol is coming from the United States in the play; this helps me to understand how the Maya peasant envisions Cancún as a kind of United States. This is an encounter between two Maya who were born in the same village and who share the same ethnic background. The characters' decision whether to migrate or to stay makes them representatives of two different worlds. In other words, *No Hay Novedad* is a scenographic representation of Chan Kom. Enjoying the performance of *No Hay Novedad* leads me to observe three different social scenarios all at once: the community scenario that I share with the Maya everyday, placed in a context of clashes and frictions between two groups, social scenario of the festivity improvised to celebrate *la Velada*, and finally, the theatrical scenario in *No Hay Novedad*, created to portray the social schism.

Although the theatrical scenario takes place in Chan Kom, a majority of peasant communities in the world could have used the expressive device of the performance to denounce migration as the commonly accepted social and economic catalyst of transformation. This Maya community exhibits the emblem of "the peasant community in transformation" with which Robert Redfield and Alfonso Villa Rojas initiated its ethnographic record during the early 1930s. Maya teachers and students rehearse and perform this emblem at the time when the young Mayas are ready to face the job market, the work world. The complex articulation of different systems of production that characterizes Chan Kom in the 1990's promotes, for the young Maya, the existence of a broader range of professional activities and roles other than being a *milpero* (peasant who cultivates the *milpa*⁴, the corn field also called *col* in Maya language), or mothers and wives devoted to domestic affairs, as their elders were.

The two characters who introduce *No Hay Novedad* represent the social and productive composition of the community, the peasant Chan Kom and the migrant Chan Kom, and the world views of Chan Kom's social actors. Current transformations in community life are encapsulated in the people's general perception of being in crisis.

> ¡Dios sabe cuántos años tocan de crisis! Cuando llega la hora, pues eso sucede. Esos más antiguos, en tiempos de los antiguos hubo buen elote. Pero los señores trabajaban con los *Yuntziles*, que traen las lluvias; ellos les piden su bendición con el *saca'*. Como se estan llevando bien con los *Yuntziles*, por eso tienen comida en sus milpas, hasta hacen el *ch'a chaac*, y cumplen con sus ofrendas. Pero hoy ya hay muchos que no lo hacen: es falta de nosotros. Sólo comer queremos, y no cumplen. Los grandes lo saben; los grandes dicen que dice el Señor Dios: "Y a los Cristianos se les dio la tierra pa' que la trabajan, y pa' que recuerden al Señor Dios." Pero ahorita toca el tiempo de crisis. Este tiempo duele. Estamos de crisis. (Narrator: Don Juan, Chan Kom)

> Only God knows how many years there are for crisis! When it comes, it comes. In the times of the oldest elders there was good harvest of corn. But these people work with the *Yuntziles* (Maya spirits of the skies and forests), who bring the rains. They ask the gods for a benediction with

saca' (ceremonial drink made with maize). As they are getting along well with the *Yuntziles* that is why they have a good harvest in their *milpas* (the fields to grow maize); they even perform the *ch'a chaac* (ceremony to bring the rain). They pay tribute to the gods with their offerings. But today, many do not make the offerings; it is our fault. We want only to eat and not to do our duty. The elders know it; the elders say that God says: "The Christians were given the land to till, and to remember God, the Father." But now, the time of crisis is at hand. This time hurts. We are in crisis. (Narrator: Don Juan, Chan Kom)

No Hay Novedad expresses the current clash of Maya worldviews, mainly via migration to Cancún. The "time that hurts" emerges from the change in the current Maya attitude toward the Maya supernatural forces and God, via *milpa* work[5]. It seems that there is a direct link between migration and people's perception of crisis, and changes in the way Maya deal with the *milpa*.

This book unravels the social intricacies and the symbolic complexities embedded in this Maya perception of crisis that affects both ethnic representation and changes in socioeconomic practices. Although it is written from the perspective of a Maya community in Yucatán, the book addresses the worldwide phenomenon of migration, socioeconomic transformation, and changes in representations of identity.

The demands and rewards of rapid industrialization stimulate massive migration from rural areas to the urban centers. Peasant societies are immersed in a process of change that exposes them to intercultural conflicts, class stratification, and other phenomena generated by the dominant political and cultural system; for these reasons, pressing contemporary issues figure prominently in my analysis. Among the more salient issues are inflation, monetarization of commercial transactions, changing moral standards, interethnic relations, accelerated internal migration, and an increasing role of government in local affairs. All of these factors are encoded in the Maya social construction of reality and in the new symbolic formula they use to identify themselves within the national system of ideology.

The point of departure in this study is the Maya perception of crisis, which becomes the key ideological character through which the actors, the Maya, express their current transformations. Via migration, Chan Kom connects, in particular ways, with the broader system of state and national politics and economics. As such, it can be argued that the broader system's socioeconomic, political, and cultural dimensions are active forces in the revision of world views and in the recreation of an ethnic identity that is neither homogeneous nor static. The economic and political experiences of different social groups, whether they exist within the community or within the dominant system's social arenas, motivate the elaboration of different signals of identity. A key figure, *milpa* work, helps shape the complexity of interrelations between the community's socioeconomic composition and the different Maya identity representations. Today, people use *milpa* as the insight and guide for their ideological legitimacy as *verdaderos Mayas* (true Maya). It means that the essence of "Mayaness" comes from people's involvement in *milpa* work. That is, they (Mayas) are what they work on (*milpas*). If being *milpero* is a major force in identifying "Mayaness", how does *milpa* become the economic and ethnic symbol for other groups that are not economically centered on *milpa* production? And, in Chan Kom today, what are the underlying dynamics of the competition between migrants and peasants, both involved in a sometimes passionate ideological battle to possess *milpa* as their representation of ethnic identity?

It is the purpose of this book to provide explanations for such questions, which address the interpretive and socioeconomic analyses enmeshed in the articulation of peasant, capitalist, and tourist economic systems. Therefore, the approach that guides this ethnography on Chan Kom in crisis integrates interpretive theory and methodology with a political economic orientation. In developing this particular means to conduct this study, I draw from other ethnographers who have attempted to combine socioeconomic analysis with symbolic interpretation in order to grasp the intricacies of any group's social experience (Bloch 1986; Comaroff 1985; Good 1988; Greenberg 1987; Nash 1979; Taussig 1986; Warren 1989; Rosenbaum 1992; Roseberry 1991, among others). The key point here is to show that the Mayas' various exegetical readings of their social reality oversimplify the situation and hide an intriguing social complexity embedded in rural-urban transformations. The key political element within this set of mutual relationships is *power*, which forms the core of social relations and identity elaborations. I use the term *interactive* to describe the approach that uses this set of mutual relationships between meanings and action as an operative principle.

This interactive approach becomes a theoretical and methodological device to study interrelations at three levels of inquiry: a) the relations between the local system and the regional and national contexts, b) the constant interplay between socioeconomic and political transformations and cultural redefinitions, and c) the intimate relationship between what is spoken openly and what remains unsaid, but is implied in ideological elaborations.

Recognizing that migration is a social process that emerges from the interaction with a broader world system, I address two basic questions: First, what motivates the migration process? This question requires an analysis of the Mexican government's political strategies for development and its intervention in native community affairs. Second, how is the native community facing the pressures to migrate? To examine these questions, I consider the effects and manifestations of the larger socioeconomic and political system upon the community, and, in turn, the cultural strategies operating to resist or adjust to these macro forces. Then, the main task of this study is to identify the real-world events, phenomena, and processes that are contributing to the Maya's present sense of crisis.

As a community study, this analysis falls into a broad and productive body of research on peasant societies, initiated by one of the giants on Mesoamerican ethnography, Robert Redfield (1934, 1941, 1950, 1960). Redfield arrived in 1930 at Chichen Itza, the archaeological site that the Carnegie Institution of Washington was exploring. Sylvanus Morely encouraged Redfield to study Chan Kom as a peasant community. Morley had already met Alfonso Villa Rojas, who at that time was the school teacher in the village. Morley recommended Alfonso Villa Rojas as assistant, and with that he created one of the most productive and inspiring research marriages of Mesoamerican ethnography. Certainly, Redfield laid the foundation for the community study approach that for four decades has guided most of the ethnographic research on Mesoamerica (Hawkins 1983). Although he started conceptualizing the community as an idyllic folk society (1941), Redfield moved (1960) towards the formulation of the "little community" that comes into regular contact with the city or wider civilization, and, as such, becomes part of it.

The Maya Lowlands, which became a research laboratory for the study of the past civilization and the present culture of the Indians and peasants, were increasingly being exposed to a world that was beginning to impinge upon them. Likewise, the Pan American highway and the INI's (Instituto Nacional Indigenista) programs, aimed at facilitating the adaptation of the Tzotzil and Tzeltal Indians to the "modern" world, established the seeds for the creation of another ethnographic research laboratory on community studies in Mesoamerica. It was the Harvard Chiapas project, directed by Evon Vogt, that took the lead in studying continuity and change in Chiapas (Vogt 1992). Eric Wolf's work, the other masterpiece in Mesoamerican community studies, was initiated with the formulation of closed corporate communities (1957). As it happened in the Redfieldian production, Wolf also moved from the emphasis on the autonomous, hermetically sealed character of certain peasant villages into a more global and national focus on the level of integration with larger entities (Wolf 1982).

The seminal work that the Carnegie Institution and the Chiapas Project provided for the creation of the two Mesoamerican research areas has been a continuing inspiration for the ethnographic productions of the Maya Lowlands (Burns 1973, 1977, 1980, 1983; Bricker 1977, 1981;

Elmendorf 1970, 1972; Hanks 1990; Kintz 1990; Press 1968, 1975, 1977; Sullivan 1985, 1989; Thompson 1974, among many others), as well as of the Maya Highlands (Cancian 1965, 1989; Carmack 1973, 1976, 1981; Earl 1990; Eber 1991; Gossen 1974, 1986a, 1986b, 1989; Nash 1970; Rosembaun 1993, among many others)

Here, I explore the interweaving of the interactive approach and the understanding of the position and role of the Maya peasants and migrants of Chan Kom as an example case of community in modern Latin America. The notion of "community" in this study is taken to mean a social space that extends beyond the rural dimension to encompass the urban arena. Although people in a community share a cultural tradition, the native symbolic system is open; consequently, it may represent and, at the same time, distort the reality it is intended to reflect. Thus, this ethnographic analysis builds upon the idea that the symbolic components identifying any community are subject to constant manipulation and competing interpretations. Central to this argument is the consideration of community as a cummulative association of socioeconomic, political, and cultural processes that are recreated and reimagined through generations of contexts of meanings.

My purpose is to present an anthropological, interpretive view of the Maya's own accounts of Chan Kom in crisis, and also to portray the Chan Kom Maya as active members in, and products of what is often called "postmodernity" (Knauft 1994; Harvey 1990; Jameson 1984). This is a current trend in socioeconomic and cultural develoaplment of late capitalism, which compresses a world of broad politico-economic changes, being these correlated with the creation of new images and representations to cope with these transformations. How do power and representation relate with each other? How do people assert meanings? are a few contemporary issues of the "postmodern condition" (Harvey 1990). The experimental postmodern mood characterizing some ethnographies is criticized because they are solipsistic or hard to read, which becomes detrimental in getting their theoretical, political, or human messages through (in Knauft 1994:28). This ethnography on Chan Kom is a postmodern product because it focuses on the interplay between local and broader politico-economic changes, which are transformed into inspiring sources of cultural and ideological representations. Certainly, in dealing with issues of the postmodern condition, this ethnography on Chan Kom is written in a mood that embraces a reflexive critique in the examination of history, politics, and the voice of the author conversing with other voices and with the texts they produce through action. To avoid the criticism of the difficulty of conveying the messages in experimental postmodern exercises, I state clearly the theoretical, political, and human messages that I convey through this ethnographic writing. Once the interactive approach is in action, the theoretical message deals with the enriching holistic results of the ethnographic analysis. The political message pinpoints the dialectical relationship between meaning and power. The human message alludes to my efforts "to render reality as if it was lived while being observed" (Condominas 1977:xix). The human message pervades the other two via ethnographic writing, since the goal is to present the reader with a "living" ethnography. In sum, this ethnographic account advocates a form of writing that presents the social crisis of Chan Kom in process, through the reconstruction of every actor's voice, including the voice of my authorship, "because ethnography is both a product and a process, our lives as ethnographers are embedded within field experience." (Tedlock 1991). The enriching experimental perspective of the postmodern mood in this ethnographic writing has forced me to grapple with disconcerting juxtapositions of diverse identities, voices, and versions of events. The resulting intertextuality, encapsulated in the "we-talk," belongs neither to the realm of objectivity nor to that of subjectivity, but rather to human intersubjectivity (Tedlock 1991:71).

Therefore, this ethnographic presentation of Chan Kom as both part and a product of the postmodernity that we all share, along with the postmodern style of the ethnographic writing, is this book's contribution to community studies and to the anthropological knowledge in general. From this perspective, this ethnographic analysis and conclusions are far removed from what Redfield encapsulated in the *ethos* of the community, that is, the comforting model of a coherent society with a consistent and shared identity (see 1960:63–65).

Chan Kom, a Maya Village (1934) and *Chan Kom Revisited* (1950) are the Redfieldian ethnographic products of a particular sociocultural milieu that nurtured anthropology more than half a century ago. *The Two Milpas of Chan Kom* is the product of a much different sociocultural context. The European migration waves that the United States received during the first quarter of the century represented the sociocultural phenomenon of that time. Will all these migrants lose their traditions as they accommodate to the dominant North American culture? What does happen when so many different cultures come into contact and conflict? Through the intellectual-anthropological effervescence motivated by such an important phenomenon, the idea of the "melting pot," conceptualized by the theorists led by Park at the University of Chicago, emerged as the predominant answer for that social inquiry (see Steinberg 1981). Redfield, as a product of this intellectual milieu, transferred this explanation of sociocultural change into the Maya sociocultural context. Ultimately he conceptualized the so-called "folk-urban continuum" as a device to explain change through different levels of contact with the dominant culture. Today, migration within and outside nations provokes an intricate map of borderlines. This confusing postmodern world of sociopolitical transformations, embroidered with reformulations of cultural identity, is the context for this new approach to the study of the Maya experience of change. Thus, I focus on the words and symbols that the Maya use to channel their perception, experience, and practice of change. Sometimes cultural symbols are brought from the past to explain present circumstances, or to foretell the future; at other times, the present inspires symbolic tools to revise the past. I strongly emphasize the process-oriented nature of this analysis, which looks at how the people of Chan Kom reimagine the past and interpret the present in accordance with current socioeconomic, political, and religious contexts in order to define what it means to be Maya in our contemporary world. Commonly, the Maya respond, react to, and act upon their contextualized social reality in public arenas such as ritual performances, elaboration of oral tradition, and the conversations found in everyday life.[6]

Book Outline

The Maya of Chan Kom used the performance of *No Hay Novedad* as an expressive device to show the social clash tangled with the current changes in Maya representations. Accordingly, this book is formatted as a theatrical performance. The title of the drama pinpoints the analytical purpose of this ethnography: Chan Kom in crisis. The drama metaphor also allows us to integrate the ethnographer's experience in the field into the discussion and analysis. The role of ethnographer has many aspects—that of the descriptive narrator, that of the active participant as a character in the community under study, and that of the critic who analyzes and explains. This drama metaphor is developed and elaborated through the various chapters of the book, which is organized into three parts. The first part is aimed at getting the reader acquainted with both the sociocultural landscape of contemporary Chan Kom and the theoretical framework used to understand the community (chapters 1 and 2). Because my orientation is toward process, I use the succession of field experiences intertwined with their theoretical formulations in order to show the combination of data and theoretical concerns in the final elaboration of the interactive approach that I apply throughout this research.

The next section comprises two parts. The first part (chapters 3, 4, and 5) is intended to show Chan Kom as depicted by the various factions within the Maya community. Chapter 3 is an introduction to the village and the current situation of crisis, as described and interpreted by the inhabitants. Chapter 4 addresses the division of the community in both its social and ideological aspects. Oral tradition, rumor, gossip, and other forms of symbolic expression are employed to describe a leader from each of the two social groups. This analysis shows that the character traits attributed to these men by their supporters and opponents mirror people's perspectives of the groups as a whole. The two leaders are symbols of the larger groups they represent. The goal here is to present the opposition of two worlds: *los Antiguos* and *los de Cancún*. Chapter 5 traces the history of these two groups back to the founding of the village. A Maya narration on the history of Chan Kom since its origin to the present is the guide for the analysis of the socioeconomic development in the village. This review of recent village history provides a basis for understanding the social complexity of Chan Kom and the analysis that follows.

The second part within the second section (Chapters 6 and 7) is the heart of the interactive analysis. Chapter 6 uncovers a dimension of the crisis that is not expressed in the self-representation of Chan Kom as divided into two sectors. The interaction of interpretive and economic analyses discloses a social inequality hidden in the bifurcated social reality presented in the preceding chapters. I also explore the socioeconomic repercussions for the village of the community's expansion into Cancún, including the effects of the urban class structure on social positions in the village. Simple statistical comparisons analyze the mutual relations of urban and rural socioeconomic structures. In order to define the meaning of "Mayaness," chapter 7 returns to the social complexity of the urban-rural community in our postmodern world. The social complexity analysed in Chapter 6 propels Chapter 7's discussion of the incongruities embedded in a "meta-Maya" identity. Finally, Chapter 7 emphasizes the distinctive urban-rural Maya identities as they are perceived within the Maya "community" and by nonMaya people. Chan Kom is viewed as a microcosm of the postmodern world, with a multifaceted identity. Although very short, the last section (Chapter 8) recaptures the ethnographic analysis and frames it in a theatrical fashion in order to encompass the main scenarios presented within the book. These different theater settings embrace the community everyday social scenario, Chan Kom's interpretation of its social reality expressed in *No Hay Novedad,* and the author's *Two Milpas of Chan Kom: Scenarios of a Maya Village Life.*

Chapter 2

Community, Ethnographer, and the Ethnography: A Search for Models

> *Chan Kom was a remote village, scarcely known by outsiders and inhabited only by Mayan Indians, chained to their language and to the ways of their ancient tradition; these latter were structured to a degree that, using Redfield's terminology, they could be described as "a body of conventional values," which suggested that the way one person understood life had to be the way all did. The ethos then existing was characterized by its adherence to work, austerity, sobriety and religious devotion. (Villa Rojas's description of Chan Kom around 1930, in Elmendorf 1977:xii)*

Chan Kom is located at the heart of the north-central part of the Yucatán peninsula, which is a low limestone shelf without channeled watercourses on the surface. The filtered rain water eroding the rock creates caves and *cenotes*, natural wells formed by the collapse of the limestone shelf, which are tourists' delights. For the Maya, these caves and *cenotes* were the primary water sources. Chan Kom is named for its central *cenote* ("chan" in Yucatec means "little", and "kom" means "kettle"). Robert Redfield and Alfonso Villa Rojas outline the history of Chan Kom's settlement in their ethnography *Chan Kom, a Maya Village* (1934). Remnents from the preHispanic past are visible on the stones from masonry buildings, in the low mounds dispersed around the corn fields, and in the fragments of pottery and obsidian that appear during house constructions. Redfield and Villa Rojas report that the first inhabi-

12

tants of Chan Kom were descendants of the Maya that took the side of the Yucatecan government during the Caste War of 1848. Need for land pressed some people from Ebtún, 45 kilometers away, to plant *milperíos* in this unoccupied area. A *milperío* is a field far away from the village; the *milpero* sets up camp at the field site during periods of agricultural labor. By 1880, a group of huts was well established at Chan Kom; the site had become a *ranchería*—a small group of home sites in a rural area. During the Mexican Revolution (1910–1920), the settlement attracted refugees from other communities. The agrarian reform promulgated by the Revolution required the distribution of communal lands (*ejido*) to peasant villages throughout México.

In 1926, Chan Kom received its first legal grant of *ejido* property (2,400 hectares); it also was assigned *pueblo* status (Redfield and Villa Rojas 1934:26,28) as a legal and political entity independent from Ebtún. Chan Kom was under the jurisdiction of the *municipalidad* (township) of Valladolid (the principal city of eastern Yucatán). In 1935, the local area became a *municipio libre* (free township), with Chan Kom as its center or *cabecera*. A group of peripheral hamlets, *comisarías*, were represented by officials, *comisarías*, who were subordinate to the political and administrative offices of the *cabecera*. When Chan Kom became the township's center in 1935, the township received another 2,303 hectares of *ejido* land.

The community is flanked by two impressive archaeological sites, as it is located about 14 kilometers south of Chichen Itza and about 90 kilometers west of Coba. Nine kilometers of a narrow, paved road connects Chan Kom with the Mérida-Cancún highway (about 322 kilometers) From the highway, 132 kilometers connect the village with Mérida toward the west, and 290 kilometers toward the east connects it with Cancún. Valladolid, 26 kilometers away, is the closest urban center where the Maya, mostly in times of scarcity, sell their agricultural produce (that is, corn, squash, beans) and animal products (chickens, turkeys, pigs). When the migratory boom to Cancún started around 1970, there was a regular bus between Chan Kom and Cancún. There was no bus service for this route during my 1989–90 field work. However, although there was no regular bus line between Chan Kom and Valladolid, there was daily access to the town by trucks and other sporadic rides. Crowded buses and taxis from Valladolid delivered the Maya labor to Cancún, mostly at the beginning of the week, after the migrants had spent the weekend at their villages. The bus line was reestablished in 1991. Chan Kom started with 251 inhabitants in 1930 (Redfield and Villa Rojas 1934:13); population reached 530 by 1972 (Elmendorf and Merril 1977, 1978) and increased again to 682, according to the census I collected during 1989–90.

The flat topography and the buffering effect of the ocean ensure uniformity of temperatures year round; however, the rainfall regime is irregular. The wet-dry seasonal cycle dictates the steps in the agricultural cycle. As in most rural villages of eastern Yucatán, the predominant and traditional economic activity in Chan Kom is slash-and-burn (*milpa*) agriculture. The principal crop is maize, mixed with beans and squash. Beekeeping is also an important economic activity. From May to October the rains fall to feed the fields that have just become pregnant with the corn, squash, and bean seeds. The nurturing rainy season is interrupted by a short drought, *la Canícula*, from mid-July to mid-August, followed by hurricanes and tropical storms in September and October. After the threat of *la Canícula* is overcome and the young corn plants demonstrate once again their ferrous spirit for survival, the rainy season continues until October, when the precipitation decreases dramatically. By then, the green corn is already harvested to be consumed fresh. The *haanli kol*, the thanksgiving ritual for this first harvest, is performed. Then, the *milpero* folds over the maize stalk (*hutz'-dobla*), and leaves the ears of corn to dry in the fields. The dried corn is harvested in December. This is the time to look for new fertile lands in the forest—to start the new agricultural cycle. The *milpa* cycle in Maya conception begins with the measuring of the square land; this is the same imagery which begins the Quiché *Popol Vuh*, when the first grandparents measure out the four corners of a *milpa* (see Tedlock 1985). In addition, the oral tradition in many Maya Yucatec villages pinpoints the existence of a box which is said to contain the center of the world; the box often contains a measuring twine for marking off milpa (Burns, personal communication).

Once the harvest is over, around December and January, there is a resting time in the agricultural activities; the peasant may migrate to Cancún seeking temporary jobs. March and April are the driest months, the time to burn the fields to enhance the nutrients of the poor Yucatec soil. Then, the *milperos* have to wait for the first rains to plant the corn seeds. Until the rains come, the peasant may migrate again to Cancún to obtain some cash to complement the peasant economy. Precipitation is highly variable in timing, quantity, and spatial distribution; this unpredictability presents the greatest risk to both agriculture and agricultural production (Contreras Arias 1959). One *milpa* plot may receive rain while another, nearby, remains dry. Other factors affecting agricultural production are the poor, thin soils, unusual topography, and access to water.

At the time of Redfield and Villa Rojas' study in 1927, the village political organization was a combination of traditional notions of leadership and Mexican and Yucatecan statutory law, established in 1921. The villagers could select local officers: a *comisario* (executive), and the officers of the *agrarian committee* (the tax collecting body), which included

The hutz'-dobla. The milpero folds over the maize
stalk, and leaves the ears of corn to dry in the fields

the president, secretary and treasurer. The *comisario*, head of the municipal government, tended to be the leader of the village. He exercised
many powers, including the settlement of simple judicial matters. The
most serious conflicts, however, were handled by external state authorities. According to Redfield and Villa Rojas, both the *comisario* and the
agrarian committee were elected annually. The *liga local* encompassed
all the adult males of the village and was organized under the laws of the
Socialist Government established after the Mexican Revolution.

Redfield reanalyzed Chan Kom in *A Village that Chose Progress*
(1960) in order to follow changes in the village since his first study. Although he notes some transformations, the study is mainly guided by his
model of a peasant community as socially homogeneous, with a particular inherent ethos of collective peasant enterprise.

In the 1960s, Goldkind (1965, 1966) revised the information collected by Redfield to focus on a particular phenomena: a social and religious schism that resulted in the expulsion of the Protestants from Chan

Recycling of tree branches and shrubs at the milpa
for firewood.

Kom during the 1950s. Goldkind is especially interested in the competition between the *comisario ejidal* and the municipal president for political control of the village.

After Redfield's first study, Chan Kom's political organization underwent significant transformations: the *comisario*'s duties were restricted to *ejido* matters, while the municipal president's authority over internal community affairs increased substantially. In Goldkind's analysis, this transformation and the competition between the two offices had enormous relevance for the understanding of socioeconomic differences and religious disputes within the village. Goldkind presents a different picture from the homogeneous peasant community described by Redfield: "There is a persisting conflict in the community with respect to position in the system of social stratification, i.e., conflict over the means to economic wealth, social prestige, preferred style of life, and political power (Goldkind 1966:341).

The contemporary social divisions in Chan Kom are represented in this longstanding competition between the *comisario ejidal* and the *presidente municipal*. The township of Chan Kom has 2,606 people; 682 live in the *cabecera*. The main political offices are the president, secretary, and treasurer, which have been held by *los de Cancún* (migrant group) since the political elections of 1987. *Los Antiguos*—who stress their identity as *ejidatarios*, members of the *ejido*—refuse to transfer the office of *comisa-*

rio to the election winner, a member of *los de Cancún* group (see below for definitions of these terms). The relationships among the different levels of Chan Kom political organization—state, *cabecera* (center), and *comisarías* (hamlets)—are relevant to understanding the social and political circumstances of the current crisis situation in the community. The present-day social and political competition within Chan Kom village is related to political mandates imposed by the state and national governments, and relates as well to attempts by the two social groups in the center to control and manipulate the *comisarías* to their own political advantage.

Due in part to the long ethnographic record on Chan Kom, the issue of social change dominates research in the village. Mary Elmendorf (1970, 1972, 1979) with Devora Merrill (1977, 1978) examine the modernization of Chan Kom through the lives and experiences of Maya women. Halperin (1976) uses the ethnographic data collected by Redfield, Villa Rojas, and Goldkind in a comparative study of different political models among Mexican peasant systems. More recently, Devora Merril (1985) has used Chan Kom as the analytical example for her study on the economic role of commercial beekeeping within the peasant economy of Yucatán.

Chan Kom, for particular reasons, has related to Redfield's classic research and evolved as anthropology's archetype of a peasant community. The village has a long tradition of ethnographic research that both documents and is a part of an even longer history of influences and transformations from the colonial period through independent statehood, up to contemporary national and international policies. Therefore, Chan Kom is an excellent ethnographic laboratory to explore, first, the general conditions of peasant communities in contemporary times, and second, the social and ideological complexities of a community driven by a flux of urban and rural transformations via migration. In sum, Chan Kom encapsulates an encyclopedic ethnographic knowledge, accumulated for more than half a century. This historical dimension, documenting socioeconomic, political, and cultural transformations, makes Chan Kom particularly suitable as a laboratory for research on social change.

Today, Chan Kom is characterized by its inhabitants as both a *pueblo de campesinos* (peasant community) and *pueblo de Mayas* (Maya community). Increasing numbers of Chan Kom Maya choose to migrate to Cancún in search of wage labor, the main economic alternative to the risks and dangers of the traditional slash-and-burn agricultural system still practiced today. Migration and participation in a cash economy are intimately related to the formation of two socieconomic groups: Maya who migrate, *los de Cancún*, and Maya peasants who refuse to leave their village, referred to as *los Antiguos*. The Maya perception of the community in crisis is in response to this social division that instigates serious confrontations and conflicts between the two social groups.

The rise of these two social groups promotes the creation and usage of symbols intended to identify each group in opposition to the other. *Los Antiguos* call themselves *milperos*, the workers of *la milpa* or maize field. To *los Antiguos*, the *milpa* image identifies them as *campesinos* (peasants), participants in the cultural tradition of their ancestors. That image is in opposition to that of *los de Cancún*, who are changing their values and priorities to reflect an urban rather than a rural life. These migrants frequently fail to fulfill the ceremonial requirements necessary to live in agreement with the gods. They also, however, manipulate the *milpa* symbol, adjusting it to their new urban experience as proletarians; they consider their place of work as an urban *milpa*. Through these re-formulations of ethnic identity, Maya legitimize the changes in their world views, as well as in their social and political arrangements.

The Ethnographer and Field Experience

How do the Maya of Chan Kom make sense of themselves within the larger world in which their lives are embedded? This question points out

Going to the milpa in Chan Kom.

Going to the milpa in Cancún.

the interaction of both the ideational and social realms that affect the understanding of people's actions and perceptions of their social reality. Recognizing the significance of "production of culture" (Canclini 1989) based on an interrelationship of socioeconomic transformations and symbolic reproductions, I apply this interactive approach to the study of social change in Chan Kom.

The interactive orientation that I use derives from work by Murphy (1971) and Geertz (1973), and interrelates the ideational aspects of culture and social action. Within this general theoretical line, Bourdieu's (1977) analysis of the mediation of culture in social relationships based on class inequality has been very helpful. Another school of thought that has influenced my thinking is Marxism, particularly the political economy approach as it applies to cultural analysis (Geertz 1973; Sahlins 1976; Fabian 1983; Taussig 1980; Nash 1979). This Marxist orientation focuses on analyzing of the process of production and its corresponding relations to power and the conflicting interests of classes or social groups; it also embraces the symbolic and ideological components of culture, but only as vehicles used to express the social and political realms. I try to combine these insights with those of scholars who have written about peasantry, ethnicity, and social transformations in general (Arizpe 1972, 1978; Good 1988; Warren 1989; Greenberg 1981; Earl 1990; among others). The active role of the Maya in expressing the transformations of community life is required. In this regard, I am indebted to the insights of other scholars (Gossen 1993; Warren 1991; Silverblatt 1987) for pioneering this advocacy in ethnographic research.

The interactive approach flavored by the active role of the Mayas—the actors in this ethnographic account—is reinforced by a third element that defines the theoretical frame within which this book is written. This third element also calls for dynamics and process. It is my field experience, the basis for the genesis and development of my theoretical approach. To demonstrate how these theoretical components interrelate, I propose to narrate the stages of my field work. This account reveals the interaction of my agenda with that of the Maya, and it explains how the appearance of new environmental, sociopolitical, and cultural phenomena lead me to revise my initial theoretical model. Fieldwork, examined through this light, places the scholar in a position "to see people not simply as passive reactors to and enactors of the system, but as active agents and subjects in their own history" (Ortner 1984:143). The interactive approach used here, however, uncovers many historical versions, depending on the social and ideological positions of the actors.

The following is a chronological account guided by the sequence of my field experiences and the evolution of my theoretical orientation. The first section relates my introduction to the community during two short field seasons, in the summers of 1986 and 1987, and it includes my initial research interests. The second part is devoted to the discussion of my extended fieldwork, April, 1989 through July, 1990, during which I refined my theoretical approach.

First Encounters: The Courtship with the Cultural "Other"

My first encounter with Chan Kom was in the summer of 1986. After years of acquainting myself with Maya culture through written texts, a research fellowship allowed me to see an actual Maya village and to experience Maya daily life. As a novice ethnographer with a passion to discover a different culture, I was moved most by the symbols contained in Maya culture. During this six-week field season I immersed myself in Maya cultural tradition, collecting stories from Maya oral tradition, observing, learning, and participating in some rituals as a strategy to better understand these people. That is, the emphasis of the field work was on what Pelto calls "event analysis" (1970:239).

I knew Chan Kom through the ethnographic work of Redfield (1941, 1950, 1960) Villa Rojas (1934), and Goldkind (1965, 1966). A Maya tourist guide, Don José Ocampo, was the only source of networking information at my arrival at the Yucatán Peninsula. He happened to be the owner of a store in X-Calacop, on the road to Mérida, 2 kilometers from Chichen Itza, and 12 kilometers away from Chan Kom. He was aquainted with a few families in the village through his commercial transactions. He was bringing the cloth and threads to the Maya women in Chan Kom, who embroider the *huipiles* that he would later sell in his store or to another sellers in Cancún. After introducing several families at the village to me, I asked to stay at Doña Emilia's, who was living in a small hatch Maya house covered by a *huano* (large-leafed palm used as thatch) roof, with electricity, but without running water. She was a widow living with a single son, Raimundo, and a recently married son, Casildo, and his wife, Anacleta. They received Don José with a big smile on their faces, shaking hands. Doña Emilia was surprised. Don José was not bringing more materials for her; instead, he brought a *xunan* (white woman) dressed *a la gringa*. The interior was dark; I pictured it as a museum of hanging things: plastic bags with seeds, cooking pots, clothes were dripping from the ceiling. Doña Emilia offered Don José the hammock; they took a chair from the hanging museum and offered it to me. The considerable difference in height and sitting in the chair made me appear much taller than the rest of the group, all of whom were ensconced in hammocks. The conversations were in Maya Yucatec; I did not understand the language. I was feeling more and more uncomfortable; I wanted to disappear into the air, but my position in the chair was as such that I was 'at the top of the hill'; even more than that, I was the center of the conversation. Doña Emilia brought a fresh watermelon from the garden that she grows in the patio or *solar*[7] of the house. However, their eternal smiles formed the relaxing embrace that my heart was craving for in such a turmoil of awkward, uncomfortable feelings of marginality. In exchange for such nurturing smiles, I promised to write a book devoted to "the people of the eternal smile". Certainly they are the main characters of this ethnography.

From the beginning, because I am a woman, I was initiated in the ritual of learning female chores. This allowed me to become more deeply involved in everyday village life, and at the same time to acquire communication skills in the Maya language. It was also my introduction to a culture in which female activity is centered in the domestic domain, while male activity is primarily focused on *milpa* work. Narratives and rituals provide the symbolic imagery that legitimizes the sexual division of labor in Maya social organization. For instance, the popular *X-tabay* of the Maya oral tradition is a beautiful Maya woman who appears at night and seduces any man found wandering around the village. She transgresses the female spatial limits by taking the man into *el monte* (the forest). No one knows exactly what happens, but, according to the story, the poor man's corpse eventually appears in the wilderness. The *X-tabay* encapsulates the Maya moral advice that male deviant behavior is punished through similarly deviant female behavior.[8]

The sexual roles are ingrained in the individual's life cycle, beginning with the *hetzmek* (Maya baptism).[9] The *hetzmek* is the means through which the newborn is recognized as a productive member of the community. Females are three months old, and males are four months old when the *hetzmek* is performed. The number three is associated with the female domain. The small table where women pat out tortillas has three legs, and three big stones hold the *comal* (griddle), where the tortillas are baked over a fire. The number three ties the female Maya to her social role as "tortilla-maker." For the male, four is a critical number. The *milpa* has four corners representing the cardinal points and the boundaries of the sky. Four defines the male social role as worker of the *milpa*, agricultural producer.

Everyday praxis, narratives, and ritual contexts helped me to comprehend the community's socioeconomic basis, which is centered on maize production. Dependence on maize structures male-female roles: while men create maize from nature by working in the fields, women transform it into edible food. Maize becomes *santa gracia* (holy grace) when women prepare it; before that, it is *ixi'im* (plain corn). I discovered that for Maya, maize is a symbol for life, and I attempted to trace the meanings of that metaphor in all aspects of Maya life.

At any gathering in the store, in church, during my visits or in any ritual context, the Maya referred to the previous anthropologists who had lived with them. Redfield was mentioned by the elders of the Cimé family who live around the plaza, particularly because Redfield lived at the house of Don Eus Cimé, who at that time was the *cacique* (traditional leader) of Chan Kom. *El maestro Villa*, Alfonso Villa Rojas, was always remembered by younger and older generations as Chan Kom's first teacher. The name of *Doña Maria*, Mary Elmendorf, was usually brought up in conversations with Maya women who lived around the plaza of the village; these are the women who Mary Elmendorf worked very closely with these women in the elaboration of her *Nine Maya Women*.

One morning, the president of the village came with a big book, very carefully covered by a thick paper to protect it. He said: "Aqui esta la historia de Chan Kom" (Here is the history of Chan Kom). It was the first edition of *Chan Kom, A Maya Village*. It became my ethnographic reference for the six weeks I spent in the village; it was a priviledged anthropological circumstance: I had the portrait of a village in its seminal stage through Redfield's eyes, and the Chan Kom in the 80's in the seminal stage of becoming an ethnography through my eyes. The ethnographic privilege was to have the Maya voices as the agents contrasting Redfield's descriptions and understandings of the community, and their own version of what has happened since that time. Doña Emilia's house was at a certain distance from the plaza, where the closest descendants of the founding Cimé family live. At that time, I started reflecting on the implications of the location of the anthropologist while the research is being conducted. Does the fact that Redfield lived with the *cacique*'s family, at the center of the village, influence his ethnographic perspective? Will my location at the periphery influence my findings and analysis?

Most of my professional training had emphasized a symbolic approach to anthropological analysis. I tended to look for multiple networks of meaning carried by words, acts, and other symbolic forms. The interpretive metaphor of culture as a text (Geertz, 1973) permeated the way I viewed Maya society. I could grasp the meaning of social activities through an interpretive model. Methodologically, this approach implied a significant contribution by the Maya as actors and interpreters of their own cultural texts.

I stayed in Chan Kom from July to August of 1986. In mid-July, the term *tiempo de peligro* (dangerous time), also called *la Canícula*, appeared in people's conversations. *La Canícula* is a month of long drought within the rainy season, which poses a serious threat to the *milpa*. The Maya perceive it as a time for diseases; in fact, the incidence of intestinal infection—diarrhea, dysentery, and vomiting—does increase (Re Cruz; n.d.). Healing rituals are performed to overcome the dangers that beset both the body and the *milpa*. As Clifford Geertz (1973) indicates, when something grabs the attention of the anthropologist, the ethnographic descriptive mechanism is activated in order to inform readers in the ethnographer's own culture about meanings in the culture under study. Certainly, what struck me in Chan Kom was *la Canícula*.

The second visit to Chan Kom was during *la Canícula* of 1987. I could not stay at Doña Emilia's this time; with a new member of the family, Anacleta's baby, the small thatch Maya house did not have enough room for me. Doña Emilia wanted to have me close, though. She asked me to stay at Charo's, her twenty-nine-year-old daughter, who was pregnant and had four children at that time. Her husband was working in Cancún and was coming home every other weekend. Charo was full of joy to know that I was willing to live with them. She was very afraid, especially at night, "with so many evil winds around"; now she had a companion.

The hostility in the social environment of the community was immediately apparent. A political election was to be held in November and for the first time a ballot box would be used. In the past, the new office holders were nominated by the outgoing officers and unanimously approved by a public voice vote. This time, two community leaders were running for the presidency and their campaign activities were causing considerable tension in the village. One leader was supported by Maya migrants who work in Cancún as wage laborers. His opponent was a defender of the full-time residents of the village, who support themselves through traditional agricultural practices. In addition to the political tensions, *la Canícula* of 1987 was severe, and scarcity or loss of the harvest threatened the survival of some Maya villagers. In the village, people interpreted this danger as divine punishment: God was angry with them because they were divided politically, and no longer a unified, interdependent group of His children. Given this sociopolitical context, I considered it necessary to analyze the implications of the migratory movement in community affairs. This required enlarging my theoretical framework in order to incorporate Geertz's "hard surfaces of reality" into the analysis.

At this stage, my research required a search for theoretical models that could explain how cultural forms work to mediate social relations among populations embedded in a wider system. My question became: How is this crisis period linked with the political and socioeconomic environment of the community? I found the political economic orientation to be an important analytical tool, as it led me to inquire further into the interests and mutual relationships of political processes and economic activity at a global level.

I also discovered that, although both social groups in Chan Kom are Maya, each group is involved in the process of creating identity signals to define itself in opposition to the other. Symbols embedded in the oral tradition and ritual contexts are laden with new or different meanings, according to the social group manipulating them. Therefore, socioeconomic change, transformation of cultural symbols to express that change, and appropriation of those meanings and symbols are interrelated processes that must be considered together in order to understand the social fabric of Chan Kom. In sum, my analysis of *la Canícula*, perceived by the Maya as a crisis time and characterized by social conflict, required a theoretical dialogue between the interpretive and the political economy approaches.

The study of the cultural and socioeconomic implications of historic political economic systems, such as capitalism, in the complexity of local situations, has been one of the focuses of contemporary ethnography. Michael Taussig's *The Devil and Commodity Fetishism in South America* (1980) and June Nash's *We Eat the Mines and the Mines Eat Us* (1979), studies of indigenous workers in the mines and plantations of Colombia, are mentioned as important experimental attempts to combine the political economy and interpretive approaches in anthropological research (see Marcus and Fisher 1986:88). Also, in *From Blessing to Violence* (1986), Maurice Bloch applies symbolic analysis to a general model of Marxist theory of ideology in order to explain the meaning of circumcision among the Merina of Madagascar. The originality of this study rests in the combination of both strategies, the sociological and the symbolic, to show how religion is involved in the rise of states, colonial rule, and disestablishment, and how it is connected to power, authority, and violence.

These attempts to understand culture and transformation of meanings in cultural symbols through the prism of political economy have focused on a single symbolic context: in folklore, the image of the devil (Taussig), or the Tio (Nash), and in ritual, the circumcision ceremony. Although falling within this theoretical orientation, I proposed to analyze the symbols in action, whether from ritual, oral tradition, or other cultural systems, as they express the current transformations. My interest then, was on the interaction of symbols-metaphors and political and economic transformations in all aspects of Maya life.

As for the previous research experience, the field work model followed during the short term in summer of 1987 had an emphasis on the event analysis. For that, information was gathered through informal conversations, observance and active participation in everyday life and ritual events, gathering gossip and other forms of popular narrative, and oral tradition. Assisting the school teachers in the collection of the population census of Chan Kom exposed me to new houses and families, to a diversified socioeconomic composition of the Mayas in Chan Kom.

In conclusion, out of my experiences during these two short field seasons, I developed a general theoretical framework for my research anchored in an interactive relationship between society and culture. Within this, Victor Turner's strategy (1957, 1967, 1968) of considering the ritual context as a social drama was a fruitful device for the analysis of *la Canícula* as the liminal time or "the antistructure" in the Maya annual cycle. However, in order to understand the exuberant display of symbols during this period, I needed to study the rest of the cycle, that is, "the structure" of the sociocultural system. The long-term fieldwork was planned to search for these goals.

Understanding a Community in Crisis: Symbols in Action and Action Through Symbols

My long-term fieldwork was conducted from April to July 1990. I returned at the beginning of this field stay to find Chan Kom in a state of acute social distress. The expression *estamos de crisis* (we are in crisis) appeared in every conversation, associated mostly with *la llegada de la Política* (the arrival of "la Política"). Why were the people going through such a period of social agony? What did the native perception of crisis entail? What did the term *La Política* mean to the people and how was it related to the perception of crisis?

My earlier research, through the integration of interpretive and political economy paradigms, focused on a specific seasonal, cultural phenomenon, *la Canícula*. My next step was to consider the broader temporal and social spectrum of which *la Canícula* is a part. I learned from my previous visits that migration to Cancún is currently perceived as the main source of socioeconomic transformation in the community, and, as such, it is provoking maladjustments and changes in contemporary Maya world views. The analysis of the migratory process was paramount for understanding the current community's social environment. Through migration, more members of the community experience the urban environment. Thus, the Maya are compelled to see themselves as members of a community that is simultaneously rural and urban, and as participants in a larger politico-economic system. The Maya respond to this set of current social and economic relations by redefining the symbols used to represent their own identity.

This case study of the Maya in Chan Kom is not an example of assimilation and disappearance of the native community due to macro-area encroachments upon it. Rather, it represents the complexity of community social and ethnic relations, particularly when they are confronted with a social class system and face social class conflicts. Chan Kom today is the epitome of a Maya peasant community submerged in an intricate process of interchange with the social pluralism of the macro-area. Migrants' experiences provoke intersocial and economic adjustments. These accommodations, involving the incorporation of Maya migrants into an urban class system and the transformation of social inequality among people within the community, are intimately connected with ethnicity. Socioeconomic transformations lead to the redefinition of preexisting social groups and the creation of new ones that arise from the Mayas' social position within the urban class structure. Thus, through migration, the community experiences the socioeconomic and ideological features of a pluralist, capitalist system.

The Maya represent Chan Kom as divided between two social groups, each involved in a process of self-ethnic redefinition. Migrants are viewed as cultural betrayers (nonMaya) by *los Antiguos*, because they abandon the *milpa* rituals to become *Mayas de la ciudad* (Maya from the city). On the other hand, the migrants consider their urban workplace as their *milpa*. In this way, they have incorporated the urban spatial and social environment into a Maya cultural system. The migrants see *los Antiguos* as an obstacle to progress. Therefore, migration not only involves socioeconomic transformations, but is the basis for a redefinition of what being Maya means for the people of present-day Chan Kom. However, this process of identity redefinitions is pointing out the traditional Maya work, the *milpa*, as the unique metaphor to define "Mayaness." It will be the sociocultural relations embedded in this particular system of production that will identify the urban and rural workers of the *milpa*. This implies that one is what one does.

All inhabitants in Chan Kom are Maya. This is not a biethnic community of *dzulo'ob*[10] (whites) and Maya (indigenous people). This social division corresponds to the Maya's own perception of their community as divided into two social groups, each competing to be considered *verdadero Maya* (true Maya).

I arrived at Charo's house and stayed there until the end of this field session. My being part of a family in which the head of the household is a migrant facilitated my analysis of the migration phenomena at the household and community levels. At the household level, it directly exposed me to the dynamics of the economic articulation between the *milpa* system and migratory work. At the community level, my living at Charo's opened the arena for me to observe the struggle that the migrants in the community go through in reassuring their identity, given *los Antiguos*'s efforts to castrate their identity as Mayas. I already knew that in this battle for Maya identification, the *milpa* operates as the metaphorical arbitrer. I decided to work my own *milpa*, in order to more closely follow *los Antiguos*'s discourse on "Mayaness". Raimundo and I made an agreement: he would have to teach me the agricultural tasks of the slash-and-burn system, and work in my *milpa* first; after a few hours, in reciprocity, we would go to his *milpa* and work in his field together. Raimundo taught me more than how to work the *milpa*. Our morning conversations, embroidering village gossips, events, and questions about our communities, our families, our expectations in life, our views of the world, were unique lessons of cross-cultural conversational understanding that still reverberate in my mind. I thought of devoting part of my ethnographic writing to something that I would title *Conversations with Raimundo at the Milpa*. Certainly these conversations are the foundational data upon which this ethnography on Chan Kom is built.

I collected the 1989–90 socioeconomic data of the community; this data base is the prime material for the very simple statistical analysis that demonstrates the more diverse and complex socioeconomic spectrum of the village, beyond just the dichotomic *los de Cancún* and *los Antiguos* social differentiation. This elaboration of the census led me to the migrant Chan Kom. After facing the fact that a large group of people migrate to Cancún on a temporary or permanent basis, I felt the push to ethnographically document the migratory move from Chan Kom to Cancún. Thus, once my *milpa* was harvested, I devoted the rest of the field session (1990) to following the migratory circuit (Chan Kom-Cancún). I lived with Consuelo's family (Charo's sister) in Cancún, and worked in the time-sharing promotion in one of the hotels that hired three Mayas from Chan Kom.

The interactive approach presents a number of methodological problems. How does one combine and integrate symbolic-interpretive analysis with the socioeconomic and political dimension of community transformations? The solution I propose comprises, first, an interpretation of the community self-representation as crisis. This interpretation involves the analysis of the predominant symbols embedded in oral tradition, ritual contexts, and everyday life experiences. I basically follow a phenomenological procedure that allows an examination of the practice of symbolic usage and manipulation by the social groups. This analysis discloses the existence of the two social groups, *los de Cancún* and *los Antiguos*.

The second methodological step is an analysis of socioeconomic information that I collected in a census taken during the 1989–90 field season. Using simple statistical methods, and my own observation and participation in the community life, I show that the actual social reality contradicts the ideological propaganda spread by the elite. The elite of both groups, *los Antiguos* and *los de Cancún*, promote this dualistic social division but the situation is much more complex. In the final methodological step, I integrate the statistical and interpretive analyses toward an understanding of the various ways that Maya represent themselves according to their differing rural and urban experiences.

Then, how does one undertake the analysis of "la crisis de Chan Kom", a crisis that embodies different ways to represent "Mayaness," which is in relation to socioeconomic changes, mostly perceived as deriving from the migration process to Cancún? The ethnographic literature on Mesoamerica provides different models to deal with changes and transformations in peasant communities, such as Robert Redfield's folk-urban continuum and Eric Wolf's closed corporate community model. The World System Theory and Dependency Theorists, and the Pluralist model as applied by Clifford Geertz, are also main theoretical sources in applying ways to relate the community to the broader socioeconomic and political systems.

Community, Ethnic Identity, and Peasant Economy

The intellectual father of the folk-urban continuum, Robert Redfield (1941), has been the target of criticisms mainly provoked by the independent variables of isolation and social homogeneity and the lack of historical dimension implied in that model (see Dumond 1970; Strickon 1965; Press 1977; Goldkind 1965, 1966). However, little emphasis has been placed on the development of Redfield's work, mainly on his later productions. In his final research on Chan Kom (1950), more than two decades after he formulated the folk-urban continuum, the author discredits his own model. Redfield demonstrates that the community did not disintegrate with the advances of modernity emanating from the city (1960:108). Besides, in this later work, Redfield attempts to incorporate in his conceptual model the history of the "little" community from the inside view. He points out the significance of the people's own story and their conception of their world, for the understanding of the holistic nature of little communities (1960:165).

Despite criticism of Redfield's analysis, his contributions to the study of peasant communities in the modern world are significant. First, Redfield pointed out the issue of how social changes shape peasant community life within a regional context. The analysis of communities as part of macro-areas is indebted to his belief that the community is a part of several more inclusive wholes: regions, areas, or nations (Redfield 1960:158). Second, Redfield contributed to the understanding of change by integrating the cultural and social systems. Following a Weberian perspective, he considers the social milieu as a configuration of diverse factors, social, economic, and institutional. Finally, he explored the methodological device of collecting native narratives to increase our understanding of communities. These efforts anticipate recent anthropological thought on incorporating native voices in the anthropological analysis.

My own approach develops from the three principles described above. Considering cultural expressions as symbolic tokens used to understand global-local communication, this approach adds a process-oriented, explanatory component to Redfield's model. As such, people's voices, perceptions, and representations are incorporated into the analysis as primary sources of information.

The Redfieldian "folk" or "little community" transforms into "the close corporate community" for Eric Wolf (1957). Rather than a remnant of ancient civilizations, Wolf's community is in active response to ongoing political and economic processes. Wolf (1966) defines peasants as rural producers whose surpluses are appropriated by a dominant group. There is, then, an unequal structural relationship that determines the peasants' way of life, survival, and development. Wolf suggests that the culture and identity of the community are closely tied to its survival; therefore, ideology is an integral part of the peasant way of life. For instance, religious sanctions are necesary in order to protect the solidarity of the group. Therefore, the examination of the relations of production also requires the study of general aspects of social organization and ideology. Wolf does not, however, specify the process through which the closed corporate community transforms its identity in accordance with the changes in its relationship with the macro-system. He was more interested in how the members of Indian communities are assimilated into the national culture through private forms of land tenure, cultivation of cash crops, and the development of internal class differences (1955:456). Ultimately, for Wolf, the persistence of Indian culture depends on the maintenance of the community's social structure. Therefore, with the introduction of a class structure, the closed corporate community will disappear. Furthermore, Wolf does not propose a model to deal with social differences within the uni-ethnic community, for instance, between rural and urban Maya communities or among Maya migrants in the urban context. In other words, if Wolf's model explains how global forces affect local social formations, it cannot, however, explain how the expansion of capitalism proceeds within the social formations it generates. By the same token, the process of ideological transformation at both the micro- and macro-levels is not an integral part of the model. Certainly, some aspects of the closed corporate community model are relevant to this study, particularly those relating to the community's internal social and cultural systems, and to the connection between the community and the larger society. I advocate, however, that the interplay between the global and local systems is more dynamic and that this reciprocal interaction accounts for the community's social heterogeneity.

Wolf's latest works (1982, 1986) represent a significant shift from his earlier formulations. First, he realizes that, in spite of capitalist expansion, peasants continue to exist and are a constituent part of the world-wide process (1982). Then, he highlights the interrelations among the economy, social relations, and culture (1986). This latest perspective is similar to my own theoretical position in this study.

For the world system and dependency theorists, the understanding of peasant culture and village life at the local level depends on the economic controlling mechanism of the dominant capitalist system (see Wallerstein 1974a, 1974b). These scholars focus on the social whole, that is, the world system, which is integrated economically, rather than politically. Following their arguments, peasants' social processes can be understood only within the larger world system. As such, case studies are considered the raw material that serves to validate the general theory and broader models of social phenomena. This analytical perspective raises an important methodological problem: how does one study local systems in terms of broader, national, and international factors? Wallerstein, for example, deals with this issue by concentrating on the world system without emphasizing the social dynamics of local systems.

From the world system perspective, Chan Kom, on the periphery, appears as profoundly influenced by the capitalist core, mainly via migration to Cancún. There are major aspects of the community's economic, social, and cultural life, however, that cannot be explained through this unidirectional core-periphery contact. In order to understand the economic and political components of the core (Cancún), particularly as these components relate to the migrants, it is necessary to consider the socioeconomic and ideological features of the Maya community. By the same token, the periphery (Chan Kom) is not a static entity. The economic and political accommodations imposed by the core demand a response that sometimes takes the form of resistance by the periphery. Certainly the world system and dependency approaches place Chan Kom within the wider contemporary world, which is also my goal. However, while the world system approach would consider Chan Kom as peripheral, restricted to the rural context, I view it as an extended community composed of both urban and rural environments, which are in constant socioeconomic and ideological interaction. I use the term "extended" in the sense of "extended family" from kinship terminology, to mean the expansion of community patterns into the urban area via migration.

The Geertzian interpretive approach, when applied to societies where change is a characteristic, can also provide ways to deal with the micro- and macro-levels of analysis. In his classic example of the interpretive approach, *Ritual and Social Change: A Javanese Example*, Geertz analyzes a "transitional society in which the traditional forms of rural living are being steadily dissolved and new forms steadily reconstructed" (1973:150). He demonstrates that social groups, when integrated into the pluralist structure of the global system, are defined by a broad range of social factors—class, occupation, ethnicity, religion, and the like. Geertz also shows that ritual performance can be a symbolic catalyst of social conflicts that arise out of drastic social transformations. As such, he advances the idea that cultural symbols change meaning according to a given social context. In sum, Geertz's model proposes that sociopolitical transformations are accompanied by changes in symbolic meanings. Therefore, the analysis of these meanings can clarify the nature of the transformations in the social group as the group becomes part of a more complex, multi-ethnic society.

I am particularly interested in this analysis of complex, ethnically diverse societies, referred to as multiple or plural societies (Nash 1957; Smith 1969). The Maya migrants become a constituent part of the pluralist Cancún social environment. This environment comprises diverse ethnic groups from all over the country, as well as national and international tourist groups. Cancún is unique in that it was specifically constructed for and is dependent on tourism as its principal industry. The presence of visitors from all over the world, and the necessity to meet their varying needs, gives Cancún a distinct social class formation. Peasant Maya are not peripheral to this complex core; they too are an integral part of the pluralist Mexican and international landscape. Therefore, I analyze images, representations, and symbols to show variations in their meanings and values, according to the different socioeconomic and political positions of both rural and urban Maya.

In sum, I recognize the methodological value of analyzing an ethnically diverse context through the cultural and social complexities embedded in the experience and practice of a ritual context. In my study, I extend this methodological device to other cultural practices and productions, such as the reinvention of oral tradition and the creation of narratives and gossip about recent events.

The Legacy of Peasant Community Studies Applied to Mexican Anthropology

Mexican anthropologists have developed various models to understand peasant societies within the specific context of the political economy of México. Earlier works are marked by the North American trends in anthropology. Boas and the structural-functionalism influenced the studies on change and its implications among Indian communitites. To a large extent, Redfield's model, which analysed the community as a remnant of the historical process in which modernization is imposed by outside forces, stamped part of this anthropological production. This model promoted the conceptualization of the Latin America society as a dual coin with two faces. One of these is the "archaic" social face, which originated in the colonial epoch as the remnant of ancient social and cultural elements. The other face is the "modern", oriented towards change and development. This social stereotype derived from models which imply social dualism (Mestizo or Ladino versus Indian, feudalism versus capitalism) is denounced by Stavenhagen as one of the first fallacies about Latin America (1968).

Wolf's model of closed corporate community was broadly applied during the sixties. Because the model's emphasis is on the confrontation between peasant society and the larger socioeconomic system, the issues of social change and acculturation processes became the most common topics of anthropological discussion. Stavenhagen (1963), for instance, looked at the native community as isolated, with a social and cultural identity separated from the capitalist system.

The global and national sociopolitical turmoil in the sixties contributed to an intellectual effervescence that is reflected in the Mexican anthropological production. The Cuban revolution, the expanding influence of the dependency-theory debate, and the critique of social and cultural imperialism called for the need to critically revise the theoretical and practical bases in Mexican anthropology (see Krotz 1991). Marxism was broadly applied during the 1970s. According to this model, the Indian peasantry was transformed ultimately into an urban proletariat; with accommodation to the capitalist development, native cultures enter into a moribund stage until reaching their own extinction (Pozas and Pozas 1971).

As Krotz (1991:184) points out, numerous anthropological productions in the sixties and seventies are stamped with cultural ecology, neo-evoultionism and above all, Marxism. These scholars (Stavenhagen 1969; Pozas and Pozas 1971; Bartra 1974; Warman 1976; Palerm 1976) show a particular advocacy on behalf of the "objects of study." There are differing views, however, within the general Marxist orientation. Bartra (1974) predicts the total proletarization of the peasantry, while another school (Stavenhagen 1976; Warman 1972, 1980; Palerm 1980) emphasizes the strength of the peasantry in overcoming the inherent contradictions existing in the Mexican dependent economy.

The eighties are marked by the incorporation of new topics in the Mexican anthropological debate. Internal migration, migration to the USA, the role of peasant women and other sectors of the rural populations, urbanization and urban poverty, are among the most common phenomena of rural and urban life. There is a new twist in the anthropological research that focuses on the dynamism and complexity of Indian peasants' interactions with capitalism. As such, Canclini (1989) analyzes popular culture in relation to the conflicts among social classes, and the exploitative conditions in which these social sectors produce and consume. Good (1988) undertakes a Marxist analysis based on the articulation of the peasantry and the capitalist mode of production among people in Ameyaltepec, Oaxaca, who are also involved in migration. Along this analytical line, which focuses on the social rather than the economic structure, Arizpe's (1972) work is relevant. She examines the role of kinship in determining patterns of migration and their effects on rural community life.

The most common discussion topics in present Mexican anthropological research deal with reproduction of identities interwoven with rural communities, migration processes and formation of urban settlements. Most recently, the Maya revolt in Chiapas and the implications of the NAFTA agreement among indigenous communities have provoked an impetuous anthropological and political debate on the contemporary position of indigenous populations. The 1994 presentations at the meetings of the Sociedad Mexicana de Antropologia, celebrated in Villahermosa, Tabasco, expressed the need to develop new anthropological strategies, mechanisms, and models not only to understand the indigenous situations, but also to bring the anthropological knowledge and experience to their service. As Allan Burns stated in his presentation for this congress, "the principle of the anthropologist's ethic code is upon the security and wellbeing of the people who we are working with."

Other Peasant Studies in Yucatán

The anthropological literature regarding the Maya of Yucatan provides abundant data on the diversification of regional economic production (Labreque and Breton 1982) and economic organization (Littlefield 1976). In the above economic analyses, the Maya peasant is seen to provide the labor force for the larger system, but remains at the periphery in receiving economic benefits. Other research in Yucatán emphasizes the intimate connection between the peasant and the state, which promotes the image of the Maya as a marginal entity within the class system (Anda Vela 1984; Baños Ramirez 1989). Strickon (1965) follows a cultural ecology approach, focusing on people's relations with the environment, in order to interpret economic and social phenomena.

Since Redfield's research, the issue of change among the Maya has been addressed repeatedly, evoking either state policies or the urban environment as sources of transformation (Thompson 1974; Press 1968; 1877; Elmendorf 1970, 1972, 1979; Elmendorf and Merrill 1977, 1978; Kintz 1990). Agricultural change in the peasant economy is also emphasized in the light of technological advancements (Hernandez X. 1980; Varguez Pasos 1981). The rapid increase of tourism in Yucatán has led to the development of points of interest—which include archaeological sites (for example, Chichen Itzá, Uxmal) and beaches (Cancún). Several anthropologists have been motivated to study the effects of tourism among the peasants (Lee 1977; Peraza and Rejón 1989).

Finally, I would mention the recent efforts among some Yucatec scholars to focus their analyses on the current, active involvement of the Maya people in the sociopolitical and cultural environments of the regional and national environments. Various research projects undertaken by the National Institute of Anthropology and History (INAH) highlight the transformations in artesan production, *milpa* production, and the Maya community in general that are responses to the spread of the tourist industry (see Morales et al. 1992). Another area of interest to Yucatec scholars is the dialogue between the religious system and peasant economic transformations. These studies reveal tensions between Catholicism and Protestantism (Cardiel and Villalobos 1989). In my analysis of Chan Kom, I address this conflict between Catholicism and Protestantism and its relationship to recent socioeconomic and religious transformations. I show how the Maya manipulate the symbolic corpus of the religious system to express their self-identified goals.

Conclusion: Community and the Interactive Approach at Work

Peasant society has not been eradicated by the expansion of various national or international economic development plans. We find a variety of ways in which peasant societies respond today to capitalism. We also find that the exchange between the peasant economy and capitalism activates a complex set of social formations in both the rural (peasants, rural proletarians, and rural capitalists) and the urban (urban proletarians and social classes) realms.

If we are to understand what "peasant" means today, we have to examine the peasant community's social and cultural adjustments to the urban environment. To this end, I believe that studying the usage of cultural symbols is important, because these symbols are the primary vehicles for political action. My analysis focuses on the way symbols help to shape the perception and representation of class and ethnic identity. The ideological system does not merely reflect social activity; it may also contradict and distort behavioral reality (Murphy 1971:158). This dialectical relationship between the ideological aspects of culture and social behavior is the central organizing concept of my approach. In taking this approach, I join other scholars who work with the Maya in the Highlands (Earl 1990; Greenberg 1987, 1990, Rosenbaum 1993, among others) and in Yucatán (Sullivan 1985, 1989; Bartolomé 1988; Kintz 1990, among others). Following Canclini's (1989) example in *Las Culturas Populares en el Capitalismo*, I look for the mechanisms through which symbols are used to defend the economic and political interests of social groups and/or classes.

At this point, I must define the term "peasant" in reference to the actors of this study. Under this term, I include those who live in or near the village and participate in the traditional, agrarian economy of the rural community, and those who, although residing and working in the city, still have an active role in the local village affairs. The community extends into the urban environment, and is spatially transferred to the *colonias populares*, the urban poor, marginal neighborhoods where the migrants settle. In this way, the rural community becomes part of the urban class structure.

This definition of peasant raises some specific issues that are discussed throughout this book: 1) the interrelation among social groups, class formations, ethnic identity, and the political potential of cultural symbols; and 2) the current relationship between the community analyzed here and the larger political economy of nation-states. To develop these issues, I maintain that social stratification and class formation are the critical variables for understanding the socioeconomic and political dynamics of cultural and ideological productions in the Chan Kom community.

The peasant community is in constant interaction with the global system, which imposes demands on the community's social system but also generates certain needs within it. The community's response to this relationship is the production of culture (ritual, oral tradition, gossip, ethnic identity) (Canclini 1989), which results in the redefinition and/or invention of symbols that incorporate the changing social environment.

Chapter 3

The Political Era: Modern Times and the Winds of Transformation

> *On September 15, 1810, the Creole priest Miguel Hidalgo summoned his parishioners to the village church (in Dolores, Guanajuato) and called on them to rise up against the oppressive government of the Spanish colony of México, thus catalyzing a bloody revolt. Over a century and a half later, on each September 15 at exactly 11:00 P.M.*—the hour when Hidalgo issued his call to rebellion—the president of México steps onto the balcony of the National Palace in México City, bearing the nation's tricolored flag. Above a central plaza packed with celebrating citizens, he bellows the ceremonial shout: "¡Viva la Independencia! ¡Viva Hidalgo! ¡Viva Morelos! ¡Viva Juarez! ¡Viva México!" A thunderous "¡Viva!" from the euphoric crowd greets each phrase as his amplified voice resounds through the plaza. Stepping aside, the president rings the palace bells, which are soon joined by those of the National Cathedral. Fireworks light the heavens; the final glowing colors in the sky form the face of Father Hidalgo as he shouted his original "¡Viva!" in that obscure church so many years ago.
>
> (Kertzer 1988:1)

Every September 15, Indian and nonIndian communities, towns and cities dotting the Mexican landscape, celebrate the independence of the

36

nation from the foreigner, Spanish imperial rule. In 1988, Chan Kom celebrated *el día del Grito,* as the Mexican independence day is popularly known, in a very particular way. A group of Maya assaulted the municipal palace as a way to express their opposition to the current political *cargos* (offices). For the Maya of Chan Kom this event represented the climax of a longstanding series of clashes between *los de Cancún* and *los Antiguos.* Why did this revolt, the highest expression of social crisis, occur on September 15, 1988? The explanations need to be drawn from the interrelation among political, ideological, and socioeconomic factors weaving the social context from which the revolt emerged.

This chapter's account of Chan Kom presents the factual material on which chapters 4–7 are built. The Maya revolt occurred on September 15, 1988, six months before my arrival. Thus, the vivid reconstruction of the event is based on the different versions I could gather through conversations. The purpose here is to show the role of phenomenology in this research and to introduce the sources of information and analytical tools used in the study. The emphasis is on the actors' roles as subject-creators of the perception of a community in crisis and as authors of their versions and interpretations of the events. As Sullivan states, "Ordinary conversations involve people who know they are conversing, who know who they are and in what relation they stand to one another, where they are in significant time and space, what they are talking about, why they are talking about that, and, when it is over what has been said" (1989:xxv). Following Geertz's use of the image of the "flow of events," I choose everyday forms of community expression to present the social scenario designed by these ordinary conversations, and to identify the principal characters in this social performance.

I begin with a description of my arrival in Chan Kom in 1989, when the fields were being burned in preparation for a new agricultural cycle, and use the description to introduce the social scenario. The material, primarily obtained from people's perception of community life, expressed through their conversations, pinpoints two phenomena that are seen as factors exacerbating their social crisis: *la Política* and *el Gilberto.* These are the main characters that people allude to when they recreate the social scenario of the Maya revolt; their roles and significance varies according to the role and position of the author of the version in the event. *La Política* refers to the crisis of authority and power in the village initiated by the increasing interference of external government forces in community affairs. The devastation caused by *el Gilberto* (Hurricane Gilbert) perpetuated the existing perception of crisis. These political and ecological pressures coincided with the national celebration of Mexican Independence. September 15, 1988 stands out in the recent historical memory of the community as the ironic zenith of the social crisis. This date is the reference point from which they construct the discourse about their current lives and fortunes. The Maya of Chan Kom, as a way to make sense of and to take action in their current social crisis, bring the intimate relationship between the political and ecological crises into the national historical process.

The Community: The Crisis at Work

It is the beginning of April, 1989, and I am apprehensive of the welcome I will receive in Chan Kom. I recall my farewell of Doña Emilia in the summer of 1987. We had watched the burning tropical sun begin to set, its brillant rays reflecting off the white cement houses in the plaza, as I set out on the shimmering, winding road that connects Chan Kom to the outside world. Now, after sunset, as I return along that same road, both excitement and forbeoding fill my heart. Many times I have thought of the village and longed for the faces of the people, I have not seen in almost two years. How will I find them? Will some be lost through death or migration to the city? These questions run through my mind again and again.

This time I have a specific academic purpose for being in Chan Kom: to understand socioeconomic transformations through cultural symbols. Because the Maya diet is based on maize, *milpa* production is the most important economic activity in the village, and it is highly ritualistic. I intend to analyze the symbolic significance of the *milpa*, both economically and in ritual performance, in order to achieve my goals. Therefore, the observation of and participation in agricultural rituals are methodological necessities. The best way to enact my methodology, I have decided, is to plant my own *milpa*. This decision awakens voices of alarm and anxiety in me: Maya men, not women, are the producers of the *milpa*. I am already acquainted with stories that associate men with the domain of the wilderness where the *milpas* are located; only men are considered strong enough to face the hidden dangers of the forest. How will the community react when I propose to cultivate my own maize? I am in turmoil over these issues as I approach the feeble, electric lights of the plaza.

To get to Charo's house, I have to cross the eastern side of the plaza from north to south. I recognize some faces among the group of Maya men sitting at Don David's store, at the northeastern corner of the plaza. The men have returned from their *milpas*, and taken their customary bath to purify themselves from the evil winds that surround them in the wilderness. After dressing in clean clothes, men often gather on street corners, under street lights, or in the village stores. In these gatherings they engage in many kinds of activities: they contract helpers to clear or plant cornfields; they arrange transportation for the next day; but mostly they converse and tell stories. As I pass the group of men, they look inquiringly at the car, undoubtedly wondering who the visitor might be.

I glance at the plaza and the streets: A group of young Maya are playing basketball in the plaza; some are bicycling around it; others are strolling past. Something catches my attention: most of the people wear caps, t-shirts with English words and messages printed on them, and sneakers. I remember that it is Friday evening, the beginning of the weekend, when the workers in Cancún return to the village. These migrants come to visit their familes, to inspect the work done in their *milpas* by hired *milperos*, and to attend to other family and *milpa* matters. At the southeastern corner of the plaza I notice another group of men; they are leaning against a wall that displays the colors and emblems of the PRI (The Institutional Revolutionary Party), the national political party of México. All the walls around the *palacio municipal*, the government office building, have a new look. They are freshly painted white, embellished with the green, white, and, red colors of the national flag, and sport political messages urging Maya cooperation and support of government programs (for instance, in collecting information for the 1990 census).

I turn left at the corner, and my heart skips when I see the light at the entrance of the familiar blue masonry house—Charo must still live there. Excited and nervous over our reunion, I start toward the one-room house. The car noise has alerted the family to a visitor. The younger children run to meet this woman dressed in a *huipil*. Charito, Charo's eldest daughter, is holding a new family member, a six-month-old baby, Charo's sixth child. As soon as she sees me, she runs into the kitchen to escape the evil winds I may bring from the outside—winds that could make the baby ill.

Doña Emilia, the children's grandmother, is visiting. She does not move from the hammock, where she swings to create a breeze, relieving herself from the hot April evening. She says: "I dreamed about you last night. I knew you were coming."

Charo is preparing dinner. The smell of warm *tortillas* on the *comal* (griddle) evokes a calming sense of home; I begin to relax. When she notices the children's agitation, she runs from the kitchen to meet me. Once again, my soul is filled by her eternal laughter and the tears running down her golden cheeks.

I feel that the nostalgia I have had for my village home is relieved by the dinner-time scene around the small kitchen table. With ears only for Charo's conversation, I ask her for all the news since I left. She seems eager to satisfy my demands, knowing that I am her most avid listener. First, she asks if I have noticed the new acquisitions—a refrigerator used exclusively to store Coca-Cola bottles and other beverages to sell, and a new TV. Her husband, Don Carlos, is working very hard in Cancún, and she can't complain regarding her sewing; she is the most famous seamstress in the village. They saved enough money to buy the new appliances. Besides, investing in the refrigerator is good business: they pay all the bills from the profits they make selling Coca-Cola.

Charo expresses worries about her eldest son. Jorge has just turned sixteen and will graduate from the *secundaria* (high school) in June. Don Carlos wants to take him to Cancún so that Jorge can contribute to the family's earnings. He has already started to make job arrangements for his son with some restaurant managers. Charo tells stories about people who have been assaulted in Cancún (in one case a woman was raped and murdered) and about people who have been robbed of all their belongings. "Cancún está mucho peligro" (Cancún is much danger) is a constant refrain throughout the conversation.

After bringing me up to date on family news, which is colored by her pride in their gradual modernization and improvements, Charo describes changes in the larger community. That discourse was my introduction to the creative process through which the story of a village in crisis is constructed: a story with many different versions; a story narrated mostly in tragic tones, whose main character, *La Política*, symbolically encapsulates the current misfortunes of Chan Kom.

> Todo se fastidió cuando empezaron a pelear la Política. El partido de Eduardo ganó, y pusieron a Martín de presidente, pero ellos no lo quieren. Cuando pasó el Gilberto, y todo estaba oscuro, esos cabrones entraron en el palacio y agarraron todo lo que había en su paso: máquina de escribir, fotografías, dinero, papeles, . . . Buscaron a Martín para matarlo con sus armas, pero él se había ido a las comisarías para ver lo que había hecho el Gilberto allí. El diputado vino a Chan Kom para ver lo que había pasado, y le rompieron una llanta del coche, y lo quisieron pegar con palo. Desde entonces andamos de cabeza, estamos en crisis. (Narrator: Charo, Chan Kom)

> Everything was ruined when they started fighting *la Política*. Eduardo's party won and they appointed Martin, but they don't like him. When *el Gilberto* came and everything was dark, those bastards got into the palace and took everything in sight: typewriter, photographs, money, papers . . . They looked for Martin to kill him with their guns, but he had gone to the *comisarías* to see what *Gilberto* had done there. The deputy came to Chan Kom to see what had happened, and they slashed one of the tires on his car, and they tried to beat him with sticks. Since then, our world is turned upside down, we are in crisis. (Narrator: Charo, Chan Kom)

When I left Chan Kom in 1987, I was aware of the political tension in the village from the approaching political election. Charo's discourse, however, disclosed a much deeper social rift, dramatically changing my image of the community. To me, it seemed as if the community had exploded into a drastic social schism expressed in terms of "we" and "they."

The fire is extinguished, and only grey ashes remain under the cold *comal*, but Charo is still vividly documenting the events that took place during my absence. Suddenly there is commotion in the darkened house, where the children are sleeping. Don Carlos has returned from Cancún to spend the weekend with his family. He is completely drunk. He enters the house, stumbling and mumbling some words. In his arms is a huge tape player that he bought in Cancún. Extremely loud music invades the room, making the babies cry.

A similar scene would be repeated every Friday night that Don Carlos appeared. Charo would relight the fire to make those delicious country *tortillas* that workers in the city dream about and to heat the beans left over from lunch, and probably from the day before. Sometimes Don Carlos would vent his frustration with the workplace (frictions with coworkers, arguments with the boss, veiled complaints of injustice, and feelings of exploitation). At other times, in long, barely understandable speeches, he would relate events in the city, until, finally, he fell asleep.

After my extended absence, since 1987, my first greetings were filled with inquiries about myself, my family, and my country. There was, however, a new, recurrent query within the familiar repertoire of greeting-questions. "Is there crisis in your country, as well?"

Through these initial conversations, I became acquainted with expressions such as: "*estamos de castigo*" (we are being punished), "*este tiempo duele*" (these times hurt), "*tiempo de peligro*" (time of danger), "*los tiempos están cambiando*" (times are changing), and "*tiempo de cambio*" (a time of change). These statements convey people's concerns over the degenerative political, economic, social, and ecological processes that they believe are responsible for their perceived chaotic existence. When asked what is causing the chaos, their explanations and interpretations focus on two main phenomena that have already been personified through repeated use: *la Política* and *el Gilberto*.[11] People in Chan Kom believe they are being punished for deviating from God's mandates. Because of their failings, they must suffer these two plagues that God has sent them.

The following is an analysis and discussion of the native epistemological view of their present chaotic existence. That perception of their social reality confirms the recent social, economic, and political transformations in the community, which are catalyzed in the native construction of *La Política* and their vision of *El Gilberto*.

Power and Authority Crisis: La Democracia
Comes to Chan Kom

I left Chan Kom in the summer of 1987, on the eve of an election for the political offices of the community. Two groups of candidates were running for office: one consisted mostly of Maya who live permanently in the village; the other was formed by Maya who work on a permanent or temporary basis in the city of Cancún. Both groups belonged to the same political party, the PRI, but had different leaders. The political representative of the first group was a young teacher of the Pech family. The second group was led by members of the first generation of migrants, who had provided the labor to build the tourist center of Cancún. Although the final vote was not held until November, the political campaigns had begun in July.

In July, agricultural activities in the fields stop; the *milpero* waits for the rain to come, for the "sacred water" to bless the maize. *La Canícula* threatens the *milpa* and the people with the appearance of sicknesses in the form of drought for the *milpa* and of intestinal infections for the Maya. In 1987, the tension and confrontations between the two Maya groups competing for political control of the community added to the perception of crisis during *la Canícula*. Both the actual sociological pressures and the symbolic view of *la Canícula* created a feeling of social division within the population.

The Cimé family,[12] the founders of Chan Kom, epitomizes the social division in the modern village. Today, the descendants of the Cimé family are the leaders of the two sociopolitical groups. This family split emphasizes the image of crisis: the Cimé family, which used to represent the political unity of the people, is no longer the decision-making head of the community. Rather, this family has become a symbol of community disunity and chaos.

I left Chan Kom in 1987 not knowing the results of the election. During those first conversations of 1989, I learned the outcome and subsequent events occasioned by the presence of *la Política* in the community.

The political group, headed by the school teacher and supported by the majority of *milperos*, cattle raisers, and beekeepers in the village, preferred the traditional election system. In this system, the outgoing president proposes someone as his successor. A meeting is held in the *cabecera* (head) of the *municipio* (township), Chan Kom; the representation of the *comisarías* (outlying hamlets) is not necessary. The public congregates at the plaza to voice their approval of the outgoing president's nominee and to demonstrate their respect for his wisdom and good intentions for the welfare of the community.

In 1987, however, the migrant group, supported by government mandates, imposed a new system—the ballot box. The migrant group leaders were more acquainted with political strategies such as political campaigns. Taking advantage of the weakest point in the traditional pattern, they tried to attract the votes of the *comisarías*, who had little or no say under the old system. The head of the migrant group was a member of a Cancún trade union associated with the PRI; this connection facilitated the group's efforts to attract more votes through campaign promises of social improvements. As a result, the migrant group won the election with the support of the majority of the *comisarías*. The defeated group, however, received most of the votes of the *cabecera*.

The election was the beginning of a new era in Chan Kom: *la Política*. It signaled the end of the power monopoly held by the traditional group of the community, and signalled as well the beginning of a period of social conflict. New sociopolitical ironies characterize the now enlarged, political arena. While the political offices are still located in the *cabecera*, they are held by migrant leaders whose main support is outside of the village. They have galvanized two untapped sources of support: the peripheral hamlets of the township (the *comisarías*) and the external resources of the national political party (the PRI). The migrant group, known as *los de Cancún*, defends their right to serve as political leaders of the community by presenting themselves as the local representatives of *la Democracia*. This became the political slogan of the national PRI, which synchronized with the broadly advertized United States's urges for the "democratization" of Latin America. According to the new officials in power, "lo que teníamos antes era un monopolio de *los Antiguos*. Ahora, tenemos Democracia, pero no les gusta" (what we had before was a monopoly by the *antiguos*. Now we have Democracy, but they don't like it).

The defeated group, called *los Antiguos* by the migrants, resisted the transfer of power to *los de Cancún*. They refused to accept the political success of *los de Cancún* in the election. They refused to turn over the position of *comisario ejidal* to the new group in power. Since the election, another term has arisen to denote the old elite in power, *grupo de ejidatarios* (workers of the communal land). The terms *ejidatarios* and *antiguos* are used interchangeably by the migrants to refer to their opposition. *Los Antiguos* use the expressions *modernos, los de Cancún, la otra parte* (the other part), or *el otro bando* (the other side) to refer to the migrants. There is also a Maya term in use: *Majan Kaho'ob*, which literally means "those who borrow the village to live."

The expression "crisis of power and authority" has been used repeatedly to refer to developments affecting twentieth-century peasantries (Wolf 1969; Sullivan 1985). This crisis is a pattern in which new social groups and new elites are created to oppose and compete with the old ones, which concomitantly become weaker. These new elites provide new ways to manipulate resources as commodities and follow new economic alternatives for survival. The new groups tend to disregard the old, traditional patterns and customary social obligations that once guaranteed the elite position in the rural sector.

The Maya of Chan Kom have generally shared this experience. There have been profound changes in patterns of power and authority in the community. The political arena has been enlarged to include more numerous and varied links between the local system and the national context. Further, a new social order reflecting new ways of leadership has been created in opposition to the old. The principal catalyst for this transformation is migration.

Hence, for the Maya, *la Política* embodies a process of social conflict arising from competition for political control of the community between two differentiated social groups. To the old elite (*los Antiguos*), the new group typifies the image of chaos, evil, and suffering.[13] Under the control of the new group, the world is increasingly unpredictable, and the old elite is more frequently obliged to submit to outside people's laws and demands. For *los Antiguos*, the land is not as fertile as it once was; the agricultural cycles come more irregularly every year; people do not conform to the same standards of behavior; they do not perform the agricultural rituals in a proper way; "no se cuida el santo maiz" (people do not take care of the holy maize); people do not go to Mass every Saturday afternoon; Protestantism is infiltrating the village; *los antiguos* (the elders) are not respected any more. All these observations contribute to the feeling of crisis. These are among the more significant real world referents of the processes of moral, economic, and political degeneration that many Maya in Chan Kom believe characterize their present existence.

For *los de Cancún, los Antiguos* represent an obstacle to the modernization of the village, as well as a rejection of national efforts to bring "democracy and equality" among all Mexicans. These efforts to depict the actions of *los Antiguos* as resistance and revolt against government mandates are the most effective stratagem for acquiring political support from the larger government.

The election of 1987 was the pivotal event in the development of political competition, authority crisis, and current social misfortunes. There have been other crises since then, but none as critical as Hurricane Gilbert in September, 1988.

The Environmental Crisis: Gilberto, El Arrancamonte[14]

Antes del ciclón la lluvia dió muy bien; en que vino el ciclón nos fregó a todos. Los pobres elotes crecieron bien, están dando mazorcas buenas en que vino el ciclón. Acá, los que hicieron milpa, todos tienen algo, lo que sea, porque ya mero termina la cosecha en que vino el ciclón, el 15 de Septiembre; ya mero termina, solo queda que queden sazones los elotes en que vino el ciclón. Ahorita ya está todito cambiado. (Narrator: Don Juanjo, Chan Kom)

Before the cyclone, the rain was abundant and came on time; the cyclone damaged us all. The poor ears of corn grew well, they were putting forth good green ears when the cyclone came. Here, those who planted their *milpas*, all of us had something, whatever, because the harvest was just about done when the cyclone came, the 15th of September; the only thing left was for the ears to ripen when the cyclone came. Now, everything is changed. (Narrator: Don Juanjo, Chan Kom)

Metaphors and symbols abound in Maya oral tradition, particularly in regard to agricultural practices. Maize, the primary subsistence crop, has both economic and symbolic importance in Maya culture.

Men clear the forest to make *milpa* (their fields). The forest is inhabited by spirits, supernatural beings who protect it. Through ritual performance and offerings of *atole* (corn gruel), the *milpero* petitions the spirits for permission to make *milpa*. The offering is made in the fields, on a rustic, wooden shrine. The ceremony is completed when the wooden image of the cross is placed at the center of the altar. Through ritual, the *milpero* contracts with the gods for protection of the maize crop. He commits to a series of ritual obligations that continue throughout the agricultural cycle. Failure to perform any of these obligations undermines the spirits' powers and may bring punishment, in the form of drought, natural disaster, disease, or even death. Damage or loss of the crop can lead to starvation. Maize unites the sacred and the profane. The spirits protect the maize crop, which feeds the *milpero* and his family; the *milpero* offers maize, *la santa gracia* (holy grace), in the form of *atole*, to feed the spirits. For the Maya of today, as in the past, maize is a metaphor for life (Burns 1983:8).

Maya attitudes toward maize have created a traditional code on which the welfare of the community depends. Maya believe that any deviance from this cultural code ensures that unpredictable weather patterns will threaten the crop. For this reason, Hurricane Gilbert was interpreted as an *anuncio* (announcement) of divine disapproval over the social miasma in Chan Kom.

According to people's accounts, on September 15, 1988, Hurricane Gilbert flattened the roofs and walls of peasant houses. Fierce winds uprooted and dragged whole trees meters from their original location. The furious rain, together with the wild winds, destroyed the maize plants in the fields. The villagers interpreted this disaster as divine punishment for the disunity in the community. Each group made allegations blaming the other for provoking the gods' anger. *Gilberto*, the evil wind, had overpowered the forces of good; it had deprived the people of their golden treasure (maize) waiting in the fields to be harvested. *Los Antiguos* did not hide their rage. They wanted to retaliate against *Gilberto*'s venom. People believed that *Gilberto* was retribution for the seeming acquiescence of *los Antiguos* to their defeat in the election.

Gilberto's timing became the perfect catalyst for *los Antiguos* to express their resistance to the new, political officials, who were perceived as illegitimate. When the hurricane had passed, the shocked villagers emerged from their homes to view the tragic consequences of the storm. It was evening, the electric power was out, and the streets were dark. A group of men took advantage of the confusion to invade the municipal offices. With old guns, sticks, and makeshift weapons, they broke into the building. According to the migrant group, the rebels intended to kill the municipal president. The president was visiting a nearby settlement to assess damage from the hurricane. News of the assault spread quickly from *comisaría* to *comisaría*, and the president was notified of the rebellion. The leaders of the riot waited for him in Chan Kom. Because of his location, the president could not avoid passing through Chan Kom to make his escape. A truck full of *milperos* from the *comisaría* was set up to camouflage the president; he passed through Chan Kom without being noticed. Arriving in Mérida, the state capital, he reported the sabotage to the authorities.

Meanwhile, a PRI deputy arrived in Chan Kom to examine the destruction caused by the storm. The rebels threatened him with sticks and other weapons.

> Muchas cosas sucedieron. Ese señor no tiene gente, solamente una poca que solamente está pendejando. La mayoría de la gente aquí está en contra de él. La mayoría de su gente trabaja en Cancún. Allá tiene su panadería, su conasupo, y su casa. Allá vivien esos cabrones, y no vienen más que a pendejar. Pero al final ellos se chingaron; se baño con sangre. Son los del otro bando, los de la presidencia. Se fueron a quejar al gobierno porque el cabrón es su ahijado.[15] Pero despues de eso tomaron miedo a nosotros. Nosotros, desde que amanece trabajamos, pero ellos, ni hacen milpa. (Narrator: Don Juanjo, Chan Kom)

> Many things happened. That man does not have followers, only a few that are constantly butting into people's affairs. Most of the people here are against him. Most of his followers work in Cancún. There he has his bakery, his conasupo (store) and his house. That is where those bastards live and they just come here to screw up things. But in the end, they screwed themselves; it was a blood bath. They are from the other side, the presi-

dent's followers. They went to complain to the government because the bastard (the president) has a godfather there.[15] But after that, they were afraid of us. We work from dawn to dusk but they don't even make *milpa*. (Narrator: Don Juanjo, Chan Kom)

Hence, the national celebration of independence from foreign rule inspired a local conservative rebellion against an authority that *los Antiguos* believed was imposed from the outside.

The heads of the rebellion were jailed and obliged to pay a large fine for their misdemeanors. Before September 15, *los Antiguos* group had suspected the state government of connivance and support for the group in power. Following the rebellion, *los Antiguos* knew that they would not be the children of the government, but they were still the children of God. The political offices in the village might be held by the migrant sector, but the religious offices, always associated with the Catholic Church, remained in the hands of *los Antiguos*. The social and political schism has also a religious reading, with Catholicism the metaphorical emblem that *los Antiguos* use as one of the main sources for Maya identity. Consequently, the distinction between religious and political offices also coincides with the social grouping of the community. That is, the control over community's power, via holders of the religious and political offices, is divided into *los de Cancún*'s monopoly on the community's political *cargos*, and *los Antiguos*'s monopoly on Catholic religious *cargos*.

The government promised to send some food aid each month to compensate the peasants for losses in the hurricane. When I arrived in April 1989, they had received that help only once: a truckload of supplies to make *tortillas*, beans, and milk for the children. The political officers were in charge of distributing the food among the population. During my first days in Chan Kom, the most common complaint within *los Antiguos* was that they had never received any aid from the hands of the political officials. The officials were accused of robbery against the "poor *milperos*." I was told that not only did the officials distribute the food among their own people, but they also took part of the aid to sell in Cancún.

Most accounts of these events, in *los Antiguos*' voices, implicate the family of the municipal president in this crime. The president's business and family are in Cancún. He has to divide his duties—as president of the community and as husband, father, and businessman—between Chan Kom and Cancún. He has no house in the village and must stay at his parents' home, which is located at the front corner of the municipal office building. The president's father, Don Lillo, is considered one of the wealthiest peasants in the village. Rumors accused the political officials of moving the supplies that were stored in the municipal building to Don Lillo's store. From there, at midnight, "quien sabe como" (who knows how), the goods supposedly were transported to the city. *Los de Cancún* promptly replied to this overt accusation; they alleged that *los Antiguos'* failure to cooperate with the government justified the irregular distribution of the supplies:

> Cuando llegaron los paquetes, anunciamos a la gente para venir al palacio y escribir sus nombres, a saber el número de casas que tomamos en cuenta. Ellos nunca llegaron. Dijeron que no querían nada con el Gobierno. Se negaron a cooperar. (Narrator: Don Martín, the President, Chan Kom)

> When the goods arrived, we announced to the people to come to the *palacio* (government building) and write their names on a list, in order to know the number of households we needed to take into account. They never came. They said they didn't want anything to do with the Government. They refused to cooperate. (Narrator: Don Martin, the President, Chan Kom)

The tales of Hurricane Gilbert and the subsequent events in the community—suitably embroidered, elaborated, and retold—have value beyond mere entertainment. They are a record of the ensuing war of accusations and responses between the two social groups. Accompanying these tales are symbols, summoned to express each group's image of the other. For those in political power, any action by *los Antiguos* group is seen in terms of rebellion and resistance. By denouncing this traditionalist group as resistant to government mandates, *los de Cancún* seek to ensure goverment support for themselves and to keep *los Antiguos* in a subordinate role in the struggle over political control of the community. Any mention to *los Antiguos* about the behavior of *los de Cancún* elicits a stereotyped commentary on the migrants, one which shapes them into violators of the village's social and moral codes. For the traditionalist, the migrant group represents a negative model of society, toward which *los Antiguos* are pushed against their will.

The Setting: Chan Kom's Lean Cows

> Si, estamos de crisis. Es castigo de Dios, así dice sus leyes de Jesús antes, que está andando por el mundo. Y dice ese señor:

> Adivina usted que quiere decir esa palabra que voy a decirle: "hay siete vacas gordas, hay siete vacas flacas. ¿Ya adivina usted que quiere decir?"
> —¡No maestro, no, quién sabe qué quiere decir!
> Tres veces le preguntaron esos doce discípulos.
> —Pues voy a decirles a ustedes. Esas palabras que les digo son siete años escasos de alimentos, con trabajo se va a buscar. Siete años suficientem-

ente alimento, hasta derramado en las calles, en los caminos. Eso quiere decir estas palabras.

—Está bueno maestro, ya lo entendimos.

—Otra cosa se dice. ¿Adivinan ustedes lo que quiere decir?: "la última albarrada tiene que volver al principio, el principio tiene que quedar como último."

—No maestro, no, no adivinamos.

—Pues voy a decirles a ustedes: las personas venerables tienen que dar en su mando a sus hijos, y sus hijos tienen que quedar como principio. Hay que respetar a su papá. Eso quiere decir (Narrator: don Pedro, Chan Kom)

Yes, we are in crisis. It is God's punishment; so say the laws of Jesus Christ, when He was in the world. And this man says:

—Guess what the words I am telling you mean: "there are seven fat cows, there are seven lean cows." Have you guessed yet what it is?

No, teacher, no, who knows what it means!

Three times those twelve disciples asked him.

—Well, I am going to tell you. Those words that I told you are seven years of famine; it is going to be very hard to find any food. Seven years of enough food, even spread in the streets and roads. That is what these words mean.

—It is OK teacher, we understand now.

—Another thing is said. Can you guess what it means: "the last wall has to become the beginning, and the beginning has to become the end"?

—No, teacher, we cannot guess!

—Then, I am going to tell you: the venerable people have to give orders to their sons, and their sons have to become the beginning. You must be respectful to your father. That is what it means.

(Narrator: Don Pedro, Chan Kom)

Every afternoon, around 2:30 p.m., Don David's son drives the family truck from Chan Kom to Xcalacop, on the national highway to Cancún. There he buys *pan francés* (white bread) to sell back in the village. Don David is the only one who sells bread in the village. Workers in the city are accustomed to eating white bread as a substitute for *tortillas*. White bread has also become common in the diet of the village, as has Coca-Cola.

Around 5:00 or 6:00 p.m., the villagers go to Don David's store to buy *pan francés* and *pan dulce* (sweet bread). The store is at the northeastern corner of the plaza. People who live on the west and south sides of the plaza must cross the plaza in order to get to the store. Through careful observation of daily Maya behavior, I established that neither the women nor the men living on the west and south sides of the plaza went to the store. They preferred to send children to buy whatever was needed; in that way they did not have to get into *los Antiguos* domain, at the northeast and east sides of the plaza. Among the questions I was asked during my first days back in Chan Kom was: "And where are you living, at *esta banda* (this side), or at *la otra banda* (the other side)?" Apparently, an invisible boundary had been drawn, spatially dividing the village into two halves.

A few days after my arrival, a new corn-grinding mill opened on the south side of the plaza. *Molino de la Mujer* (Woman's Mill) was the inscription on the front wall. Concha, Don Ramon's daughter, was running the business. Her father is a major supporter of the migrants' group in the village. His son, married to one of the municipal president's sisters, left the village about ten years ago; now, he and his wife own a mini-supermarket in Cancún. Concha herself spent some time in the city, working in a boutique. With her savings, she and Don Ramon were able to open the corn-grinding mill. Her parents' assistance in the store frees her to work in Cancún for short periods.

Don Chano, the owner of the first mill and *tortillería* (tortilla factory) in the village and one of the political heads of *los Antiguos*, saw his clientele diminish because of competition from *Molino de la Mujer*. Now, those living on the west and south sides do not have to cross the plaza to bring their *nixtamal*, maize soaked in water, to the mill. The mill has always been a meeting place for women, a place to socialize and share gossip. *Molino de la Mujer* provides a second, competing center for female interaction. Now, at sunset, the men, having returned from their *milpas*, gather at the plaza. There are two main groups: one at Don Chano's mill-store; the other, at Don Lillo's store.

My first Saturday in Chan Kom I am awakened by very loud music. It is coming from the municipal building. A record player has been set up to play a fashionable cumbia that is interrupted, from time to time, with an announcement:

> El diputado, representante del PRI va a venir hoy a Chan Kom; todos estan invitados a acudir a la reunión para recibir a las autoridades.

> The political deputy, representative of the PRI, is coming to Chan Kom today; everyone is invited to attend the meeting to welcome the authorities.

The president has sent several trucks to the *comisarías* to recruit people for the event. The trucks return vomiting Mayas from the neighbouring hamlets and Chan Kom's *comisarías*. In a Wolfian fashion, the scenery could be described as the invasion of the center, Chan Kom, by its periphery. It was precisely this periphery that supported the migrant's political success over the traditional *los Antiguos*'s control. And now, during the performance of such a central political event, the periphery is the representation of the audience and public of the political event. While this occurs, the majority of the center's representatives, *los Antiguos*, concentrate at their center of action, the Catholic church, the encapsulation of the power that they control.

When the deputy arrives, the people milling around the plaza begin to congregate at the spot where the political speeches will be given. Those who have come specifically for the event are clearly distinguishable; they wear shirts and caps printed with the symbols of the PRI party. While Chan Kom's president is introducing the deputy to the public, the priest from Valladolid arrives to hold the weekly mass. *Los Antiguos* have gathered at the church entrance, at the opposite side of the plaza, to await the priest.

Chan Kom's president gives a short speech; his grandfather's name, Don Eustaquio Cimé, punctuates the discourse:

> Mi abuelo, Don Eustaquio, el fundador de este pueblo ha colaborado con el PRI desde el comienzo. Gracias a eso, Chan Kom es un pueblo moderno. Tenemos la carretera que va a Cancún y a Mérida; hay electricidad, agua potable, el campo de bola . . . Quiero el progreso para este pueblo, quiero seguir los pasos de mi abuelo en este pueblo. (Narrator: Don Martín, Chan Kom's president)

> My grandfather, Don Eustaquio, the founder of this village, has collaborated with the PRI since the beginning. Thanks to that, Chan Kom is a modern village. We have the highway to get to Cancún or Mérida; we have electricity, running water, the baseball field . . . I want progress for this village, I want to follow in my grandfather's steps. (Narrator: Don Martín, Chan Kom's president)

In his speech, the president presents himself as the inheritor of Don Eustaquio's legacy. His obvious purpose is to legitimize his political position, both in the village and with the PRI, by citing his grandfather as the village founder and initiatior of good relations with the government. *Los Antiguos* interpret the president's speech as pandering—a courtship with the government.

Informants' answers to my queries about the social situation revealed that each of the social groups has its own story to tell about the establishment of the village. In contrast to the president's promotion of Don Eustaquio Cimé as village founder, *los Antiguos* emphasize the role of Don Epifanio Cimé. For *los Antiguos*, it was Don Epifanio who conducted his people to a land with an abundance of good soil to make *milpa*, and it was he who set up the moral and social principles that safeguard the welfare of the community. The narration of this story by *los Antiguos* has acquired mythological tones. Don Epifanio has become a folk hero who, guided by God's will, brought his people to the promised land, Chan

Kom. In these accounts, Don Eustaquio is, sometimes, the illegitimate son of Don Epifanio, and, at other times, merely his nephew.

As mentioned above, an invisible line separating the two groups bisects the plaza through the center of the village. The political and ideological differences between the groups are expressed physically in the structural-spatial distribution of both groups around the plaza. I discovered that the households of Don Epifanio's descendants are situated on the east and north sides of the plaza, while those of Don Eustaquio are mostly on the west and south sides. The plaza is both the physical center of the village and the center of community political power. The social schism in the community is mirrored by the spatial division through the village's center.

Conclusion: Symbols at Work

People do not experience social relations in the abstract. These relationships develop out of personal experience with specific individuals and specific events. Embedded in the recent history of social relations in the village, the concept of crisis in the community is tied to this interrelationship between the particularities of the social and personal experiences, and the specifics of the events. For this reason, I have placed the Maya stories and experiences at the center of this analysis. Their perception and interpretation of the events comprise a long braid of experiences of competition, subordination, manipulation, and oppression. These grievances thread their way through to specific targets which are reached with the weapons of stories, myths, slander, and gossip. Sometimes the strands of the braid are woven too tightly, and it needs to be destroyed to avoid the pain; as such, the accumulation of grievances may grow so intense that it may result in a collective act such as the Maya revolt in Chan Kom during the 1988 celebration of *el día del grito*. When members of the same community do not share the same experiences, they may manipulate commonly understood symbols in new ways, in order to accentuate their difference.

In Chan Kom, changes in the socioeconomic circumstances of one group of villagers have led to social and political conflict with more traditional members of the community. This conflict has created both social and spatial divisions within the community and the village. Both groups have turned to symbols from a shared ideology in order to justify their competing positions. The groups are engaged in a contest of symbols, which is expressed through threats and propaganda. Thus, the founding of Chan Kom is recreated in mythological terms. These myths serve as a metaphor for the conflict that pervades all spheres of Chan Kom society: economic, social, political, and ideological.

Los de Cancún have usurped political power in the village by manipulating old resentments held by the *comisarías* toward the center, as well as by establishing political connections in the cities with the state government. This group also has economic power because its members participate in the city's cash economy. These migrants are trying to impose their ideas of social and economic reform on the more traditional village residents. They portray any opposition to their reforms as an act of rebellion against the larger government.

Los Antiguos resent the loss of political power and the corresponding loss of control of community material resources. They believe that the political situation, *la Política*, represents an attempt by state government to intrude into internal community affairs. *Los Antiguos* invoke moral and religious expectations to denounce the behavior of their opposition and use social sanction, through gossip and slander, to undermine the position of the migrant group. They interpret the devastation brought by Hurricane Gilbert, *el Gilberto*, as retribution against the community for its abandonment of traditional ways.

For the people of Chan Kom, *La Canícula* of 1989 was "the most severe drought they remember in the last twenty-five years." They believe that divine intervention was playing an important role, intensifying the crisis by sending the drought. "No está bien; Dios no le gusta que estemos así, odear los unos con los otros" (This is not right. God does not like to see us like this, hating one another.).

Chapter 4

One Community and Two Worlds

> *Esos son del grupo de los antiguos; no más
> quieren el poder, no piensan, no entienden, no
> quieren superación, no quieren progreso,
> estan atrasados. (Voice from* los de Cancún)
>
> *They are from the* los Antiguos *group; they
> only want power, they don't think, they don't
> understand, they don't want to get ahead, they
> don't want progress, they are backward. (Voice
> from* los de Cancún).
>
> *Muchos solo adoran su dinero . . . son esos, los
> que se viran de religión, de evangélicos. Nunca
> van a la iglesia, ni les da gracias a Dios por
> tener dinero . . . no hacen milpa, no agradecen
> a Dios. (Voice from* los Antiguos).
>
> *Many only worship their money . . . they are
> the ones who change their religion, become
> evangelicals. They never go to church, nor do
> they give thanks to God for their money . . .
> they don't make milpa, they don't thank God
> for their blessings. (Voice from* los Antiguos).

After introducing *la Política* and *el Gilberto* as the promoting factors
for the social crisis context of Chan Kom, this chapter is devoted to the
ethnographic analysis of the competing social groups, *los Antiguos* and
los de Cancún, which are engaged in a duel for the representation of
what to be Maya means. To understand the context of the competition
between *los Antiguos* and *los de Cancún*, an analysis of their socioeco-

54

nomic and cultural milieus is necessary. Each group employs socioeconomic, cultural, and political arguments to defend its views of itself, the community, and the world. Taking "Mayaness" as the encapsulation of these views, that is, as the emblem of Maya identity, each group's definition of "Mayaness" is influenced by its socioeconomic and political positions.

Here, the self-representations of *los Antiguos* and *los de Cancún*, along with the way in which they view each other, are presented through the profiles of two characters, a leader from each group. These profiles are constructed from narrations, ritual contexts, and stories of everyday events. I show that the roles of these men, and their reputations among the people, model the new social and spatial mapping of the community brought about by the conflict between *los Antiguos* and *los de Cancún*. My analysis follows the methodological track that Scott (1985) uses to uncover the silent and anonymous forms of class struggle that typify the peasantry of his study case.

The concept of power is important to any understanding of the exchange between *los de Cancún* and *los Antiguos*, and especially so in matters of identity. I address the notion of power in relation to the groups' experiences of subordination or domination when competing or striving for power. As Michel Foucault (1983) has shown, power is all-pervasive; through the manipulation of resources and ideas, powerholders can enforce personal and social identities and can affect their own and their opposition's self-images.

The other concept that pervades this analysis is "opposition ideology," which I use here in the way Schwimmer (1972) borrows it from the field of social psychology. Schwimmer applies the concept to societies that include indigenous groups, which, according to him, are "peripheral to the basic political and economic decision-making institutions in the society" (1972:118). The cases chosen by Schwimmer to operationalize the "opposition ideology" are the New Zealand Maori and the Canadian Indians. Opposition ideology refers to "a relation of negative reciprocity holding between a dominant and a subordinate group" (1972:120). In these cases, the peripheral or subordinated groups are the Canadian Indians and the New Zealand Maories; the whites represent the dominant group in both cases. The "opposition ideology" concept is also related to what Warren refers to as "negotiability of subordination and separatism" (1989:48) among Guatemalan Maya Indians. In this case, Indian identity is linked to the Indians' relations of subordination with the dominant Non-Indian social group, or *Ladinos*. In these two examples (Warren's and Schwimmer's), the subordinate group, the Indians, is opposed to the dominant, the Whites or *Ladinos*. In both cases, the ideological construction is examined through the various ways in which the Indians negotiate toward separatism from the Whites' or *Ladinos'* system of values.

The concept that people create their own identity based on a referential other, or opposite, from which they are trying to differentiate themselves, is central to this analysis. My approach differs from that of Warren and Schwimmer in that I focus on the dynamics of internal, ideological competition between two social groups, both of which are Maya. In Chan Kom there are no Whites, the dominant group in Schwimmer's cases, or *Ladinos*, the dominant group in Warren's case, which will be the *Dzulo'ob*[16] in the social composition of Yucatan. All the inhabitants in the community are Indians or Maya. I also point out a broader corpus of relations embedded in this negotiation of ethnic identities. *Los Antiguos* use various cultural symbols to define their identity, but they tend to emphasize that identity in opposition to *los de Cancún*. The migrants employ the same Maya cultural symbols as *los Antiguos* to represent themselves, but they invest these symbols with different meanings, according to their new experiences.

In this analysis, I demonstrate that the subordinate-dominant roles are not attached to one group or the other; these roles are malleable, and fluctuate according to changes in the socioeconomic and political positions of each group at any particular point in time.

Los Antiguos de Chan Kom

The character that is considered *el mero* (the best one), the leader of *los Antiguos*, is Don Chano, one of the wealthiest Maya in the community. He is about sixty-five years old and a descendant of Don Epifanio Cimé, whom *los Antiguos* recognize as the principal founder of Chan Kom. Once Don Eustaquio Cimé, the old *cacique* (village leader) retired from the *"monopolio municipal"* (as Don Chano says), Don Chano took over political control of the community. He was president twice and *comisario ejidal* three times. Besides 8 hectares (200 mecates) of *ejido* land, he owns 28 hectares (700 mecates) of the *yaxkas*, the most fertile land of the *ejidos*. He keeps thirty head of cattle on the Santa Cecilia Ranch, where other members of his family have their cattle. He also owns a combination store and corn-grinding mill for *tortilla* flour. His house and mill-store are located at the eastern side of the plaza. With the destruction of the harvest by Hurricane Gilbert in 1988, those who depended on their own maize for subsistence were forced to work on other people's lands or to migrate to the city in search of wages with which to buy food (particularly *masa* [corn dough] or ready-made tortillas). Don Chano's mill-store was the only one in the village that sold dough or *tortillas*.

Don Chano's physical appearance is a cause for popular derision among the migrants. He is the skinniest man in the village, a physical feature shared by most of Don Epifanio's descendants. Don Chano's lean physique is transformed by his opponents into a personality trait, miserliness. He always wears the same clothes. Although he is one of the richest men in the village, it is rumored that his family eats only beans and tortillas at every meal, and sometimes skips dinner.

Don Chano is, as the people say, *grande*, meaning a person who, because of age, has knowledge on various matters. Younger men ask him for advice, mainly regarding agricultural activities: when to start burning or planting the fields, the type of seed to use, and other such questions. His economic situation is prosperous enough to allow him to serve as the sponsor of religious rituals that require the expenditure of a great deal of money.[17]

"La Santa Cruz que Jesús nos dejó para que le acordáramos" (*"The Holy Cross that Jesus gave us to remember him"*). (*Don Juanjo, Chan Kom*)

It is May 3, the day of the Holy Cross. It is Wednesday, 6:00 A.M., and there is a lot of activity at the plaza. A stream of people coming from the northeastern side of the village and a concentration of men at Don Chano's store indicate that a ceremony is to be celebrated at his house.

By the beginning of May, in a normal agricultural cycle, the fields have been burned and the maize, bean, and squash seeds are waiting for the rain to fall and prepare the soil, or already have been planted. In any case, rainwater is needed, either to nurture the soil, or for the seed to germinate; a dry spell will kill seedlings or give the birds a chance to dig up the seeds and eat them. This is the time to pray to the Holy Cross for rain or to thank it for the blessing of the *santa lluvia* (holy rain) already received. Although it is Wednesday, the comings and goings from Don Chano's house denote the transformation of a normal work day into a holiday. Today, the male participants in the celebration have replaced the old, tattered clothes that they wear everyday to the *milpa* with clean, neat long-sleeved shirts and pants. Men and women have arrived very early at Don Chano's. The Maya men had to open the *pib* (a pit in the ground in which coals and food are placed and then covered with earth) where *relleno negro*, the ceremonial meal, was placed the day before. Today, the Maya women, participants in the ceremony, are released from their everyday domestic activities. They will not make the usual *chocomilk*, the commercial substitute of the traditional chocolate, for the kids; they will not eat the traditional *frijoles* with *tortillas* for breakfast. Before the sunrise, they normally would have been making the *tortillas* for their husbands' breakfast at the house and lunch at the *milpa*. The Maya women, the *prestadas* at Don Chano's, will have to postpone two of their daily domestic activities, namely, feeding the chickens, turkeys and pigs, which they can use in festivities or sell as an extra source of cash, and taking care of their home gardens.

The large kitchen at Don Chano's is crowded by groups of women devoted to different cooking tasks. There are two large circles of seven or eight Maya grouped around low tables, where they make the *tortillas*, which finally reach the *comal*, going hand to hand, at the end of the circuit. Another group is devoted to cutting the onions, tomatoes and chillis, into small, regular pieces; the vegetables will flavor the palate of the people when they eat the ceremonial meal. Three or four Maya women are getting buckets of water to wash all the dishes and glasses collected to serve the tables at the meal time, after the *novena* (a recitation of the rosary).

Every year, *u novenai u kinu kaba* (novena on the name of the day) is performed before the Holy Cross celebration day. Although all the community participated in a single celebration in the old times (Redfield and Villa Rojas 1934:148), there are several *dueños*[18] (owners) of crosses today. Among these *dueños*, Don Chano is known as the *más antiguo dueño-cargador* (the oldest owner-holder) of the Holy Cross in the village. His father found this particular cross buried in the *milpa* soil when he was planting maize in the early years of the community.

Some form of the cross is present in any Maya ritual context. The main role of the cross is to sanctify and to protect from evil (Redfield and Villa Rojas 1934:110–11). As such, Chan Kom has four village crosses, each of them placed at the outskirts of the community and oriented towards the four directions. These four crosses mark the border between the protected space, sanctified by the crosses, and the wilderness, all of which is non-village space and the source of unknown and evil forces. The Maya use the sign of the cross in order to bring divine forces against the evil winds, the source of people's maladies. Thus, the cross is used in a variety of situations to protect or rescue any space, activity, or person from evil (Redfield and Villa Rojas 1934:110–11.) May 3, the day of the Holy Cross, is also celebrated in the urban arena (Cancún, Mérida) in which it becomes *la patrona de los albañiles* (the saint patron of the construction workers.)

In 1989, the celebration of the day of the Holy Cross had special overtones in Chan Kom: a drought was threatening the corn fields. Most of Don Chano's group had already planted their *milpas*; now they needed rain desperately. If the seed did not germinate soon, the birds would eat it, and the *milpero* would have to invest not only time in a new planting but money to buy new seed. The anxiety over the condition of the *milpa* was powerfully expressed in the prayers offered to the Holy Cross.

Chan Kom has four village crosses, each of them placed at the outskirts of the community, oriented towards the four directions. These crosses mark the border between the protected space, sanctified by the crosses, and the wilderness.

The male head of the household is in charge of the organization of the ceremony. He arranges for the *maestro cantor*[19] and invites friends and neighbors, the *prestados* (the borrowed people), who will help with the labor chores. The wife is in charge of inviting Maya women who, together, will take care of preparing the cooked offerings for the saint. (Redfield and Villa Rojas 1934:150)

The celebration culminates in a feast. A pig, chickens, and turkeys are killed to prepare the *relleno negro* (a ritual meal) to be offered to the saint and to be shared in communion by all the participants in the ceremony. The owner of the saint is responsible for all the feast expenses. This year Don Chano is, once again, as he has for more than forty years, holding the festivity at his house. This time, however, there will not be *el baile de la cabeza de cochino*[20] (the dance of the pig's head) as in the old, more prosperous times.

It is early in the morning when I arrive at Don Chano's store. The altar placed at the northeastern side of the storeroom is arranged for the last set of prayers in honor of the Holy Cross, the last *novena*. Don Chano's wife comes from the kitchen to light the candles that are placed at the front of the altar. A large, wooden cross is at the center of the table, dressed in a colorful *sudadura* (type of dress covering the cross). Other ritual paraphernalia surround the cross on the altar, constructed especially for this ritual. At sunrise, the *relleno negro* had been dug up, and a large pot of that dish is arranged on the altar as the main offering for the Holy Cross.

The *Maestro Cantor* arrives and the thirteen church *rezadoras*[21] are ready to start the *novena*. Murmurs come from the kitchen, where women are preparing food and making tortillas. The meal will be offered to the Holy Cross before it is shared by the people. Other whispered conversations come from outside, where the men are gathered. When the *rezadoras* and the *maestro cantor* finish the prayers for the Holy Cross, they wait for the *dueños* to enter the living room and share the meal with the other guests. As in other Maya ritual meals, people eat at the

(Description of the altar) A large wooden cross is at the
center of the table, dressed in a colorful sudadura.
Other ritual parphernalia surround the cross on the
altar, . . . the relleno negro had been dug up, and a large
pot of that dish is arranged on the altar as the main
offering for the Holy Cross

table in shifts. The men eat first, followed by the children, and finally by the women, who have been cooking and serving.

As important as the meal itself is the pleasure of socializing. Gossip, stories, and accounts of recent community events are shared. I am invited to eat with the men during their turn at the table. It is the first time that I have been in the private area of Don Chano's house. The inside is immense, composed of one room after another. In the back is a large yard where his wife keeps chickens, pigs, and turkeys, and where she grows a small plot of vegetables. Familiar with the traditional, small, one-room, thatch Maya house, I am amazed by the vastness of Don Chano's home. When I express my admiration of the large rooms and elegant interiors, he comments that it was one of the first houses to appear on the plaza and was built by his father, Don Epifanio. In spite of its size, Don Chano's house is furnished simply, with no display of luxury in furniture or adornments. Nevertheless, such an enormous house is a sign of Don Chano's high social status in the village.

Men finish eating the *relleno negro* and move toward the door, as if to leave. They gather in the doorway and begin to chat. The conversation revolves around the anomalous weather that, once again, threatens the harvest. This year the rains have come early. The end of March was very hot and dry and some peasants, particularly *los Antiguos*, took advantage of the weather to burn their fields, acting on advice from the elders. Maya peasants use a divinatory device, *las cabañuelas*[22], to predict the weather through the year. The elders have the knowledge and experience to interpret the signs, and the younger generations rely on the elders' advice to time major agricultural tasks such as burning, planting, and harvesting. Don Chano knows how to interpret *las cabañuelas*, and is one of the main consultants on agricultural matters.

As the conversation continues, mocking references are made to *los del otro bando,* the migrants. Most of the migrants have failed to burn their *milpas*. They did not expect the anomalous cycle and were working in Cancún when conditions were right for burning; this reinforces their image in the community as natives forgetful individuals of peasant knowledge and neglectful of *milpa* care. *Los Antiguos* comment that the migrants no longer know how to interpret the weather signs and did not consider the disruptive effects caused by Hurricane Gilbert. The failure of the migrants to burn and sow before the rains is seen as fair punishment for their refusal to share the government food package with *los Antiguos*. As Don Luis, one of the religious officially, says jokingly, "Ellos agarraron todo el maiz que dio el Gobierno, y ahora no pueden sembrar el suyo" (They grabbed all the government's corn and now they can't grow their own). He continuing on a more serious note: "Eso pasa porque ya se olvidaron de Dios, no hacen las primicias, no le agradecen al

Señor Dios; son mormones" (This happened because they forgot all about God, they don't perform the *primicias*[23], they don't give thanks to God, they are mormons).

This is the first time I have heard the word "mormon" associated with the migrants. A few days later, my daily informal conversations with Raimundo[24] in the *milpa* reveal the contextual meaning of mormon. *Los Antiguos* believe that when mormons perform a ritual, a monkey jumps up on the altar and eats the offerings. I interpret this connection that *los Antiguos* establish between monkeys and mormons in the following terms: "Monkey" in Spanish is *mono* and the Maya use the phonetic similarity between *mono* and *mormones* to associate them in a ritual context. Furthermore, the "r" sound is not used in the Maya language, so it is often not heard in words borrowed into Maya; for example, *mormon* is heard as *"mohmon"* (Burns, personal communication). A monkey eating the offerings is a very difficult image to picture in any Maya ritual setting. Offerings may not be eaten until they are blessed by the saint through prayer. Most Maya ritual offerings are based on maize (*atole, saca'*, ears of corn), which in itself is considered sacred. The image of a monkey eating the sacred corn that awaits blessing is doubly blasphemous. *Los Antiguos'* condemnation of the migrants for deviance from the socioeconomic traditions of the *milpero*-peasant finds expression in the religious context through accusations of heresy.

Raimundo is a sacristan in the Catholic Church and a *maestro cantor*. He reads the Bible and enjoys retelling Biblical stories. In July, as we are planting maize seed in my *milpa*, we take the customary break to drink *saca'*, a ceremonial beverage made with corn dough. Earlier, we had placed the *saca'* on the wooden altar in the *milpa*, to thank God and the lords of the forest for allowing us to work the land. Inspired by the idea of "creating my own maize" through the action of planting seed, I ask Raimundo about the creation of the world. He says:

> Esto lo dice el Antiguo Testamento, porque es el tiempo de los antiguos, cuando estaban vivos los Mayas. Pues al principio los monos es igual con nosotros, los hicieron con nosotros, con personas. Está peleando Jesús con el diablo; está ganando el diablo, entonces así puso a los monos; tienen puro pelo, el diablo los hizo. Nosotros, Dios nos hizo. (Narrator: Raimundo, Chan Kom)

> This is what the Old Testament says, because it is of the time of the elders, when the Mayas were alive. At the beginning, the monkeys are our equals, they were created with us, with people. Jesus Christ and the devil are fighting; the devil is winning, then he puts the monkeys first; they just have hair, the devil created them. We, God created us. (Narrator: Raimundo, Chan Kom)

From Raimundo's reply, I interpret the choice of the term *mormon* by *los Antiguos* as their attempt to radically differentiate themselves from the migrants. Therefore, the usage and manipulation of *mormon* not only express the current experience of transformation, but also demonstrate *los Antiguos'* efforts to explain the present by integrating it with a mythological past.

A large number of people are invited to Don Chano's house to celebrate the Holy Cross Day. The celebration helps me to identify those Maya who support Don Chano's leadership. These gatherings for celebrations and the daily congregation of men at Don Chano's doorway can be considered a political show of *los Antiguos'* group solidarity. As more people join the group gathering at the entrance of Don Chano's store, another contingent of Maya loiter in front of Don Lillo's store, at the other side of the plaza. Someone from Don Chano's party points out the group and makes some comments regarding their laziness. At this point, the conversation turns to Cancún:

> En Cancún se gana bastante, mucho, pero el pasaje esta muy caro, la comida, la renta . . . todo esta muy caro, y cuando tu llegas aca, pues ya te queda muy poco. A veces dejas unos cuantos pesos en tu casa, y tienes que volver a agarrar ese dinero para tu pasaje, y para que te sostengas una quincena hasta que vuelvas a cobrar. Por eso, los que viven aca estan mucho mejor, descansar, nadie les obliga; en cambio alla, pues si, tienes que estar al horario, y pendiente; te pasaste, y no te dejan entrar o te rebajan el sueldo. En cambio aca, un señor se puede quedar tres días a dormir, pero él no depende de nadie, porque hay milpa, abejas, ganado; aqui puedes hacer lo que uno guste, puedes dedicarte a lo que quieras. Alli, trabajas, pero tienes deudas; lo que ganas, ahi se va, y no te queda nada, hasta la quincena. (Narrador: Don Luis, Chan Kom)

> You can earn a lot of money in Cancún, but the bus ticket is very expensive, the meals, the rent . . . and when you get to the village, there is little left. Sometimes you leave a few pesos at your home and you have to take it for your return bus ticket, and to support yourself for the two weeks until you get your pay. On the other hand, those who live here, if they want, they can rest for three days, no one controls them. On the contrary, there you have to fit a schedule (in Cancún); if you are late, they do not let you in to work or they take some money from your pay. Here (in Chan Kom) we don't depend upon anyone else. Here you have *milpa*, bees, cattle, you can devote yourself to whatever you want. There (Cancún) even though you earn money, you have many debts; when you get paid, you have to pay your debts, and you end up with nothing, until the next paycheck. (Narrator: Don Luis, Chan Kom)

Then the conversation rambles on to the way money was saved by the elders, who hid their savings inside pots or buried them in the soil.

Stories are told about people who have found buried gold and silver coins. Don Pablo adds a moral to the stories:

> El dinero siempre es malo; si lo encuentras, siempre tu lo vas a sufrir. Después de que entierras tu dinero, cuando mueras, si alguien lo encuentra, se asoma en forma de fuego, o en caballo, en lo que sea, porque es espíritu . . . El dinero también es pasajero, no se queda; tu puedes tener bastante dinero, pero no se te queda. Si encuentras dinero, siempre tienes que enterrar una parte porque si no, siempre te lo van a acordar más tarde. (Narrator: Don Pablo, Chan Kom)

> Money is always bad; if you find it, every time you are bound to suffer. After you bury your money, when you die, if someone finds it, it transforms into fire or a horse, or whatever, because it is a spirit . . . Money also is fleeting; it never stays with you in one place. You may have a lot of money but it never stays. If you find money, you always have to bury part of it, otherwise someone will remind it to you later (meaning that you will be punished). (Narrator: Don Pablo, Chan Kom)

Certainly, money, as described through this conversation among *los Antiguos*, is invested with magic and fetish-like properties that bring it close, symbolically, to the evil forces. These voices also express different considerations of money. According to the tradition, whenever money is found, it must be shared with the lords of the land. Found money it also can be used as a commodity, as the migrants use it.

Don Chano, a Social Profile: From Thief to "Holy Man"

Various stories concerning Don Chano's ambition and his achievement of economic and political power, circulate among his opposition, the migrants. For the migrants, Don Chano represents the essence of traditional Maya wealth, a dead end that they do not consider worth aspiring to. The Maya migrants, who now control the community's political power, seek *superación y progreso* (improvement and progress) in the accumulation of capital through their urban jobs.

In particular, the migrants tell stories related to moneylending and credit practices in order to explain how Don Chano acquired all his land and properties. According to these accounts, Don Chano is the worst usurer in the village. Before planting season, particularly if the previous harvest was poor, the *milpero* must borrow money to buy seed. Lack of money for medical expenses in the event of illness or accident is a source of anxiety for many people. Depending on the type of illness, the peasant may have to pay for the services of a *h-men* (curer), a doctor, or a midwife, as well as for medicines. The village fiesta also involves monetary expenditure; Maya are expected to spend money on new clothes, entertainment (such as *la corrida*, a bull-fight), on drinking, and other ways to honor the patron saint. The above are just a few examples of events in peasants' lives that require accumulation of capital or some other method to obtain cash.

Pawning is a strategy the peasant uses to survive when the maize reserves are gone and the next harvest is still to come. It is also a handy mechanism they use to cope with the expenses and obligations mentioned above (religious and secular celebrations, medical care, and school materials). Pieces of jewelry, given to a woman upon her marriage, are the most suitable pieces for pawn. If the peasant can afford it, cattle may also be sold or pawned. The property is recovered if the peasant can pay the interest on the money borrowed. Most of the time the interest is so high that he loses his property.

In addition to usury, Don Chano is accused of using his political position illegally for personal economic gain (for instance selling wood collected from communal lands). In these stories, presented by *los de Cancún*, Don Chano is the embodiment of "the other side" of the social spectrum; he dwells within the enemy's domain. He is seen as a transgressor of the moral and political code of the community. The purpose of this narrative propaganda against him is to undermine any attempt by Don Chano to regain political control of the township. By accusations of disreputable behavior while in office, his opposition, *los de Cancún*, promote their moral right to hold political office.

Don Chano, as a Maya landowner, owner of the corn mill, cattle owner, and bee keeper, has amassed sufficient capital to be one of the main financial contributors to the local Catholic church. He is seen as a righteous man among his own social group, but is reviled by his opponents for violating the community standard for a religious man's behavior. Rumors, slander, gossip, and narrative stories originating with "the other side" represent Don Chano as the apotheosis of falseness posing under a guise of saintliness. Hurricane Gilbert left the people without maize; those who depended on their *milpa* for subsistence had to buy their tortillas and *masa* at Don Chano's store. Most of the *los Antiguos* group saw Don Chano as a benefactor—the only person in the community who helped the poor peasants by providing them with maize, so necessary to the Maya diet. *Los de Cancún* point out that he also was enlarging his economic empire in the midst of human misery.

Don Chano could not compete politically against *los de Cancún*, who had outside government support and protection. He was becoming, however, an increasingly powerful economic adversary. His growing reputation in the community as the benefactor of the poor *milperos*, along with the vigor of his already-developed economic power, prompted new accusations by his opponents. His more immediate political competitors, particularly the other line of the Cimé family, expanded their depiction of him as a shameless and greedy man. During those days of uncertain weather, when the light rain was insufficient for planting, yet an obstacle to burning the fields, large numbers of mosquitoes and big flies plagued the village. People feared that the insects would spread disease and cause food to rot. Several times I was told that Don Chano's mill was the source of bad odors that attracted these *porquerías* (filth). The *nixtamal* water used to soak and wash maize before milling is thrown out in his backyard. This dirty water becomes putrid when exposed to the sun's heat. By these accounts, Don Chano's shameless efforts to feed his greed, via increasing production of *masa* and tortillas, put the welfare of the entire community in danger. While *los de Cancún* elaborate on Don Chano's representation as a greedy man who takes advantage of the poor *milperos, los Antiguos* promote his reputation as a good Catholic and provider of maize in times of scarcity.

In sum, Don Chano's enemies deluge him with an inexhaustible torrent of abuse in their conversations. The political and economic threats that he embodies, particularly for those in power, hasten this outpouring of vituperative stories. These narrations are more than entertainment or popular derision; they encapsulate, in the image of Don Chano, the migrants' perception of *los Antiguos* group in the village. Don Chano, with some of his brothers and nephews, works the lands of the Santa Cecilia Ranch. There they keep their cattle, make their *milpas*, and keep bees. The name "Santa Cecilia Rancho" is loaded with connotations for Chan Kom's peasantry. It exemplifies the symbiotic relations among the three principal agricultural activities in Chan Kom: *milpa*, cattle, bees. Maize provides subsistence for people, cattle, and bees: maize flowers feed the bees, and cattle can eat the maize plant after the harvest. Santa Cecilia is also the site of ancient Maya ruins that are visible in the form of big, stony hills. Maya believe that the *alux*[25], a character in Yucatec Maya oral tradition, owns the forest and *milpas*; he lives "where our ancestors lived." These archaeological remains are called *muulo'ob*, and they are always associated with the ancestors. Peasants in Chan Kom think that there are not as many *aluxo'ob* as before; however, Santa Cecilia is still considered their home. A Maya peasant describes the *alux* in the following terms:

> Dicen que el alux son las imágenes de los antiguos de hace tiempo, los antiguos Mayas. Dicen que son sus imágenes, sus santos, son sus dioses de los antiguos. Y ya se murieron los antiguos, las imágenes quedaron, y se quedaron alux. (Narrator: Don Luis, Chan Kom)

> They say that the *alux* are the images of the ancestors, the ancient Maya. They say that they are their images, their saints, they are the gods of the

ancestors. The ancestors have died but their images remained, and they
became *alux*. (Narrator, Don Luis, Chan Kom)

Today *los Antiguos* attribute to the *alux* features comparable to those
of a saint. Most of the traditional group plant *ejido* or communal land;
however, the leaders of *los Antiguos* group are spatially identified with
Santa Cecilia Ranch. Although Santa Cecilia is *ejido* land, it was held first
by Don Epifanio and today by Don Chano and other descendants of Don
Epifanio. Don Epifanio's heirs work this land as if it were their private
property.

A reflection on Los Antiguos in the light of Don Chano's social profile

For *los Antiguos* in Chan Kom, the symbols embedded in both myth
and daily discourse express their views of the social reality; a social reality
divided between the Catholic moral code and the social inequities that
they perceive as a result of "modern influences from the city." For them,
the order of nature depends upon Christ's law, and contrasts with the
domains of Satan that promote chaos. Oral tradition and ritual context
display a variety of cultural symbols, which are actualized and reinterpreted to depict the domain and features of "the other"—the evil, *los de
Cancún*.

Los Antiguos, who controlled the political sphere in the past, express
a world view in which they see their power as limited because of the
current, political competition. Denied their political power, they use symbolic weapons in their propaganda against *los de Cancún*—the representatives of Satan, those who brought *la Política*, the social crisis.

As explained in the previous chapter, the spatial distribution of people can become symbolic of social groups and their interrelationships.
Los Antiguos in Chan Kom live mostly along the eastern side of the plaza.
They have appropriated symbolism associated with the cardinal direction
east to legitimize their social and political actions. In Maya tradition,
lakin (the east) is the sacred corner of the skies; it is the place where
Jesus Christ is reborn every day. The cross is oriented toward the *lakin*
in the shrines used in the *milpa* ceremonies. Christ, sun, and *milpa* are
joined in the meaning of *lakin* and used by *los Antiguos* to assert their
identity as the "true Maya."

Los de Cancún Maya of Chan Kom: Don Lillo,
 a Social Profile

The epitome of *los de Cancún* group in the village is Don Lillo. Don
Lillo, one of Don Eustaquio's older sons, makes his living as a store
owner and by renting out his various properties. That store is a masterpiece of a merchandise pastiche: one can find sandals, bicycle wheels,

shirts, nails, machetes, candy, cookies, potatoes, rice, and so forth. He no longer plants a *milpa* and he sold his cattle a few years ago, in part to pay the expenses incurred in his son's last political campaign. Besides the store, Don Lillo owns several houses in the village. Today, he maintains these houses, sometimes empty, sometimes rented to teachers or government officials. He is used to saying, however, that a house for each of his children's families awaits their return. Someday, he hopes his children will live together again in the village.

A few years ago, during the last presidential term held by Don Chano, the political officials prepared a document that denied *ejido* lands to the migrants working in Cancún. The list included the new political officials elected in 1987. The former officials attempted to dispossess these people, in a legal way, of the most significant source of their identification as Maya: their right to make *milpa* on the *ejido* lands. One of the allegations contained in this document was that these migrants do not live on a permanent basis in the village, and some of them do not have houses there. For *los Antiguos*, a house and *milpa* in the village are the ideological foundations for being Maya, and a member of the community. Don Lillo tried to circumvent the intent of the document, insisting that his properties were to be his sons' and daughters' homes upon their return to the village. The document was declared invalid after a group of migrants complained to the government.

The stories that circulate in the village about Don Lillo concern his lifestyle and his miserliness. He has never ventured into the outside world. I have never seen him more than two steps away from his store. Don Lillo's store is his kingdom, from which he looks out on the world. It seems odd that this shabby, disorganized shop should be the source of Don Lillo's reputation as one of the richest men in the village. The building itself sags under many layers of paint, which are very noticeable where there are holes in the wall. A thick coat of accumulated dirt enhances the darkness of the store's main room. The merchandise is arranged in such a disorderly fashion that Don Lillo often spends several minutes rummaging through piles of clothes or boxes in search of a requested item. Don Lillo contributes to the decrepit atmosphere by his dress; he is often seen without a shirt, in bare feet, a piece of cord holding up his pants. The rumor goes that although he could afford to escape from the *milpero* diet, principally tortillas and beans, he eats nothing else.

Don Lillo's name comes up in any discussion of moneylending and credit practices in the village. Don Lillo maintains a notebook in which he keeps track of his clients' debts. He advances cash, repayable at a fixed interest rate, that sometimes approaches 60 percent. In fact, as some villagers claim, he acquired part of his properties through the failure of clients to pay the high interest. Such moneylending practices are a main cause of the permanent impoverishment of some *milperos*.

Both Don Lillo and Don Chano exemplify, the image of the pawnbroker as a local merchant who trades in a great variety of goods: candles, grain, clothes, and alcohol. The pawnbroker not only makes money by charging an exorbitant interest rate, but also by selling subsistence items to the borrower at elevated prices. These various practices allow the moneylender to rapidly increase his wealth. This economic power adds to his social and political prestige. As Arturo Warman (1988:71) notes, the mexican peasant is caught in an endless cycle: if he produces any surplus, the usurer takes it; if there is no surplus, his debt increases and he is forced to sell his labor as a rural or urban proletarian.

From his store, Don Lillo can see the plaza and observe the movements of the people. His store is the center of activity for *los de Cancún* group. He owns the only video player in the village, and most Saturday evenings, at the same time as the church service, he shows a movie attended primarily by the weekend contingent from Cancún.

The Modern Uayes

Ellos tienen estudio, solo volar hacen. Pueden ir hasta en Estados Unidos, hasta en México. Van a la ciudad a visitar, se viran y vuelan. ¡Cuando el Uay Kot vuela, uyhh!, ¡si vieras cómo vuela!, como un avión, hasta cuando pasa por aquí, es como si lloviznara. Entonces, cuando se va, buscamercancías en otros lugares. (Narrator: Don Luis, Chan Kom)

They are learned people, they spend most of their time just flying about. They can go as far as the United States, even to Mexico City. They go to the city to visit; they transform themselves and fly. When the *Uay Kot* flies, uyhh!, you have to see how he does it, like a plane, so that when he passes through here, it is as if it was drizzling. Then, when he goes, he looks for merchandise in other places. (Narrator: Don Luis, Chan Kom)

When I remarked on the great variety of items available at Don Lillo's store, people's explanations turned to folk stories. More than once, when the issue of Don Lillo's store was involved in the conversation, I was told the story of the *uay kot*. Among the mythological creatures of Chan Kom folklore is the *Uay*[26], a half-human, half-animal character. *Kot* in Maya language means "eagle." Then, the *uay kot* transforms himself into an eagle. Operating via deals with the evil forces, who provide him with incantations, the *uay* is able to transform himself into an animal. The *uay*, like all souls and beings who are not "Christian," wander around the village at night. They enter peoples' homes and handle food, poisoning it. The next day, when the food is eaten, the people become sick and sometimes even die.

The people of Chan Kom always associate the *uay kot* with storeowners and businessmen. Although villagers did not often refer openly to Don Lillo as *uay kot*, they used his description to account for the mystery of a man who never took two steps away from his store and yet enriched himself with such success. This mystery led the people to connect Don Lillo with evil forces that must be helping him to enlarge his economic empire. Don Lillo's reputation as the *uay* of Chan Kom fits well with *los Antiguos'* manipulation of the religious symbolism to criticize *los de Cancún* group. By accusing Don Lillo of intrigue with evil, and by ostracizing him, *los Antiguos* deny him and the migrant group membership in the moral and religious program of the community.

Rumors started by and exaggerated among *los Antiguos* blamed Don Lillo for their not having received their share of food aid sent by the government after hurricane Gilbert. They accused Don Lillo of being a *uay*. They insisted that the location of his store—just in front of the municipal building, where the aid was stored—and the fact that he is the president's father gave him and his family easy access to the supplies. The rumors claimed that Don Lillo transferred items, always at night, to his house-store, then took the goods to Cancún where he or his family sold them.

The amassed capital attributed to Don Lillo inspired other stories that connect him with the fires of hell. These stories concern the origins of his wealth. A long time ago, Don Lillo hired a peasant to do some work in the yard of a house he had just purchased. The worker was digging a hole when he uncovered a large ceramic pot. He opened it and discovered silver and gold coins. The worker hesitated, but eventually decided to tell Don Lillo about the find. Don Lillo's eyes flashed with excitement upon hearing the news. Immediately, however, he regained his composure and explained to the worker that he himself had buried that money a few weeks ago. He compensated the worker with a few pesos and never called on him again.

Los Antiguos believe that anything found buried in the earth belongs to the ancestors. When someone makes a find, part of the treasure must remain buried, and prayers of thanksgiving are required. For *los Antiguos*, Don Lillo violated village ethics by keeping all the money that belonged to the ancestors.

Stories about Don Lillo dominate conversation in the village, particularly during periods of extreme competition between *los Antiguos* and *los de Cancún*; for instance, during the 1990 campaign for the municipal presidency, a torrent of vituperative stories were easy to elicit at any gathering of *los Antiguos*. Don Lillo was always portrayed socially as the epitome of miserliness, responsible for poverty in the village and opposed to Catholicism. For *los Antiguos*, he followed the steps of the devil, and the entire *los de Cancún* group modeled their behavior after him. In contrast to his image of asceticism and his contacts with the evil forces promulgated by *los Antiguos*, however, is the great expense Don Lillo assumes in the celebration of Santa Fátima, for which he and his wife are responsible.

The celebration of La Virgen de Fátima (The Virgin of Fátima): *Los de Cancún's social profile at work.*

> La virgen de Fátima apareció allá, en Fátima, no se, . . . es nombre de México, una ciudad o no se como, . . . Dicen que apareció en un cerro, en una ruina por alla, por México. Es como una persona. La encontraron viva tres muchachos. El 13 de Mayo es cuando apareció; después, los tres muchachos murieron. Es virgen, por eso está vestida de blanco. (Narrator: Don Pil, Chan Kom)

> The Virgin of Fátima appeared there, in Fátima, I do not know, . . . it is a Mexican name, a city, or, I do not know. . . . It is said that she appeared on a small hill, in a ruin there, in Mexico. She is like a person. Three boys found her alive. The 13th of May she appeared. After that, the three boys died. She is a virgin, because of that she is dressed in white. (Narrator: Don Pil, Chan Kom)

Following the day of the Holy Cross, the next major religious celebration in Chan Kom is May 13, the day of Santa Fátima. People began to venerate Santa Fátima very recently, probably under the influence of the last missionary campaigns in the area.

Although both are female symbols in the Catholic-Maya pantheon, the Holy Cross and Santa Fátima have different meanings. Those who own a cross usually know stories of how the cross was found. In most of the tales, as Don Chano explains, the *milpero* is working in the field and miraculously finds the cross next to a tree, or hidden in a cave; sometimes it is the draft horse that inexplicably leads the *milpero* to the cross.

As Raimundo, the principal *maestro cantor* of the community states, "the cross is holy because Jesus Christ died there, and he left it to us, to remember him and his sufferings on the earth." The cross is present in any kind of ritual related to the cyclical agricultural or Catholic calendars. It is always placed first, at the center of the altar. Sometimes, the cross is dressed with a *huipil*, the female indigenous dress. In contrast, the imagery associated with Santa Fátima is much closer to the Catholic paraphernalia more common among the *dzulo'ob* (whites) cultural system: the image of a white virgin, covered by a long and elaborate white dress. Santa Fátima's images are usually bought in the city or from merchants who sporadically pass through Chan Kom.

The *novena* for Santa Fátima begins on May 5, at the home of Don

Lillo. This occasion is one of the few opportunities during the year when all Don Lillo's children are able to leave their businesses and jobs in Cancún to return to the community and participate in the family's celebration. Most of Don Lillo's sons and daughters left the village at a very early age; some of them did not even finish elementary school in Chan Kom. Today his children are small entrepreneurs. When they talk about how they created, developed, and nurtured their economic and social position in the city, they do not hesitate to point out the initial hardships and sufferings they endured. They are the first generation of young Maya to migrate to Cancún. As pioneers, they created a "civilized" space, a tourist center, from the hostile, wild forest that was Cancún twenty years ago. They were the construction workers whose hands built the hotels admired by tourists today.

The big-celebration day of Santa Fátima is May 14. Don Lillo has adjusted the date to coincide with the weekend, in order to accommodate his children's schedules. He is severely criticized by *los Antiguos* for changing the religious festival to suit his convenience.

This weekend, the climax of the festivity, Don Lillo has plenty of hands to kill the pigs, chickens, and turkeys—the basic meat ingredients for the *relleno negro*. He has enough men to dig the *pib* and make *chicharra* (pork rind). The women have already burnt the *chile*, which flavors and gives the black color to the *relleno negro*.

Chan Kom is very crowded that weekend. All Don Lillo's sons and daughters, with their wives, husbands, and children, have returned to the village. Also, many of the president's followers, who work in Cancún, come with their families. The women, dressed in the latest fashion— high-heeled shoes, permed hair makeup on their faces— attract the glances of both the men and women of the village. The men, by their dress—the latest fashion sneakers, colorful T-shirts, and jeans—advertise themselves as "men from the city." Obviously, they want to differentiate themselves from the village *Antiguos*, who wear ordinary blue pants, simple shirts, and *huaraches* (sandals). They present themselves as men who favor modernity and progress. Most of Don Lillo's relatives from Cancún arrive around noon on Saturday. The *prestados* for the ceremony have killed and butchered the pig at sunrise. The men are in charge of *la chicharra*, while the women prepare the beans and tortillas. This time, the women do not have to be at the *comal* for too long; someone brought ready-made tortillas from Cancún. Men dig the *pib* where, late in the afternoon, the big pots with the *relleno negro* will be buried and left to cook until the next morning. Don Lillo's daughters and daughters-in-law bring purified water and special food items from Cancún for their children. They are accompanied by non-Maya maids who supervise the children throughout the day.

The next day is Sunday, the day of the celebration. Just at sunrise, the strains of the Mexican song *Las Mañanitas*[27] fill the village. Don Lillo's sons have hired a band from Cancún to play a serenade to honor their mother and the Virgin of Fátima. This is not customary in Chan Kom for the celebration of any saint's day festivity.

The *pib* is opened and the *relleno negro* carried to the altar at Don Lillo's home. The food is placed before the image of the Virgin of Fátima in order to be blessed. Most of the objects on the altar are brought from Cancún: postcards with scenes of the beach; a big clock that turns color alternately from red, to green, to white, the Mexican flag colors; Christ-

(Description of the altar) Most of the objects on the
altar are brought from Cancún. The image of the virgin
is flanked by flowers brought directly
from Cancún.

mas lights on the wall; four white-red-green garlands hang from the upper part of the altar. The image of the Virgin, covered by a fancy white dress and lace veil, is flanked by dozens of flowers, white gladioli and tuberoses, brought directly from Cancún. At the top of this monumental altar, stretching from the wall to the ceiling, is the national flag. The red, green, and white of the national flag and the PRI, coordinate all the ceremonial paraphernalia.

Once the *novena* is over and the ritual food blessed, the plates with the *relleno negro* are served at the table and bottles of beer are distributed among the men. One of Don Lillo's relatives in the village has opened a *cantina* recently and the beer is his contribution to the celebration.

As a special guest, I am invited to sit at the table with the men. The men are discussing a note to the president from officials in Mérida. The PRI plans to send a representative to the village in the next few days to get peasant signatures for support of governmental development programs in the area. The men are considering the demands they will present to the PRI authorities in exchange for Chan Kom's support. Don Casiano, one of the president's elderly uncles, is at the table. At a very early age he had filled in as village leader for his father, Don Eustaquio. Improvising a speech, Don Casiano expresses his opinions in the following political diatribe:

> Mi papá, Don Eus, fundó este pueblo. Desde el comienzo el PRI le ayudó. Primero abrieron el camino blanco, después se hizo la carretera, se puso electricidad . . . Así fue prosperando, así vamos hacia el progreso. Fuimos y seguiremos siendo del PRI (Narrator: Don Casiano, Chan Kom)

> My father, Don Eus, founded this village. Since the beginning, the PRI helped him. First, they open the white road, then, the paved road was built, electricity was installed . . . That was the way to prosperity, that is how we are going toward progress. We were and we will continue being PRI. (Narrator: Don Casiano, Chan Kom)

To celebrate, the men will drink all day long. Some Maya women will not expect their husbands to return home until late at night. Some of the men will get involved in fights, and some will get hurt. Alcohol, beer, shouting and yelling, and loud cumbia music will fill the plaza that night. Some of Don Lillo's guests will leave for Cancún that evening; others will wait until they recover from their hangovers.

Saints as expressing forces of competition

May 15 is the celebration of San Isidro Labrador in the Catholic calendar. San Isidro Labrador is the patron saint of the *milperos* in Yucatán.

San Isidro Labrador es un trabajador, es lo que llaman honal santo porque tiene que trabajar, tiene su xul, su calabaso . . . todo tiene . . . tiene hasta su mazcab . . . Cuando llega el día 15 tiene que llover pa' que siembre uno. (Narrator: Don Pil, Chan Kom)

San Isidro Labrador is a worker, he is called *honal Santo* because he has to work; he has a digging stick (the *xul*), a water gourd (*chuh*), . . . his machete (*mazcab*) . . . When the 15th of May comes it has to rain in order to seed the fields. (Narrator: Don Pil, Chan Kom)

Don Pil, a very strong defender of *los Antiguos* group, traditionally holds this celebration at his house. In any saint's day celebration, the offerings are cooked one day in advance. Because Don Lillo has postponed the celebration of the Virgin of Fátima saint's day until May 14, the two celebrations are going on simultaneously. As *los Antiguos* gather at Don Pil's home to kill the pigs and to eat *chicharra, los de Cancún* enjoy the *relleno negro* at Don Lillo's. Once again the two competing social forces are spatially separated in the village; this time, the division is expressed in a ritual context.

The continuing lack of rain following these May celebrations increases anxiety among the peasants. It seems that the gods are angry at their children. Soon, conversations turn pessimistic, stating the futility of planting the *milpas* this year. A spirit of defeatism and a resignation to the "time of punishment" permeate the village. The approach of the year 2,000 is also cited as a factor contributing to the general feeling of chaos.[28]

El problema es que hay muchas cantinas, mucho crimen allí, en México, en todas partes, mucho vicio, y fumar mariguana, ahorita el Presidente de México esta pendiente de agarrar el contrabando de mariguana . . . Es que va a acabar el mundo cuando llegue el 2,000; solo Jesús sabe lo que va a pasar. (Narrator: Don Max, Chan Kom)

The problem is that there are a lot of cantinas, a lot of crime there, in Mexico, everywhere, a lot of vice, and smoking marijuana; now, the Mexican president is anxious to catch the marijuana contraband in the country . . . The world is going to end when the year 2,000 comes; only Jesus Christ knows what will happen. (Narrator: Don Max, Chan Kom)

Los Antiguos assert their Maya identity by invoking the Holy Cross, which they consider a Maya peasant saint. *Milpa* symbolism distinguishes them from the opposing group, *los de Cancún*. Partly in response to criticism by *los Antiguos, Los de Cancún*, make constant efforts to create and demonstrate their self-representation of Maya. They try to show that they also deserve divine protection, by continuing to venerate the saints through *novenas*. They overcompensate, however, in their efforts to overcome their public image as betrayers of their own tradition. Alterations in the traditional ritual paraphernalia—fancy flowers, displays of other so-called "luxury" items on the altar, incorporation of *Las Mañanitas* into the celebration— all are assertions of their self-representation as "más verdaderos Mayas" (more true Maya) than *los Antiguos*. *Los de Cancún* seek public recognition as "true Mayas" by openly flaunting the glamour of their economic and political power. This public display by *los de Cancún* catalyizes *los Antiguos* reaction; the latter resist a political power that they consider foreign, as well as an economic power fostered by prostituting the Maya labor force to outsiders.

Conclusion: Milpa, *The Sacred and Profane of Maya Identity*

The above descriptions acknowledge two different ways to assert control over the community. These vivid and accessible examples of everyday life expose the socioeconomic and religious contexts in which different models of community and identity and different ways of experiencing a subordination/domination relationship are negotiated. The stories that circulate in Chan Kom about Don Chano and Don Lillo are an effective propaganda for the construction of the bifurcated Maya identity in the community.

The social reality of the community, as viewed through my account on the oral compositions, presents a social dichotomy. As the notions of "opposition ideology" (Schimmer's) and "separatism" (Warren's) imply, it seems that in this self-representation of Chan Kom, the scenario is overrun by two social groups whose endeavor is the construction of different identity choices.

Los de Cancún, because they control the political offices, assert a dominant position over *los Antiguos*. The majority of the village population, however, are on *los Antiguos'* side. *Los Antiguos* focus on the symbolic, social, and economic levels of the *milpa* system to define "true Mayaness." The definition of Maya identity in these terms immediately places *los de Cancún* as outcasts who now are devoted to other economic activities centered on money. *Los Antiguos'* attempt to deny *los de Cancún* their ethnic identity serves as a mechanism for *los Antiguos* to surmount their own subordinate political position.

Unlike the case Scott (1973) analyzes, Chan Kom's social dualism is not a struggle between rich and poor. Rather, the representations of Don Chano and Don Lillo reveal a community caught in a competition between the powerful, elite, social groups who are struggling for political control of the community.

The socioeconomic context that ignites efforts to create an ideological separation between *los Antiguos* and *los de Cancún* is the confrontation between two types of Maya wealth: those whose wealth is invested in cattle and private land in the village, and those who are rich in liquid assests mostly obtained from wages and business in Cancún. *Los Antiguos'* accumulation of capital is portrayed as more in harmony with nature: "tenemos ganado, tenemos *milpa*, tenemos abejas" (we have cattle, we have *milpa*, we have bees). Their investment in material goods is principally in tools and other equipment related to this tripartite economic activity. On the other hand, *los de Cancún*, with their accumulated capital in cash, invest in the creation of business and in building their own houses in the city. As the new political officials show, this group's propaganda consists of publicly demonstrating that they have the economic power to assert their already achieved political power. With their liquid assets, they can buy the pigs necessary to perform the *novenas*; they can pay musicians to sing *Las Mañanitas* to the Virgin; they can pay the *h-men's* services in the Maya rituals. This deliberate demonstration of their economic strength seems intended to prove their right to political power. *Los Antiguos* react to this display of wealth and political power by emphasizing their adherence to the traditional Maya way of life. The ability of humans to "virarse de" (transform themselves), applied in the Yucatec folklore to the *Uay*, is recorded in ancient as well as contemporary Mesoamerican traditions. The significance of "transforming man into an eagle" (*Uay Kot*) in Chan Kom lies in the capacity of *los de Cancún* to transform themselves into a political and economic threat to those who formerly held power.

In the celebration of the *novenas* of the annual ceremonial cycle, ethnicity is again used to justify each group's position in the community. The civil-religious hierarchy and offices are under the jurisdiction of the local *Antiguos*, though they are directed by the Catholic priest who does not live in the village; the priest comes every Saturday from Valladolid for the religious service. For *los Antiguos*, Catholicism is the flag that unifies those "true Mayas." They also consider other Maya rituals (such as devotion to the *milpa*, or to curing illness) to be part of the Catholic religious code, even though these rituals are performed by the *h-men*. The celebration of ceremonies, whether within the Catholic Church or not, is, for *los Antiguos*, a reinforcement of ties to the ancestors. *Los Antiguos* consider themselves the children of whatever saint they are honoring, in the same way that they are descendants of the guardians of the forest and *milpas*. Making *milpa* shows respect for the ancestors and ensures the protection of the guardian of the land, *el alux*, who *los Antiguos* treat as a saint. *El Rancho de Santa Cecilia* exemplifies *los Antiguos'* appropriation of the *milpa* symbol to link themselves to the ancestral line, to cover their identity with a veil of sacredness, and ultimately to legitimize themselves as "true Mayas."

Once, I was chatting with a migrant Maya enterpreneur who left the village at a very young age to work in Cancún. He accompanied his boss to New York to work in his restaurant for one year. When he had made enough money, he returned to Cancún and established his own business. Today, he is the main leader of *los de Cancún* group. When I asked about his *milpa*, knowing that he had none, he replied: "Nosotros vamos todas las semanas a *la milpa*. Mi campo de trabajo es Cancún, mi *milpa*" (We go every week to our *milpas*. The field that I work is Cancún, that is my *milpa*). While *los Antiguos* invoke the traditional meaning of *milpa* to separate themselves from *los de Cancún, los de Cancún* have extended its meaning into a new context, the urban work place.

As the Chan Kom case shows, when the symbolic system collides with refractory social forces, the potential for change and transformation in the symbolic system increases greatly. This means that symbols do not simply arise spontaneously or that they are just the foundation of a continuing process of redefinition of the symbolic universe. Rather, people endow symbols with power to represent a substantial dimension of the society. Furthermore, as Foucault (1983) suggests, through the manipulation of these ideas and symbols, the powerholders enforce personal and social identities that affect the self's and the other's image. To create, redefine, transform, or recreate a symbol, or, better said, to identify a group, an ethnia, or oneself with a symbol is a way to separate from the so-called "other" (Warren 1989), to oppose the other (Schimmer 1972), or to strive for power (Foucault 1983).

The ideological and political underpinnings of the narratives and rituals examined in Chan Kom present not only a wide range of possibilities to link the individual with the society and the world; they also provide people with the tools and the means to express their different experiences, to produce and perform their different dramatizations of the social reality.

This interpretive analysis of Chan Kom's two worlds shows a collage of conflicting meanings being manipulated by the social actors. However, both social groups use the same symbols and the same strategies to mold the representation of the community as a mirror image of their mutual competing relationship. Both use religious arguments to assert their "Mayaness" and to ostracize the "other." Both are also depicted as the main usurers of the village. Are we then, to conclude that Chan Kom's social reality is as simple as the division between *los Antiguos* and *los de Cancún?*

Chapter 5

From Milperío *to* Pueblo

*Tuvieron que caminar hasta llegar aquí, y
vieron que aquí es puro monte alto, y buscaron un cenote y vieron que podían jalar agua,
y les gustó. Pues aquí hay mucho venado,
mucho jabalí, mucho pavo de monte, mucho
tepiscuente . . . Se fueron a Ebtún porque allí
vivían ellos, pero otro día vinieron para hacer
sus milpas, y cada uno vió monte para talar e
hizo su milpa. Y llegó el tiempo de la quema y
lo quemaron, el tiempo de la lluvia y empezaron a sembrar sus milpas. Pues les dió bien
año, bien logrado todo, maiz, frijol, macales,
toda semilla que sembraron les dió bien . . .*

*Y dijo el Gobierno:
"Está bien . . . ¿y ya vieron donde?"
"Si, ya es Chan Kom, y ya logramos nuestra
milpa".
"Si, está bien compañeros" —dice el Gobierno
"necesitan ustedes tierra para seguir trabajando hasta hacer un pueblo, que sigan
ustedes mejorando." (Narrator: Don Casiano,
Chan Kom)*

*They had to walk until they arrived here, And
they saw that the monte (forest) is very high,*
And they looked for a *cenote,* And they saw that
they could get water, And they liked it here.
Well, here is a lot of deer, wild boar, wild turkey, peccary . . . They went back to Ebtun, because that was where they were living. But they
came back another day to make their *milpas,*
and each one saw a place in the forest to clear

79

> to work the land. And the time to burn arrived,
> and they burned the fields; the time for rain
> arrived and they began to sow the *milpas*. They
> were given a good harvest, Everything was a
> success, Maize, beans, macales, every seed that
> they grew gave a good yield . . .
>
> And the Gobierno said:
> "It is good . . . Did you see where you want?"
> "Yes, already it is Chan Kom, and already we
> have made our *milpa*."
> "Very well," says *el Gobierno*, "You need the
> land to continue working until you create a vil-
> lage, may you continue to progress." (Narrator:
> Don Casiano, Chan Kom)

The divided Chan Kom social reality in *los Antiguos* and *los de Can-cún*, which is epitomized by the characters of Don Chano and Don Lillo, oversimplifies and masks the complexity of the social relations and the politico-economic motivations of the various social groups within the community. For example, those who are not active members in the competition for political power, and who depend on *milpa* for their survival, are not overtly represented in the dualism of the "we" and "they" categories. This ideological message does not acknowledge the socioeconomic inequalities that exist in the village. This chapter is mainly devoted to bringing those Mayas who do not have direct access to the public sphere from the wings onto the stage in this drama of Chan Kom in crisis. To do this, I present a narration of the foundation and history of Chan Kom. This account is analyzed using my own interpretation of Marxist models of modes of production and employing the concept of *milpa* as a distinctive mode of production, according to which the symbolization of *milpa* work can be manipulated to effect transformations in the social structure and economic system of the community.

So far, the development of this discussion has been guided by the ideological aspect of *milpa*, which stands at the core of the recent formulations of Maya identity. However, *milpa* also embraces an unquestionable economic aspect, which, once it is understood, helps define the ways those formulations are being expressed. During the time I lived with the Maya of Chan Kom, I frequently heard the expressions: "*milpa* es vida pero no da para más" (*milpa* provides a living but nothing more), and "tenemos que hacer la lucha", (we have to struggle). The first expresses the main goal of the peasant farmer: self-sufficiency. The *milpero* will sell only what the household does not consume. And in times of scarcity the products grown and raised by Maya women at the *solar*[29] (chickens, turkeys, pigs, chiles, squash, radishes, and so forth) are sold for money that is spent mainly on necessities (clothing, medicine, school expenses, and the like). The *milpa* satisfies the basic subsistence demands of the household, but it does not generate a surplus that could bring capital accumulation. For this reason, the *milpa* production system is sometimes considered a domestic productive system (Bartolomé 1988; Merrill 1985). The search for economic alternatives to acquiring cash is the struggle referred to in the expression *hacer la lucha.*

What kinds of economic and social phenomena are implied in *milpa* work and production in order to become such a powerful ideological weapon? What kinds of social relations does the *milpa* production promote in the Maya community? In the analysis required to answer these questions, I use the Marxist concept of mode of production because it embodies a complex set of mutually dependent relations between both ideology, as the legitimation of the social inequality, and the set of social relations and productive organization that characterize the economic system. This is not a dogmatic Marxist approach; rather, I concur with Godelier (1972) that Marxist concepts, purged of dogmatism, can illuminate aspects of the social organization, otherwise masked in the ideology. What is described and analyzed here is a look at Chan Kom's political economy, filtered through the conceptualizing of *milpa* as a mode of production. Further, to escape from any risk of falling into the quite common pattern of bringing the Marxist model and applying it to the community case, I use a native version of Chan Kom's history as the mediator between the model and the case. The narration shows how intimately *milpa* work is linked with the historical progression of sociopolitical events in Chan Kom. The storyteller describes Chan Kom's history in three stages; the story begins when Chan Kom is just a scattered seminomadic settlement (*milperío*), and proceeds with the foundation of the village and the first years, during which the inhabitants experienced increasing prosperity. The first stage ends when Chan Kom becomes a *municipio* (township). *La gran problema* (the big problem) is introduced in the second stage of the story. The last stage of the story is the contemporary period. Throughout the story, the Maya once again use the device of personalization to describe influences and pivotal events in their community history. The expression *la gran problema* refers to a religious conflict between the Catholics and the Protestants within the village; stage two ends with the Protestant exodus from the community. The last stage is characterized by the arrival of *la Política.*

This encounter with the past of Chan Kom, which is focused on the development of the *milpa* mode of production, is introduced by the native voice, via narration, and by ethnographic voices, via the literary production regarding Chan Kom. As such, Redfield's ethnographic accounts (1934, 1941) and additional comments from other studies (Goldkind 1965, 1966; Halperin 1975) contribute significant information to this analysis.

Chan Kom, A Milperío

Quiero contar a usted
los primeros hombres que fundaron Chan Kom;
fueron don Eustaquío y don Epifanio.
Esa gente vinieron de Ebtún, cerca de la ciudad de Valladolid.
Allí quitaron por falta de tierra, por falta de *ejido*,
pues ellos allí están trabajando,
pero de repente aumento la población.
Tuvieron que caminar hasta llegar aquí,
y vieron que aquí es *puro monte alto*,
y buscaron un *cenote* y vieron que podían jalar agua,
y les gustó.
Pues aquí hay mucho venado, mucho jabalí,
mucho pavo de monte, mucho tepiscuente . . .

Se fueron a Ebtún porque allí vivían ellos,
pero otro día vinieron para hacer sus milpas,
y cada uno vió monte para talar y hizo su milpa.
Y llego el tiempo de la quema y lo quemaron,
el tiempo de la lluvia y empezaron a sembrar sus milpas.
Pues les dió bien año, bien logrado todo,
maiz, frijol, macales,
toda semilla que sembraron les dió bien.

Y dijeron:
"pues está bueno, así que logramos nuestra milpa,
ya tenemos maiz, pues vamos a hacer casas."

Empezaron a hacer sus casas, como quince o veinte casas.
Pues sigue viniendo gente a hacer su milpa.
Pues ya lo están fomentando Chan Kom así.

Un día dijeron:
"Pues si aquí trabajamos, si aquí hay monte,
pues vamos a venir todos aquí.
Vamos a hacer casas, vamos a sembrar,
a hacer solar, vamos a hacer animales."

Pero cuando supieron la gente de Ebtún
y las autoridades, dijeron:
"No, no vamos a dejar que vaya ese grupo,
porque ya supimos que esa gente que van,

van a hacer su pueblo, Chan Kom,
y eso no nos conviene porque van a jalar más gente".

Y mientras, ellos siguen trabajando.
Supieron que hay leyes para dotar ejido,
pues ya tiene un número para solicitar ejido,
y fueron con el gobierno, Carrillo Puerto.

Y dijo el Gobierno:
"Está bien, les voy a dotar de tierra a ustedes
porque hay ley. ¿Y ya vieron donde?"

"Si, ya es Chan Kom, y ya logramos nuestra milpa".
"Si, está bien compañeros" -dice el Gobierno
"necesitan ustedes tierra
para seguir trabajando hasta hacer un pueblo,
que sigan ustedes mejorando."

Mientras, la gente de Ebtún ya lo supieron, y dijeron:
"No vamos a permitir a ese grupo de gente,
pues se van a separar de nosotros.
Si quieren ser milperío, está bien,
pero no para hacer su pueblo. No lo vamos a permitir."
Y llamaron a las gentes y dijeron
que no tiene derecho a separarse de Ebtún, y dijeron:
"Si no quieren ustedes obedecer,
levantamos a las gentes de Ebtún
y hubimos a quemar a ustedes allá,
ya saben ustedes, que no hagan casas allá;
si hacen que hagan un jacalito no mas,
pero no casas como de pueblo."

Pero la gente sigue haciendo sus casas.
Lo supieron en Ebtún, y dijeron:
"ustedes son desobedientes, rebeldes,
pues vamos a visitarles un día."

Pues llego el día que quieren quemar Chan Kom;
se presentaron en el centro en un momento y dijeron:
"Ustedes, si quieren hacer sus milpas no mas, pueden hacer,
pero casas no permitimos que lo hagan, que sigan en
Ebtún", así dijeron las autoridades.

Fueron a hablar con el gobernador, y se notificó
que esa gente viene a perjudicar a Chan Kom,
y interviene el Gobierno para castigar a los cabecillas.

Pero ellos siguen amenazando con quemar Chan Kom . . .
Mi papá es el lider de Chan Kom, no tiene miedo. Pues
ya vieron que Chan Kom está mejorando, y poblaron.
Xcoptei, Xcalatzonot, Ticimul, Nicteha, San Isidro,

Xbohom y otras comisarías como Xanla . . .
Los Cime y los Pat son las familias más importantes,
que son los cuñados de mi difunto papá.
Pues durante varios años esos dos grupos de gente
se llevaron muy bien, pues eran ellos los cabecillas,
los líderes . . .
Creo que en 1935 ya Chan Kom lleva bien con los demás
pueblos vecinos. Ellos dijeron que están de acuerdo en
formar municipio libre de Chan Kom. Presentaron como
quinientas gentes para crear el municipio. Pasaron un
estudio al Congreso, y el Congreso lo aprobó. Mi
difunto papa fue el primer presidente del consejo
municipal. Desde eso, empezaron a manejar el municipio,
está diendo bien. (Don Casiano, Chan Kom)

I want to tell you the first men that founded Chan Kom;
They were Don Eustaquío and Don Epifanio.
Those people came from Ebtun, near the city of
Valladolid. They left there because of lack of land,
they needed *ejido*, well, they are working there;
But suddenly, the population increased.
They had to walk until they arrived here,
And they saw that the *monte* (forest) is very high,
And they looked for a *cenote*,
And they saw that they could get water,
And they like it here.
Well, here is a lot of deer, wild boar, wild turkey peccary . . .

They went back to Ebtun, because that was where they were living,
But they came back another day to make their *milpas* and
each one saw a place in the forest to clear to work the land.
And the time to burn arrived, and they burned the fields;
The time for rain arrived and they began to sow the *milpas*.
They were given a good harvest,
Everything was a success,
Maize, beans, macales,
Every seed that they grew gave a good yield.

And they said:
"Well, it is good; so we created our *milpa*,
Now, we have maize, let us build houses." They
started to build their houses, something like fifteen
or twenty.
And more people came to make *milpa*.
And in this way, they are creating Chan Kom.

One day they said:
"If this is where we work,

If this is where there is forest,
Then let all of us come to live here.
Let us build houses, let us sow seed, Make our gardens,
Let us raise animals."

When the people from Ebtun and the authorities learned about this,

They said:
"No, we will not allow that group to leave,
Because we know that these people who go,
Are going to create their own village, Chan Kom,
And that does not suit us,
Because more people will follow them."

And meanwhile, they continue working.
They knew that there were some laws to grant *ejido* lands;
They have enough people to request the lands,
And they went to see *el Gobierno,* Carrillo Puerto.

And *el Gobierno* said:
"It is good, I am going to grant you *ejido*,
Because there is the law. Do you know where you want?"

"Yes, already it is Chan Kom,
And already we have made our *milpa*."

"Very well," says *el Gobierno*, "You need the land
To continue working until you create a village,
May you continue to progress."

Meanwhile, the people of Ebtun already knew of this,
And they said:
"We are not going to allow this group of people to separate from us.
If they want to be a *milperío*, that is fine,
But they may not be a village. We won't allow it."
And they called the people and they said,
That they do not have the right to separate from Ebtun.
And they said:
"If you do not want to obey,
We will raise all the people of Ebtun
And we will go and burn where you are;
As you already know,
You are not to build houses there;
If you build something,
Then build a *jacalito* (small straw shack) no more,
But not houses as in a village"

But the people continue building their houses.
This was known in Ebtun, and they said:
"You are disobedient, rebels,
We will visit you one day."

Well, the day arrived that they wanted to burn Chan Kom;
Soon, they appeared at the center of the settlement
And they said:
"You, if you want to make your *milpas*, nothing else, you may,
But houses we will not allow you to build,
Your homes must remain in Ebtun." So the authorities said.

They went to speak with the Governor
And they said that the people from Ebtun came to persecute Chan Kom,
And *el Gobierno* must intervene to punish their leaders.

But they continued threatening to burn Chan Kom . . .
My father (Don Eus) is the leader of Chan Kom at that
time; he is not afraid . . . So they saw that Chan Kom is
improving, and they settled Xcoptei, Xcalatzonot,
Ticimul, Nicteha, San Isidro, Xbohom and other
comisarías like Xanla . . . The Cime and the Pat are the
most important families; they (the Pat) are my father's
brothers-in-law. During several years, these two groups
of people got along well, they were the leaders . . . I
think in 1935 Chan Kom still got along with the other
neighboring villages. They (the villages) said they
were in agreement to form an independent *municipio* of
Chan Kom. About five hundred people presented
themselves to create the *municipio*. They sent a
petition to the Congress, and the Congress approved it.
My late father was the first president of the *municipal
council*. Since then, they began to lead the *municipio*. . . .
(Don Casiano, the eldest of Don Eus's sons, Chan Kom)

In this story, the qualities that make Chan Kom a community are
milpa, houses, and Catholicism, the religion of the village. The prime
motive for Maya to leave Ebtún for Chan Kom was to find land (*monte*)
where they could make *milpa*. In a manner that resembles the biblical
exodus, Don Casiano describes finding the piece of promised land that
will become Chan Kom. Land to make *milpa*, abundance of game to complement the maize diet, and the *cenote* for water—these things constituted the ecological triad for Maya survival at that time. *Milpa* guides the
development of the story: the people go in search of good land to make
milpa; several consecutive harvests convince them to transform the
milperío into a settlement.

The construction of houses in Chan Kom is the significant factor in
the winning of permanent independence from Ebtún. Finally, the abundance of land and the increasing success of maize cultivation encourages
the peasants to petition the state for more *ejido* lands. Don Eustaquio is
endowed with quasi-mythical attributes in this story. He is the promoter

of the *milperío* development; he initiates the relationship with the state; and it is Don Eustaquio who knows that "there were laws" to grant *ejido* land.

The Mexican Revolution reached Yucatán in 1915; with it came the agrarian reform program. The program altered the socioeconomic condition of the peasantry that had been tied to the henequen plantations. The abolition of debt peonage, along with the decline of the henequen industry, drove some peasants to repopulate areas of the peninsula that had been abandoned during the *Caste War*[30] of the mid-nineteenth century. The institution of the *ejido*, in which the peasant community received large tracts of land to be held in common, was established. Peasant households have rights of usufruct to *ejido* land, as long as the land continues in use. *Ejido* lands cannot be sold or rented; however, they can be passed to heirs. Felipe Carrillo Puerto, a leader of the Mexican Revolution, granted large areas of *ejido* land to Yucatán. As Don Casiano puts it, by the concession of *ejido* lands, the government supported the peasants in their assertion of independence from Ebtún. The friendship and close connection between Don Eustaquio, the leader of the community, and *el Gobierno* is fully promoted in the history of the community[31]. Associating with Don Eustaquio with the government ties the influences, actions, and intrusions of the state and the PRI national party into community affairs.

¡Con Milpas y Casas, Ya somos un pueblo!
(With *Milpas* and Houses, We are already a village!)

Since its origins, Chan Kom has participated in a money-based, market economy, mainly through maize production. At the time of Refield's research, in order to obtain cash to buy clothes, salt, sugar, soap, and other necessities, a peasant had to produce twice the corn he needed for subsistence to sell in the market (Redfield 1934:56). If a low price for maize was established by the local market, the peasant preferred to plant less and subsist on surplus from the previous harvest (Redfield 1934:51).

The *ejido* lands, although assigned to each village, are owned by the State. The official that regulates and controls the *ejido* in the community is *el comisario ejidal*, who administers the management of the land. He also requests the concession of land from the National Comittee, and distributes the land among the *ejidatarios*; the amount and quality of the land each household will receive also depends upon his criteria. The land is supposed to be distributed equally (Goldkind 1966:330). By working the *chan kax* (the forest) through a slash-and-burn agricultural system, the *milpero* improves the land and acquires the right of usufruct. The household, comprising a husband, wife, and children, is the unit of *milpa* production and consumption.

Peasants may build their houses on *ejido*, and they have the right to live there for as long as they are considered Chan Kom citizens. In return, they must perform some services for the community. Most of the community's houses were built as a communal activity. This peasant contribution to community labor, *fagina*, is described by Redfield (1934:78) as a mechanism to promote community labor exchange.[32] *La fagina*, administrated by the *comisario*, mobilizes the collective labor of the village for community projects, such as the construction of houses, plaza, and streets. Furthermore, it was established as a requirement for obtaining village citizenship (Redfield 1934:79). Then, the *fagina* service can be considered as a social institution that plays a relevant role in the formation and development of Chan Kom as a community.

The Milperío and the Initiation of the Milpa Mode of Production

> The concept of mode of production calls attention to major variations in political-economic arrangements and allows us to visualize their effect. (Wolf 1988:77).

The concept of mode of production embodies a complex set of mutually dependent relations, mainly guided by the connection between social labor and the way people organize their production. Through social organization, production is regulated, channeled, and distributed. It follows that social organization acquires particular features depending on the quality of those dependent relations.

The establishment of a quasi-nomadic camp in Chan Kom was the first step in the *milpa* production system. *Milpa* work, although family-based, promotes a particular sociopolitical organization based on solidarity and mutual cooperation. The institutions of *fagina* and *ejido* (Halperin 1975:95) are the basis for this cooperative sociopolitical organization. The *comisario ejidal* and president were the offices that controlled the political organization; they were held by members of the Cimé family, the founder family. Data provided by Redfield and Villa Rojas, along with the native narration, indicate that when Chan Kom was just a small settlement, the social relations that characterized it resembled the Marxist notion of domestic community. The domestic community is "the basic cell in a mode of production which is formed by a collection of such communities organized for the economic and social production and reproduction of the specifically domestic relations of production" (Marx 1866:257, in Meillassoux 1975:34). The domestic Maya unit is the core of *milpa* production and consumption. Since this formative *milperío* stage of Chan Kom, Maya had to strengthen their linkage as a social group to react against Ebtún opposition. Independence from Ebtún and the establishment of the settlement became the peasants' goal.

Milpa work, as the productive enterprise which requires the involvement of all members in the family unit, became the economic instrument that fomented the collective involvement of all peasants. Then, it is through *ejido* and *fagina* that the predominantly family-oriented *milpa* system becomes the productive activity that unifies and fosters the solidarity of the group.

In its *milperío* stage, Chan Kom resembled a *milpa*/domestic community; the *milpa* system received most of the producers' energy, and it determined the general social organization to which other economic, social, and political activities were subordinated (Meillassoux 1975:35). The *milpa* system generated a specific social organization based on *fagina* services and *ejido* distribution, both of which led to particular social and political activities.

Within this domestic community, the kinship pattern organized the labor activity in the fields, and it was also used to expand the scope of social and ideological links. The relationship between kinship and labor in the *milpa* was, and still is, mediated by the role that the household (Merrill 1985:307) or the domestic unit (Bartolomé 1988:278) has in the economic production.

Villa Rojas records pioneer family names other than the Cimés in the foundation of the village. Don Casiano, however, metaphorically places the foundation of Chan Kom under the monopoly of his Cime kin. The protagonist, the *cacique* or leader, is portrayed as personally responsible for the settlement's progress. He achieved his leadership by establishing connections with the government through the procedure that grants *ejido* land. He and those relatives closest to him held the *comisario* offices that controlled the communal labor and distribution of communal land. The political and administrative offices soon became affiliated with the privileged membership of "the founding family."

At this first stage of community development, kinship operated at two levels, that of the family or domestic group and that of the political order (Wolf 1982:89). This Marxist, kin-ordered mode of production is not exclusively what characterized Chan Kom at this initial stage. The political power was also being gradually concentrated in the hands of the *cacique*'s family. In the early days, the *cacique* performed the political role of *presidente*, and sometimes, *comisario municipal*, organizing and distributing the *fagina*. Thus, the *cacique* and his family controlled a strategic element in the process of *milpa* production, which they sometimes used for purposes of coercion. With the advent of this relationship, the *milpa* economic production began to resemble a tributary mode of production. Before 1958, Don Eustaquio and his close relatives held the political and administrative position of *comisario ejidal* for successive terms (Goldkind 1966:530). Since the *comisario ejidal* was in charge of *milpa* distribution, the Cimé family had the power to monopolize most of the *ejido* lands (Halperin 1975: 101), which, as I will show, further increased their political and economic status.

Redfield mentions a small accumulation of mercantile wealth, but this wealth could not be considered major capital. Maize that was not consumed by the producers could be taken to the market, to Valladolid or Mérida, and bartered for surplus products from elsewhere or sold for cash. The profit obtained in trade was mostly reinvested in the productive enterprise of *milpa*. This process did not allow the accumulation of capital; it was, however, the prelude to the transformation of those who were associated with mercantile wealth, into those who would control the future political and administrative spheres of the community.

Cattle and Milpa Production: The Advancements of Protestantism

De repente es un pueblo donde vienen los americanos, y dijeron ellos que si quiere la gente hay otra religión, pero si quieren ellos puede ser centro Chan Kom para esa religión. Ellos quieren que todo Chan Kom sea del Evangelio. Vinieron esos, los americanos, me acuerdo, era yo muy chico, que pueden hacer muchas cosas en beneficio del pueblo.

Pero aquí las gentes no estuvieron de acuerdo y se fueron a Xocenpich. Mientras, es la religión de los Pates. Mi difunto papá lo estudió y vió que puede causar problemas y lo dejó, y siguió la religión católica, y hubo un poquito de problema, pero después entendió la gente, y se tranquilizó.

La mayoría respeta al grupo evangélico. Porque me acuerdo que para celebrar Nochebuena, los católicos van a gustar lo que hacen los evangélios, y así hay unión, hay amistad. Y duró muchos años así, pero por la política agraria, dijo el presidente y el comisario ejidal que los evangelios tienen que apoyar también la ganadería. De antes hay mucho ganado aquí en la plaza, y es un peligro.

Y dijo el presidente municipal y el comisariado:
"Bueno, el que quiera seguir sus ganados es libre de todos los cenotes abandonados dentro del ejido. Allí deben llevar sus ganados".

Ese comisario ejidal dice que quiere cumplir las leyes agrarias. Pues dió órdenes el comisario para que toda persona quite su alambrado. Les dió órdenes a esos hermanos de Don Chano para que quiten el alambre. Era yo presidente municipal en ese tiempo. Vinieron los hombres del comisario ejidal y me dijeron que me ponga de acuerdo con ellos. Me dijo:

"Yo gané y soy la autoridad, yo mando por el ejido. Tu eres presidente municipal, y creo que no tienes que ver con el ejido, pero yo quiero ponerme de acuerdo contigo".

Y yo digo:
"Pero eso va en contra de mi papá, que tiene
fomentado Tikincacab, y sus hermanos tienen Santa Cecilia, y hay muchos
ganados allá. No puedo estar de acuerdo
Pues nuestro cargo no tiene que ver con el presidente, nosotros depende-
mos directamente del departamento agrario".

Y yo les digo:
"No, es que yo no me puedo poner de acuerdo
porque ustedes van a crear un gran problema, una división de gentes".

A los cuatro días ellos fueron a quitar los alambres . . . Fuimos con el
ingeniero Cárdenas y dijo que el lo ordenó; dijo que cuando los ejidatarios
formaron el ejido, nunca celebraron asamblea general, nunca celebraron
un acta para que ocuparan las tierras. Pero como esa pobre gente no sabe
leyes, como ven que hay paz, tranquilidad para trabajar el ejido, y un presidente y un comisario ejidal, se les dijo que son libres de ir a mejorar esos
pozos abandonados, pero como no saben, no celebraron nada, todo fue
verbalmente.

Pasamos después con el gobierno y dijo:
"Lástima porque mi gobierno apoya la ganadería, no debieron hacer eso".
Mientras sigue el pleito entre los dos grupos. Yo he dado mi apoyo al grupo
católico y los que tienen el ganado . . . Mientras se engrandece el problema
del ejido y de la religión. Mi papá es el presidente de la Junta de Mejoras, y
pide al gobierno el camino peinado, y el gobierno dice:

"No tengo mucho dinero pero quiero que el camino sea beneficio para
ustedes, para que el pueblo progrese".

Pero ellos hacen maldades para que suspendan los trabajos. Mientras así,
estamos trabajando en la carretera. Pues un día mi difunto papá está reun-
ido con los trabajadores de la carretera, y ellos se están molestando, y
disparan a mi papá, y le dieron solo en la oreja. El grupo de nosotros está
armado también. Esa noche hubo la balacera. Cayó herido ese Don Primitivo, el comisario ejidal, y lo llevaron a Mérida, . . . y vino el Gobierno y
los castigó . . .

Así, el grupo de ellos se desanimó a vivir acá, y se quitaron y se fueron a
Piste y a Mérida. Quedó el grupo del presidente, puro católicos, y así está
viviendo Chan Kom durante mucho tiempo. (Narrator: Don Casiano, Chan
Kom)

Suddenly, this became a village where the Americans wanted to come. And
they said that if the people so desire, there is another religion. If they want,
Chan Kom can be the center for that religion. They want to convert all
Chan Kom to Protestantism. Those came, those Americans came, I remember, I was a child. [They said] they could do a lot of things for the
benefit of the village. But here, the people did not agree, and they [the
Americans] left for Xocenpich. Meanwhile, that is the religion of the *Pats*.

My late father studied it, and he saw that it could cause problems, and he left it, to return to the the Catholic religion. And there were some problems, but then the people understood and things calmed down.

Most of the people are respectful toward the Evangelical group. Because I remember that to celebrate Christmas Eve, the Catholics like what the Evangelicals do, and in that way, there is union, there is friendship. It was like that for many years; but, because of the agrarian politics, *el presidente* and the *comisario ejidal* said that the Evangelicals had to support cattle production. Years ago, there were a lot of cattle running loose in the plaza; and they were a real danger to public welfare.

And the *presidente* and *comisario ejidal* said:
"Well, whoever wants to continue with cattle production can take advantage of the abandoned *cenotes* within the *ejido* lands. They must bring the cattle there."

In this way, Tikincacab, Acanche, and Santa Cecilia were established. They brought the cattle there so as not to cause trouble. There was agreement for this, but the *Pats* do not respect it. They send people to do bad things; meanwhile, the *comisario* supports these things; the *comisario* was an Evangelical. Within the *comisario ejidal* group, that was Evangelical, they appointed the next *comisario ejidal*. Before the assembly got together to name the new *comisario* it was already done; they convinced the people and they won the majority. Then, the new *comisario* of the Evangelical group said that all those works (measures regarding cattle) were not legal, according to the *ejido* laws, for example, all barbed wire fences. Well, they had to take down all those wires. The conflict was joined!

That *comisario ejidal* says that he wants to follow the agrarian laws. He issued orders that everyone had to take down the wires. He gave orders to those brothers of Don Chano that they should take down their wire. I was the *presidente municipal* at that time. The *comisario ejidal* men came and told me to agree with them. He told me:

"I won, I am the authority and I control the *ejido*. You are the *presidente municipal*, and I think you do not have anything to do with the *ejido*, but I want to agree with you."

And I said:
"But this is against my father who has established Tikinkakab, and his brothers have Santa Cecilia, and there is a lot of cattle there. I cannot agree. Well, our office has nothing to do with the president, we depend directly on the agrarian department."

And I told them,
"No, I cannot agree with you, because you are going to create a big problem, a division of the people."

Four days later, they went to take down the barbed wire . . . We went to the engineer, Cárdenas, and he said that he ordered it done. He said that when the *ejidatarios* formed the *ejido*, they never held a general assembly, and they never passed a formal act in order that they should occupy those lands. But since these poor people didn't know law, and since they saw that there was peace, tranquility for working the milpa, and a president and a *comisario ejidal*, I told them they were free to go and improve those abandoned wells (cenotes). But since they didn't know, they didn't formalize anything; everything was verbal. We went next to *el Gobierno*, and said:

"It is too bad, because my government supports ranching, they should not have done that."

Meanwhile, the conflict continued between the two groups. I gave my support to the Catholic group and those who had cattle . . . Meanwhile, the *ejido* problem got worse; also that of the religion. My father is the president of the Improvement Committee, and he asked the government for a graded road, and *el Gobierno* said:

"I don't have much money but I want the road as it will benefit you, so that the town will continue to progress."

But they vandalized the work so that it was suspended. Meanwhile, we were working on the highway. Well, one day my late father was together with the highway builders, and they were getting upset, and shot at my father and they hit him in the ear. Our group was also armed. That night was the shootout. Don Primitivo was injured, the *comisario ejidal*, and they took him to Mérida . . . and *el Gobierno* came, and it punished them
. . .

In this way their group lost interest in living here and they left and went to Pisté and Mérida. The president's group remained, all Catholics, and in this way Chan Kom has lived for many years. (Narrator: Don Casiano, Chan Kom)

Redfield refers to four or five enterpreneurs who started promoting progress in the village. According to Redfield, they were initiating an endless process towards progress by introducing private *ejido* holding (1950:57–58). Based on Redfield's and Villa Rojas' data, Goldkind demonstrates that there is a minority group that cultivates above the subsistence level in order to get a profit (Goldkind 1965:867). Goldkind's analysis shows that the four or five families considered the wealthiest in the village belonged to the same patrilineal group. The Cimés are the most active of this group. They were relatives of the administrators of the *ejido* system. These enterpreneurs were slowly aquiring control over the most fertile lands with nearby *cenotes*. According to Goldkind, Don Eustaquio claimed to have permission to take private, permanent possession of these *ejido* lands and pass them on to his heirs.

Goldkind observed the increasing socioeconomic differentiation in the village by the way people used the terms "rich" and "poor." "Poor" is a synonym for *milpero*, the peasant whose subsistence depends primarily on maize cultivation." "The rich" are those who have cattle, who are engaged in the buying and selling of grain, hogs, and cattle.

The Cimé family owned by far the most cattle. As the cattle increased in number, so did complaints about damaged *milpas*. Until the 1950s, the law in Yucatán favored the ranchers. It was the responsibility of the *ejidatarios-milperos* to build fences around their fields; fences of sufficient height and strength would prevent the cattle from entering the *milpa*. Since *milpas* rotate through a fallow phase as part of the slash-and-burn agricultural pattern, this requirement was completely unrealistic. Most *ejidatarios* did not fence their fields, and crops continued to be destroyed. In sum, through the action of the Cimé family, most of the Chan Kom families were deprived of direct access to the best *ejido* lands, and were restricted to the worst lands; they also received no compensation for damages caused by cattle in their *milpas*.

In the development of social stratification, the institution of *la fagina* performed a significant role. As Bonfil (1962:109) points out in his study on Sudzal, an *ejido* north of Chan Kom, *la fagina* is the main instrument used to control and exploit the peon (peasant laborer). *La fagina* obliges the peasant to work without payment. Don Eustaquio was the *cacique* and controlled the political and administrative forces of the community (Goldkind 1966:355). "His conception of his relations to the people of the village is formed on this pattern: he is the wise father; they are the dutiful children" (Redfield and Villa Rojas 1934:213). The political instrument this "good father" used to indoctrinate his children was the institution of *fagina*; through *fagina*, he judged the contributions of each of the peasants to the welfare of the community. It follows that *la fagina* could be used as a mechanism to prevent those of lower status from achieving more prestige, thereby simultaneously reinforcing the political power, social prestige, and economic position of those in control of the political institutions (Halperin 1975:109; Goldkind 1966:336).

The *cacique*'s ability to control the distribution of communal land and labor led to an escalating process of social stratification in the community. The *cacique* had the power to control the *milpa* production of the poor peasantry. His control of land distribution assured that his own family received the most productive lands and the land in closest proximity to the village. The poor peasant had to invest time walking to distant fields; he was assigned the worst fields, stony with thin soil, that remained after the distribution among the elite of the best *milpas*. By manipulating labor through the fagina, the elite could control the *milpero*'s labor investment in the field. If the peasant was obliged to devote a certain number of hours to communal service, he had less time to invest in his *milpa*. The elite used these mechanisms to affect the *milpa* production of the *milpero* so that the poor peasant could never reach the level of capital accumulation. For the poor, economically and socially confined to the "wings of the stage" in this political drama, *milpa* continues to demand most of the household's productive energies and provide most of its resources. *Milpa* does not need abundance of capital to secure subsistence; its drawback is that no matter how well the peasant works, he cannot achieve a higher standard of living. Furthermore, if drought, a hurricane, or some other ecological disaster occurs, the *milpero* is forced either to hire himself out at a low wage to the elite in the village or to migrate. When the poor peasant is faced with circumstances requiring a cash expenditure, he is forced to borrow money from these same elite, hoping that the next harvest will cover his debt. The patron and the usurer are usually the same person. The patron helps the peasant to survive by providing wages and loans. In turn, he demands loyalty from those who fall under his protection. The patron expects that the poor *milperos* will assist in the completion of elite ritual obligations (as *los prestados*, which literally means "borrowed people") and remain loyal clients of his store.

The founding families of the village, those who first settled in the Chan Kom area—the Tamays, the Pats, the Caamals, and the Cimés—constituted the high-status families in the village. By the decade of the 1940s, after Chan Kom was recognized as head of an independent township, the Cimés' political and economic control over the village had eclipsed that of the other families. The peasants were mainly devoted to securing their own survival by growing *milpa*. They looked to other high-status families for political leadership to oppose the Cimés. In turn, the majority of *milperos*, the poor, helped these leaders to win political offices. Thus, a member of the Tamay family became *municipal president* in 1947 and a Pat became *comisario ejidal* in 1958. It was during Primitivo Pat's office as *comisario ejidal* that "la gran problema sucedió" (the big problem happened). People today refer to this conflict, perceived as a religious confrontation between Protestants and Catholics, as the starting point for their current social maladies. Let me briefly summarize the history of the advance of Protestantism in Chan Kom.

"La Gran Problema Vino Cuando Esos Cabrones Quisieron Quitar Nuestra Religión" *(The Big Problem Came When Those Bastards Tried to Take Away Our Religion). (Don Juanjo, Chan Kom)*

In Don Casiano's account of Chan Kom's origins, there is a symbolic triad that codifies the qualities of pure Chan Kom Maya: the *milpa* generates the economic, social, and political relations; a *house* represents residency and membership in the community; and finally, *Catholicism* legitimates the religious code of community life (all the original inhabitants of Chan Kom were Catholics).

Catholic purity was threatened when the road to Chichen Itzá was opened and Protestant evangelical missionaries began to proselitize in Chan Kom. In Don Casiano's account, the invasion of the missionaries is associated with "cuando llegaron los americanos" (when the Americans came). These Americans were a group of scholars sent to Yucatán by the Carnegie Institution, in the 1920s and 1930s, to undertake interdisciplinary research studies. At that time, Yucatán was perceived by the larger world as a research laboratory that attracted not only archaeologists, botanists, biologists, and anthropologists, but also the missionaries of a different religion.

When the missionaries first arrived, the whole community, except the Tamay family, converted to Protestantism. As Halperin (1975:110) points out, the Protestant ethic, based on asceticism and hard work, greatly helped Don Eustaquio's efforts to get people involved in community works. As time went on, however, the Pat family, enemies of the Cimé since the foundation of the village, became the main members of the directive council of the new religion. Saints' festivities were prohibited; *jaranas*—a popular dance, generally associated with the celebration of the community fiesta—and other kinds of dances were also prohibited. A lifestyle of austerity was established.

To succeed in its efforts to transform Chan Kom into the *cabecera municipal*, head of an independent township, the Cimé needed the support and collaboration of the neighboring Catholic Maya settlements. The Protestant ethic prohibited the villagers from attending fiestas and dances in the neighboring communities. Within the context of the peasant lifestyle, these kinds of events represented for the Maya the chance to establish social and political connections. The old enmity between the Pats and the Cimés reappeared; the Cimés converted back to Catholicism.

The religious division of the community was exacerbated by the various existing networks of social allegiance maintained by the Pats and Cimés. This religious and social division was also tied to the emerging source of wealth, cattle raising. As individuals accumulated animals and increased their earnings, they started improving the tracts of *ejido* land with watering systems and fencing. Because of this investment, they regarded these *ejido* lands as private property. By 1940, according to a new law, all cattle had to be fenced in. This restricted the economic initiatives of small cattle owners because of the expensive cost of fencing. Further, while the *ejido* comission prohibited the fencing in of communal lands in most of the neighbouring villages, Chan Kom decided to allow the fencing. Consequently, the *ejido* lands that were fenced belonged to those who could sell cattle to purchase the fence. The small cattle owners opposed the fencing of the land. At the end of the 1950s, Chan Kom was preparing to elect a new *comisario ejidal*. Don Primitivo Pat was elected, in spite of Don Eustaquio's efforts to maneuver one of his own sons into the office. Don Primitivo, besides being one of the favorites of the Protestant missionaries (Redfield 1950:94), had the support of the poor *milperos*. Most members of the Pat family were small cattle owners. Don Primitivo, familiar with the *milperos'* complaints over the invasion of the cattle, favored a new plan for a common *ejido* pasture.[33] The Cimés, however, refused to withdraw control over *ejido* land that they had already fenced. Today's accounts of "la gran problema" accuse Don Primitivo Pat of ordering his men to destroy the fencing around sections of the *ejido* controlled by Don Eustaquio and Don Epifanio, "the heads of Chan Kom." Don Eustaquio reported the misdemeanor in Mérida; policemen came and arrested the Pat men. The Cimés, however, wanted more revenge, because they had not received compensation for damages.

Don Casiano's account refers to an event called *"la balacera"* (the shooting) in the Chan Kom community. *La balacera* was an open confrontation between the Cimés and the Pats, the Catholics and the Protestants. What still fires peoples' memories of these events is the fact that it was a religious battle. The heretic enemy, *el Evangelio* (Protestantism), represented by the Pat followers, was defeated in the battle. According to the present accounts, the "children of God" won. The Pat people followed a well-worn path for those who had contested the *cacique's* authority— ostracism and migration. Most of them settled in Pisté, the major closest Maya town, located on the Mérida-Cancún highway, one kilometer away from the archaeological site of Chichen Itza. The poor, who had placed great hopes in the election of Don Primitivo Pat, saw their interests subordinated.

In sum, either through *la fagina*, used as a mechanism of social control, or by actual or threatened violence, the wealthy kept their economic and political control. The Pat family, the competing high-status social group, manipulated the existing socioeconomic inequality in the village to contest the political control held by the Cimé, the *cacique's* family. These were the two groups competing for power. The political and economic schism was, however, masked by a religious confrontation between Protestants and Catholics.

Conclusion: A Religious Discourse for the Milpa Mode of Production

After the foundation of the village, Chan Kom underwent various transformations in social relations and labor expenditure; it also became increasingly involved in a process of social differentiation. Within this process, *milpa* stood for the economic activity that unifies everyone, because every household, in one way or another, depended upon *milpa* for survival. The *milpa* mode of production went through considerable modifications up to the occurrence of "la gran problema." Initially the *milpa* mode was characterized by communal cooperation in working the land, building the houses, and organizing village life; these are the features that resemble the kin-ordered mode of production required for *milpa* production. According to this model, Chan Kom was an extended family, but soon the patriarchs of this big extended family began to take over the development of political and administrative institutions. The Cimé family, these patriarchs and their closest relatives, channeled the communal work toward the development of the village's infrastructure through the manipulation of *fagina*. They took the first step in the local connection with the government. The long dialogue between the community and the state (*el Gobierno*) invoked a national political slogan of progress and modernization, a rhetoric adopted by the Cimé to promote their social and political prestige. In fact, this dialogue, under the guise of progress, was supported by a platform of patron-client relationships. As a result, the community received government assistance for improvements and development (for example, the concession of *ejido* land, the recognition of Chan Kom as a township, the road to Chichen Itzá in 1932). In turn, the state-institutionalized party now demands the peasants' support in political elections. The seeds for the local/state dialogue are ingrained in Chan Kom's origins and in the development of the *milpa* mode of production in the community. The terms, agreements, and rhythms of future Chan Kom/government exchanges depend upon these initial dialogues. *El Gobierno* will assert its influence over and will make demands on the community through those individuals and families with whom it has conversed in the past (that is, the patriarchs, the elite, the rich). As Goldkind states, "as often occurs in a stratified community, the wealthiest were able to mobilize sufficient political power to overcome any serious resistance to their economic and political dominance" (1966:341). In this process of increasing centralization of political and economic power, the state plays an important role by supporting and encouraging the elite's demands for "progress", in exchange for its interferance in the community political life.

At first, *milpa* was the reason for migration from Ebtún, and the motivation for collective efforts to create a permanent settlement. The gradual process of social differentiation proceeded through positive exchanges between the sociopolitical power to control the distribution of land and labor, and the economic resources to gain social prestige and effect political control. Under this system, the economic activities of poorer Maya were restricted to *milpa* production. These poor Maya, kept in economic poverty, are socially immobile, with neither the economic nor the political power to challenge the acts of the wealthy. Their main strategy to oppose the *cacique* is to take advantage of sociopolitical divisions among the elite, by forming a political alliance with the elite enemies of the *cacique* who are Protestant. The *cacique*'s group, Catholics, believed the defeat of the Protestants was proof that God was on their side, and they used this proof of their righteousness to attempt to mobilize the peasantry in their favor.

Chan Kom was born as a split from Ebtún; the daughter community was born out of conflict with the mother community. It is likely that most of the original settlers of Chan Kom, who years ago were considered rebels by Ebtún because they created the daughter community through their voluntary exodus to seek better land, had to suffer another exodus from Chan Kom in the 1950s because of ostracism. Those opposed to the interests of the high status group, the Cimé, followed the migration pattern to resolve the internal village schism. This schism had deep roots in the clash of economic interests between the *caciques*, cattle owners, and the emergence of an entrepreneur social group. The final reading of the social problem in religious terms was the transcendental ideological tool appropriated by the *caciques* to combat the competitors, perceived as betrayers of the community's foundational faith, Catholicism. As such, Chan Kom gave birth to another daughter community that got dispersed throughout neighbouring villages. In this case, however, their reason for leaving was their defeat in the battle for political control of the community. In this battle, religion was the provider of the ideological weapons used in the confrontation. This would not be the last time that Chan Kom Maya would resort to migration to resolve internal conflicts that are disguised in a religious context.

Chapter 6

Social Diversity in Chan Kom's Milpas

*Ahora trabajo en mantenimiento, en la "Auto-
mobil Caribe". Es una compañía grande donde
se venden coches de primera, coches de categ-
oría. Ahí esta seguro el sueldo . . . Tengo milpa,
pero pago para que me lo hagan. Si, todo pa-
gado lo hago. (voz de los "nuevos ricos" emigrantes en Cancún)*

*Actually, I am working in the maintenance de-
partment of the "Automobil Caribe." It is a
large company that sells first-class automobiles. Here, I have a permanent job that guarantees my salary . . . I have a* milpa, *but I pay
someone to take care of it. Yes, every thing is
paid for. (This is the voice of the "new rich"
migrants to Cancún)*

*Aqui damos trabajo a los pobres. Algunas veces
empleo a algunos trabajadores para que me
tumben el monte; les doy la asistencia y les
llevo la comida. Siempre doy trabajo a los que
lo necesitan. (voz de los "capitalistas rurales")*

*We offer some jobs to the poor. Sometimes I
hire some workers to clear the forest; I give
them a sort of salary and I bring them some
food. I always offer jobs to those who need it.
(This is the voice of the "rural capitalists")*

*Esto es un servir al pueblo (el narrador se re-
fiere al cargo de presidente de la comunidad).
Cuando salí de Chan Kom yo no tenía nada,
pensé salir para buscarme la vida para ver si*

100

*yo puedo lograr algo que es mío, con mi es-
fuerzo, sin la ayuda de mi papá . . . Salí de
Chan Kom porque no veía resultados de la
milpa, pues si no hay lluvia no se puede hacer
nada y me decidí a salirme pa' trabajar, pa'
buscar lo económico, para sobresalir . . . Fui
hasta los Estados Unidos . . . Los chavos de acá
que trabajan en Cancún tienen sus patrones, y
no pueden dejarlo, pero en mi caso, yo estoy
libre, tengo mi tienda, mi negocio . . . Yo también invierto aquí [Chan Kom], tengo mis ga-
naditos, mi ranchito, y doy dinero a mi papá
para que pague la milpa . . . Cancún lo tengo
como mi campo de trabajo, como mi milpa, no
más. Voy, trabajo y regreso. (voz de la nueva
burguesía originada entre los emigrantes de
Cancún)*

*This is a service for the community (he refers
to the office of president in the community).
When I left Chan Kom I did have nothing; I
thought of leaving to earn my own living, to
check if I could get something by myself with
my own effort, without my father's help. I left
Chan Kom because I did not see any benefit
from the* milpa *; if there is no rain, you cannot
do anything. And I decided to leave seeking
prosperity . . . I went to the United States . . .
The youth who work in Cancún, they have
their patrons, and they cannot leave it (he refers to their jobs); I have my store, my business
. . . I also invest here (he refers to Chan Kom),
I have cattle, my ranch and I give some money
to my father to pay for the* milpa *. . . Cancún
is like my field work, like my* milpa, *that is. I
go, I work and I return here. (This voice is
from the new bourgeoisie originating among
the Maya migrants in Cancún)*

*Yo solo tengo milpa, así también mi papá.
Estoy acostumbrado a sacar el* saca' *en la
milpa para los* yuntziles *que traen la lluvia.
Eso viven nosotros aquí. El santo elote es toda
la vida, es grande de comida. Nosotros no tenemos dinero, pero tenemos elote. Cuando
haiga santo elote es para el otro año y sem-*

*bramos otro para que haiga otro . . . (voz de
un milpero pobre)*

I only have milpa, *as my father does. I am used
to bring the* saca' *to the milpa for the* yuntziles
*who bring the rain. Those live with us, here.
The holy corn is all of our lives, it is big meal.
We do not have any money, but we have corn.
When there is the holy corn, we have for the
next year,and we plant another in order to
have another. . . . (This voice comes from the
poor* milpero)

*Pues a mí me gustaría vivir aquí [Cancún] por-
que hay dinero, pero en Chan Kom no hay dinero . . . Trabajo de albañil; tengo muchos hijos
con mi esposa; a mí me gustaría traer a mi
mujer en Cancún, pero ni modo, no hay dinero. Por ejemplo, yo no viajé esta semana, pero
envié dinero a mi esposa, una parte se quedó
para mí, para el gasto. (voz de uno de los milperos pobres que trabaja en Cancún temporal-
mente)*

*Well, I would like to live here [Cancún] be-
cause there is money, but there is no money
in Chan Kom . . . I work in construction; I have
many children with my wife. I would like to
bring my wife to Cancún, but, no way!, there
is no money. For example, I did not make a
trip this week, but I sent some money to my
wife; part of it was for me, for my own expenses. (This is the voice of one of the poor*
milperos *who is a temporal migrant in
Cancún)*

*Yo, si hago la milpa no es por dedicarme enter-
amente a ello, sino que si lo hacemos es por
bajarle el terreno a los ganados, lo talamos. Y
da buen resultado, pues además tenemos
maiz, podemos venderlo o conservar para alimento. (Voz de los "nuevos tradicionalistas"
en Chan Kom)*

If I make milpa, *I do not devote all my time to
it, but we do it to clear the forest and to weed
the land for the cattle. And this gives us good*

> *results, since it also provides us with corn*
> *which we can sell or keep for food. (This is a*
> *Maya voice that comes from the "new tradi-*
> *tionalists" group in Chan Kom)*

Up to this point, what we know about present-day Chan Kom is that there is a social schism between those who migrate to Cancún and those who refuse to leave the village. Who are those high-powered individuals, the allies of the *cacique*, today? What relations exist between those who held political control in the past, and the opposing groups existing today? How are the social inequalities, revealed by Chapter 5's historical overview, expressed in the community at the present? A brief account on the connecting events between the recent past, the Protestant exodus, and the present will bring some light to these inquiries.

In the formative stage of Chan Kom as a community, *milpa* could meet both the subsistence and commercial production goals of the peasant households. The need for cash was limited, and the yields from the *milpa* were generally good. Purchases were confined to basic commodities: salt, sugar, coffee, cocoa, cloth, clothing, sandals, shoes, machetes, bullets, thread, and candles (Redfield and Villa Rojas 1934:60). After the disturbances of the Mexican Revolution, while the regional economy was recovering, large commercial *milpas* gradually allowed accumulation of wealth. Redfield and Villa Rojas record the existence of *milpas* larger than 70 mecates (2.8 Has), representing 26% of the *milpas* in Chan Kom; these *milpas* needed to meet the subsistence and exchange needs for the households (Redfield and Villa Rojas 1934:53). With the practice and commercialization of hog-fattening, the household production activities were intensified. This economic practice prevented a peasant from selling the corn immediately after the harvest at low prices. Certainly, the commercialization of hog and *milpa* production, along with the ownership of cattle, intensified the process of social stratification that Redfield records in his final field work on Chan Kom (Redfield 1950), and that Goldkind (1965, 1966) extensively discusses in his later analyses. As a result of this process, the Cimé family emerged as the elite group in Chan Kom. This elite strengthened its political and economic position through political and socioeconomic regional alliances, particularly with the state government (Goldkind 1965, 1966; Dominguez 1980). These local-regional relations brought more demands for cash to the peasant economy. Droughts, declining land fertility, increased population, and the monopolization of some *ejido* lands by a number of elite households, contributed to the decline, by 1940, of *milpa* production (Redfield 1950).

With construction of the graded road that connects Chan Kom with the highway, in the early 1970s, the peasants could bring their products directly to the market. This is the time when the Mexican government undertook several rural development projects financed by the World Bank. Also, peasant migration to urban and tourist centers began at this time (see Elmendorf and Merrill 1977, 1978). The opening of the road created new channels of communication; the easier access to the outside markets facilitated the commercialization of local artesanies (*huipiles*, hammocks), and the possibilities of earning wages via migration to the urban centers. This does not mean that the local/national network was paralyzed before the 1970s. Elmendorf and Merrill (1977: III15–16) mention three previous avenues of communication. One was established in 1944, with the marriage of Don Eustaquio's daughter and Sylvanus Morley's guide/chauffeur. Their house in Mérida became the headquarters for the close Cimé kin group. Don Epifanio, who had been trained by the Rural Cultural Mission in masonry, bought a house in Mérida, opening with this another avenue to the capital. Despite being cofounders of Chan Kom, and members of the same kin group, Don Eustaquio's and Don Epifanio's descendants have developed as different groups since these early times, even in building their social networks with the capital. Today, Mérida is still an urban destination where some individuals, predominantly from Don Epifanio's descendants group, go to persue their high school and college education. A third avenue of communication, this time with Valladolid, comes from the connection via *compadrazgo*[34], with the doctor/gynecologist in Valladolid. Since the 1970s, Valladolid has become the closest urban center where predominately young girls, after finishing their elementary schooling, work as maids, babysitters, and in restaurants and stores. Students also may choose Valladolid as the place to pursue their education; they live with *compadres* and other relatives during the week, and return to Chan Kom during the weekends. A fourth source of outside social networking was promoted by the increasing flow of migrants to Cancún.

Certainly, the 1970s were a decade of great changes in Chan Kom: the establishment of bus service, a cooperative store, an enlarged school, a boarding school, a health clinic, and the introduction of electricity and running water (Elmendorf and Merrill 1978). As the national economic system increased its presence in the community, some of the preexisting strategies for cash production in Chan Kom were intensified (migration, cattle husbandry, artisan activities) and others were improved (for example, honey production) in order to bolster household production. On the other hand, *milpa* became oriented primarily toward meeting the basic subsistence needs of the household.

Within this context of new stress-producing conditions affecting the peasant sector, commercial beekeeping became an important alternate means to obtain cash (Merrill 1985). While *milpa* products had a use value, the products from commercial beekeeping generated an exchange value for the household. By the late 1970s, migration emerged as a competing strategy for cash accumulation (Merrill 1985:298). The village leader, Don Eustaquio Cimé, was getting old. His numerous sons inherited his great fortune based on cattle, private land ownership, and ownership of several masonry houses in the village. These houses are mostly situated at the west, northwest, and south sides of the plaza. By the mid 1970s, Don Epifanio Cimé's sons had taken control of the community's political offices. The descendants of Don Epifanio (the cofounder of Chan Kom) lived along the east side of the plaza. They had accumulated considerable capital, invested in cattle, and, at the time, in the increasingly important beekeeping enterprise. In the meantime, one of Don Eustaquio's youngest sons, Don Alito, lost most of his cattle in a widespread epidemic. He decided to migrate to Cancún to make a new future for his large family. Once he was established in Cancún, his house became the headquarters for his young nephews, who felt attracted to the possibility of progress and independence from the village's labor demands. Today, these people consider themselves the pioneers of Cancún development and the creators of Chan Kom's modern development. Maya men started working as mason's helpers, day laborers; young women worked mainly as maids in the hotels. Old men had easiest access to temporary contract in construction, while old women began to market their embroidery in the hotels[35]. Although these positions are still occupied by Maya migrants, there is a more diversified work opportunity for the migrant laborer today, which I will address later in this chapter. By 1980, Cancún was attracting increasing numbers of not only male, but also female villagers, mainly from among the younger Maya generations.

Chan Kom already had a history of migration. The community itself was born from the womb of Ebtún in the 1920s. And during its development, Chan Kom established umbilical cords with Mérida, Valladolid, and finally Cancún. The connection with Cancún had an international projection in New York which has not yet been further pursued. In the early 1970s, the descendants of the wealthiest villagers could afford to pay for the trip, and for the expensive costs of urban living in Cancún[36]. These young well-to-do were the forerunners of migration on a permanent basis. Two of these pioneer migrants, who are cousins, had the opportunity to work in a New York restaurant for one year. The One cousin's savings were invested in a mill-store in the village, and in a transportation business in Cancún that turned out to be a complete success. The other cousin's savings financed a bakery in Cancún which has turned out to be a fruitful source of capital accumulation to be invested in other small businesses. The increasing enrichment of these families did not go unnoticed by the land and cattle owners, who remained in the village and controlled the political offices. The municipal president at that time, Don Chano, demanded the presence of the migrants in the village to provide *fagina* service to the community. If these migrants desired to maintain their status as *ejidatarios*, members of the community, they would be required to fulfill the obligations and community responsibilities that such rights implied. The migrants were in a quandary. How could they leave their workplaces in Cancún or the United States in order to perform their community obligations? A new strategy appeared to resolve this dilemma: their fathers would do the *fagina* for the migrant sons. The elite in political power responded with a long list of names of those who had left to work outside. The purpose of the list was to dispossess the migrants of their *ejido* lands on a basis of nonresidency because they did not maintain houses in the township. The history of the close connections between Don Eustaquio, the old leader, and the national political party (PRI) turned out to be very helpful; the dispossessed migrants, led by Don Eustaquio's grandsons, appealed to the governor of Yucatán. Their *ejido* rights were reinstated. This episode illustrates only one event in a long story of friction between the two sides of the Cimé family, the symbol of the social schism in Chan Kom.

La Milpa es Vida. El Maiz no se puede vender porque es vida
(Milpa is Life. Corn cannot be sold because it is life)

M. Elmendorf and D. Merrill (1977:12) have already discussed the effects of opening the road in 1971, and the resulting deforestation. Men have to go farther away from the village to find good soils to make *milpa*, and they have to obtain cash to buy fertilizers, herbicides, and seeds. Incessant currency devaluations inflate local prices for agricultural implements and consumer staples. In addition, because of Yucatán's propensity for natural disasters (droughts, hurricanes, plagues), the difficulties of production (poor soils, lack of surface water sources), and the productive limits of *milpa*, the peasant can only achieve a subsistence level of production from *milpa* agriculture. As the Maya say: "La milpa es vida, pero solo da para comer; uno tiene que hacer la lucha por otra parte" (*milpa* is life but it only gives just what we can eat; one has to struggle elsewhere to achieve a better life.)

Certainly, the expansion and intensification of beekeeping brought some cash accumulation to the peasant, and protected and supplemented the household subsistence. After the 1988 ecological disaster of Hurricane Gilbert, however, and in association with the increasing migration to Cancún, beekeeping production decreased, as Figure 6.1 indicates. In order to establish an economic data reference for my 1989–90 socio-

Figure 6.1 *Percentage of Beekeeping by Household in Chan Kom*

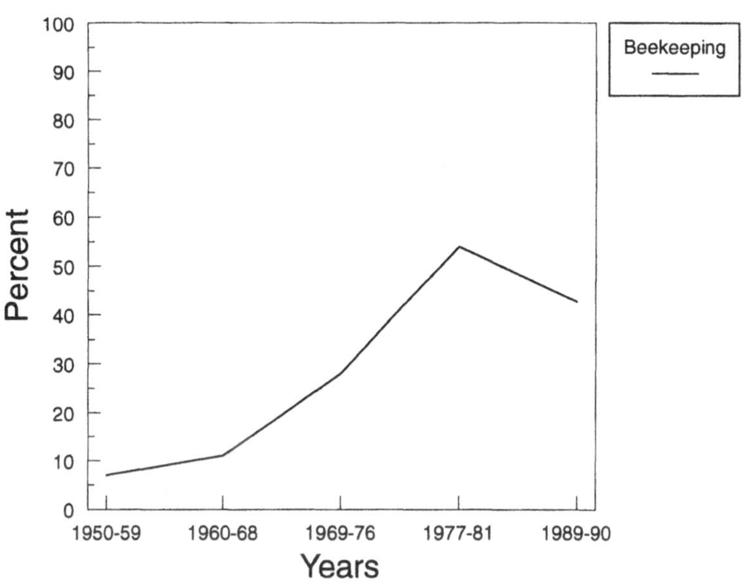

economic census, I use the statistical information of Merrill's work (1985). Merrill selects four case studies to show the variability in the role of beekeeping among similar household systems. Through my field experience in 1989–90, I could identify the peasants that Merrill used as cases. Then, extrapolating the economic information from these cases studied by Merrill, I compare them with the same cases in 1989–90, incorporating my own data. In most of the following charts, the 1980–81 data category comes from Merrill's research in Chan Kom, while the Pre-Gilbert (1988) and Post-Gilbert (1989–90) data categories refer to the census I collected. This comparison of the different chronological data allows us to scrutinize the economic impact of the hurricane. Figure 6.2 takes the information from the four case studies that Merrill (1985) addresses and traces their economic situation up to 1989–90. It indicates that the after-effects of the hurricane also affected *milpa* production. The results point out a clear decline in the size of the *milpas* after Gilbert. In half of the cases, there had been a decline in progress before Gilbert, which was exacerbated by the hurricane. Figure 6.3 reinforces this trend by showing the milpa size distribution by year. While Figure 6.2 shows the decline of the number of mecates in *milpa* production in the four cases studied, Figure 6.3 shows that the *milpas* were broken into smaller units; then, after Gilbert, there is a rise of smaller size *milpas* (less than

Figure 6.2 *Sizes of Milpa in Mecates*

Figure 6.3 *Milpa Size Distribution by Year*

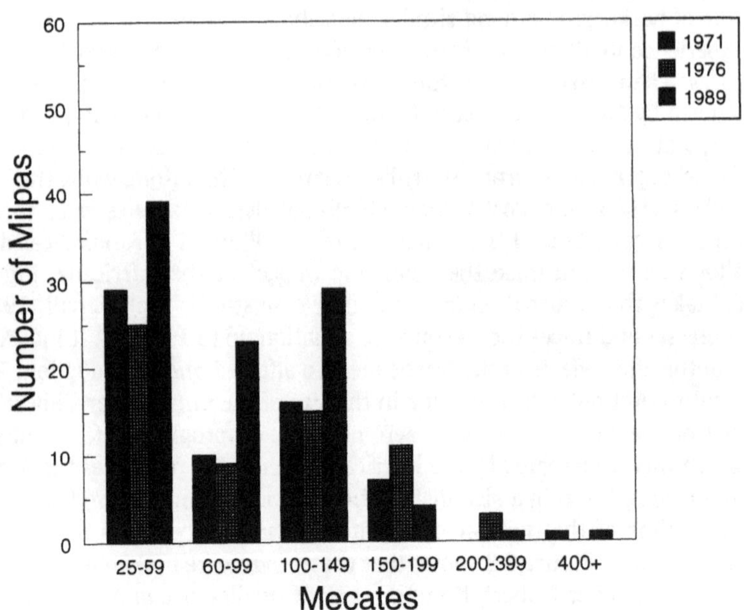

100 mecates). Figure 6.4 shows the decline in the number of beehives after Gilbert; this decline was also in progress before, although it was accelerated by the hurricane.

Today, the primary goal of *milpa* is to meet the basic consumption needs of the peasant household. As the figures from the socioeconomic census indicate, *milpa* is an economic activity shared by the vast majority of Mayas in Chan Kom.

When clearing the *monte*, the *milpero* saves the finest wood to sell, or to use for the cooking fire. Maize that has been spoiled by birds or other animals is used as feed for turkeys, chickens, and pigs. The best maize is saved for seeds, and the rest is consumed by the family. After the harvest, the maize stalks are given to the cattle. At the *milpa*, the maize and squash flowers feed the bees. The corn cobs are used to start the fire, to level the kitchen floor, and to thresh the seeds; they are also used as bottle covers, toilet paper, and in many other ways. To paraphrase Annis (1987:36), *milpa* is an agronomic system that operates by producing a large number of useful items in very small quantities. Annis also points out a very important characteristic of the *milpa* system; namely, that it absorbs resources that are abundant but otherwise wasted (1987:37). Examples of these resources are dawn hours for weeding, children's work after school hours, knowledge of flower and plant growing,

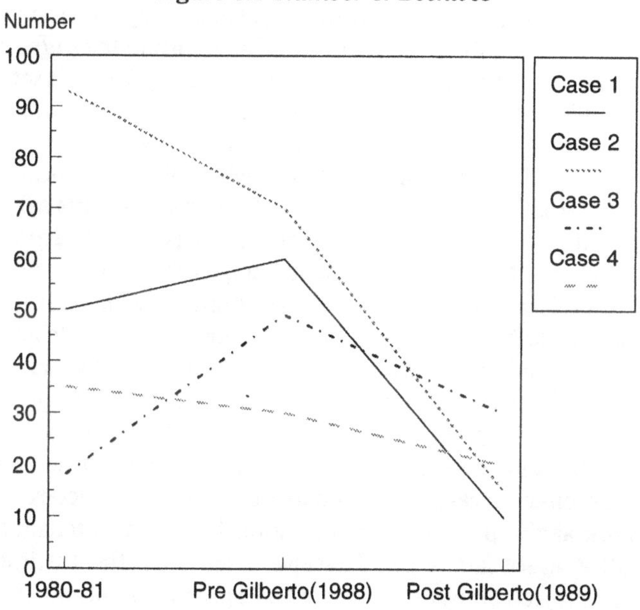

Figure 6.4 *Number of Beehives*

and the use of human and animal feces as fertilizers. A peasant does not evaluate *milpa* production in terms of labor or capital invested; rather, the *milpa* is evaluated in terms of its use value for the household (Merrill 1985; Annis 1987). This intertwined connection between the agroeconomic system and the use value of *milpa* production has been present among the Maya throughout history, particularly because it satisfies Maya economic self-sufficiency.

Figure 6.2 shows how extremely dependent *milpa* is on ecological circumstances. The trend indicated by Figure 6.3, the decrease in *milpa* size, along with the increase in number of small *milpas* after the hurricane, may indicate a social tendency for the larger *milpas* to be concentrated among a few. Although both figures suggest Gilbert as the sole cause of the decreasing size of *milpas*, other factors of economic transformation, such as cattle raising and migration, need to be addressed.

Environmental degradation of the soil presses the *milpero* to clear the forest further and further away; many prefer to migrate rather than invest more time in getting to the *milpas*, and in hard work on the land. As some Maya state, referring to those who chose migration to obtain a livelihood, "algunos no se quieren romper sus cuerpos, se estan quedando suaves" (some people do not want to break their bodies; they are becoming very soft). Local prices for consumer goods have risen dangerously due to inflation and currency devaluations. Amid such disequilibrium, *milpa* cannot provide peasants with subsistence security. In some other Maya areas, particularly in the Highlands, people introduced new mechanisms to palliate the lack of economic return in the *milpa* system. By reaching out to the national and international market for exotic fruits and vegetables, some Guatemalan communitites make the *milpa* enterprise lucrative (Allan Burns's personal communication).

This kind of commercial enterprise, which links the local and the national/international market, requires the support of external agricultural policies. In Chan Kom, this external support came through the initiative of the INI (Instituo Nacional Indigenista), which proposed an irrigation project to the villagers of Chan Kom in 1973. With the direction of an agricultural engineer, the project developed in a "cooperative" form (see Elmendorf and Merrill 1977). Through the villagers' cooperative labor, 80 hectares of land were cleared and a water storage tank was built. A well provided water via a wind-mill backed up by a pump fed with gasoline; the water was then saved in a large cement reservoir. Each family had direct access to the production of its four-hectare plot. Via their work at the plot and a contribution for the maintenance of the cooperative, every family could receive credit from the Institute. This irrigation project promoted a diversified agricultural production (fruit trees, chaya, beans, and vegetables), and contributed with additional economic benefits by selling the products outside the village. This productive mechanism encouraged women's involvement; they incorporated economic activity at the cooperative into their domestic productive performances, while men were at their *milpas* or working in Cancún. This small-scale marketing gave them the opportunity to earn cash income. Although it was a prosperous enterprise in the 1970s and 1980s, the irrigation system was not in use in 1989.

Further, when I arrived in 1989, women were not embroidering *huipiles* in the sewing cooperative, which began operating as a government development projects in the 1970s. These programs, which facilitated access to outside markets for agricultural and artisan products through cooperative enterprises, had failed by 1990. People interpret the failure as a consequence of the social schism in the village. Once the pump broke, and given the villagers' alliances with *los Antiguos* or *los de Cancún*, it was difficult to reach an agreement among the two groups to find the resources to fix the problem. Similarly, women started complaining about differences in payments for their embroidery production; the closest ones to *los Antiguos* accused the allies of *los de Cancún* of being better-reimbursed for their production by the Government agents, the intermediaries in charge of bringing the final artisan product to the national market. By 1990, with the failure of the governmental projects to obtain extra cash and the decay of beekeeping, the main economic avenues for the villagers in Chan Kom were the self-sufficient *milpa* production, the raising of cattle, and the escalating migration to Cancún. Poultry and pigs are still an important source of cash in times when a rapid expenditure is needed (for instance, expenses related to health: doctor, medicines, hospital payments).

Embroidery is also an important source of supplementary family income; the female members of the household (mother and daughters) are involved. The traditional method of being provided with the cloth and thread by an outside intermediary, who buys the final product at the end of the month, is still in practice, although new mechanisms to commercialize the embroidered *huipiles* and blouses are being introduced. Doña Casiana, one of the president's aunts, has a son working in Cancún; he got married in Chan Kom, but after several years of working in the city, the new couple settled in Cancún. Doña Casiana's son, working as waiter in a hotel, and his wife, working as a cleaner in the same hotel, were able to save enough to have their own house and a small store in Cancún. Doña Casiana, taking advantage of her son's social network in the city, started bringing *huipiles* produced in Chan Kom to Cancún to be sold at the hotel, where her son and daughter-in law worked. Doña Casiana then invested the savings of her extra cash commercial activities in a *cantina* that provides the community and other *comisarías* with beer, which is consumed, preferably, during the weekends, when the mass of village migrants return, and during ceremonial and festival celebrations. Today, migration to Cancún and the enterpreunership among some families is promoting the direct commercial transactions between Maya women in the village, who now become the intermediaries and use their social network in Cancún to commercialize the product.

Inflation contributes to jeopardizing the "egalitarian" propaganda promoted by the elites in the community, and has resulted in the current Maya perception that the community is in crisis. The *we/they* cultural categories, so widely spread among the Maya public, emanate from this perception. Interestingly, the representations that Maya groups use in the struggle for power do not imply social and economic inequality. That is, the battle to reach "true Mayaness" is set up in the discourse of *milpa* work, which is being read under a communal, egalitarian, and solidarity code. However, by raising cattle, the peasant may meet the demands of extra cash that the self-sufficiency of *milpa* work does not allow on a permanent basis. As an economic system, raising cattle demands particular productive strategies that threaten the egalitarian communal bases of *milpa* work, so over-advertised by *los Antiguos*'s elite. Back in 1975, the INI (Instituto Nacional Indigenista) promoted the creation of a cooperative cattle ranch; the goal was to assist the poor villagers in managing and learning about cattle raising. Credits would be granted by the Institute in exchange for their pooling labor; in this way, the poorer members could have access to an important supplementary source of income. Although the ranch started with 20 members (Elemdorf and Merrill 1977: III56), most of them withdrew *la sociedad de ganaderos* (cattle-owners' society), and by 1990 it had just six members. The cattle ranch was located in the same *ejido* land where *Santa Cecilia* ranch is located. Not only the location, but also the group membership of those involved in the cattle cooperative associated the *sociedad de ganaderos* with *los Antiguos*. The 29th of June is the celebration of San Pedro and San Pablo, the patron saints of the cattle. Nine days before, the participants of the saint's ceremony started the *novena* at their houses, which would conclude on the 29th with the ritualistic communal meal of *relleno negro*. This time, in 1989, since the big cattle-owners and those who belonged to the cooperative were members of *los Antiguos*, it was decided to use the image located in the Catholic church. This meant that the Saint was also honored at the Catholic church. Once again, *los Antiguos*'s succeeded in voiding *los de Cancún*'s access and participation in Catholic religious activities.

Raising cattle does not require the complete involvement of the household. Because the supply of good land in the *ejido* is so limited, the villagers who own cattle can afford to purchase lands which become private ranches. Other villagers keep their cattle within the *ejido* lands. Besides land ownership, in the case of the large ranches, cattle raising implies the need for labor investment in planting *sacate* (grazing grass) or in clearing the forest. The contrast in the relations of production between the *milpa* and the cattle systems is represented in Maya folklore by the image of *X-Juan Thul*[37], the guardian of the cattle. He has a Spanish name, Juan. The cattle-owner's name, in contrast to the *milpa* owners' Maya names (*aluxo'ob, yuntzilo'ob, . . .*) may indicate how the Maya use the filter of oral tradition to incorporate a colonial economic system into their cultural logic. *X-Juan Thul*, considered by the Mayas as "the least of the yuntzilob" (Redfield and Villa Rojas 1934:118), can get into contact with the devil and manipulate the evil winds to protect the cattle. This fact correlates somehow with the generalized competitive conflict between cattle-owners and *milperos*, between land for pasture, and lands invaded by the uncontrolled herd (Varguez Pasos 1972). The first time I was introduced to the role that *X-Juan-Thul* performs among the Maya was at *Santa Cecilia* ranch. After feeling honored by an invitation to visit the ranch, I accepted and agreed to be accompanied by one of the leaders of *los Antiguos*, Don Nato, who has his *milpas* and cattle at *Santa Cecilia*. Don Nato was very concerned, because he had lost three heads of cattle in the last month, and several more had the symptoms of some kind of infection. He recalled that the last *loh corral*[38], the ritual to drive off the evil winds, had been performed during the 1950s, "cuando pasó la balacera" (when *la balacera*[39] happened). At that time, *X-Juan-Thul* probably was angry that the cattle-owners were not paying any homage to him; this might be the reason why he had again stopped protecting the cattle from the evil winds. Don Nato then decided it was the time to ask *Santa Cecilia* and the cattle cooperative members to agree in the celebration of a *loh corral* to drive the evil winds away from *Santa Cecilia*.

Currently, the economic system is characterized by the migratory process to Cancún. The demand for labor among migrant peasants has very high seasonal variation. During the dry season, agricultural work slows and wage labor in the village is scarce; work is scarce, and many people migrate to look for wages. A few villagers opt to stay in the community to work for either the rich cattle-owners or for those who work in Cancún and cannot return to fulfill their labor chores in the *milpa*. Many Maya peasants prefer to work in temporary jobs, mainly in the construction industry, because their positions leave them free to meet the community agricultural demands during the rainy season. In the case where they cannot return to the community to fulfill their *milpa* responsibilities, they ask relatives, neighbors, friends, or other villagers for help. Reciprocity may be involved in these relationships, because the peasant knows that tomorrow he may become a migrant; in that case, he will need help from those for whom he is working today. This social labor relation, more common among relatives and *compadres*, is engrained in the old pattern of mutual help and assistance; mutual assistance is more attuned to the *milpa* ideology of egalitarianism and the formative stage of Chan Kom's history. Increasingly, however, these relations are held by contract that ends with the payment of a salary. This system enables the peasant without capital to receive a wage. Thus, during the dry months, the peasant is looking for wages either within or outside the village. After the harvest, maize is consumed little by little, and, when a surplus exists, is sold each week to cover expenses. It helps that *San Diego*, a celebration for the village patron saint, follows immediately after the harvest, when the peasant has money to spend for the *corrida* (bull fight), for contributions for the masses at church, and for other entertainment expenses.

The village celebration obliges the peasants to spend precious money and begins a cycle that drains the maize reserves. By planting time, the maize reserves are almost gone and the peasants have to ask for credit. In addition when an environmental tragedy such as Hurricane Gilbert occurs, the peasant traditionally will borrow money for survival. There is an alternative today that brings a greater degree of balance—migration. Chan Kom has 682 inhabitants; of these, 474 are older than 12 years of age (adult), and of that, 160 adults migrate. Migrants represent 33.76 percent of the adult population. According to Elmendorf and Merrill's census, Chan Kom had a population of 526 in 1976 (1977:III–2); more than 50 people, 8.4% of the total population, were working in Cancún (1977:III–63).

Many unmarried young women have emigrated to the city, where they are employed as domestic servants, as cooks in restaurants, or employees in hotels. These servant women send a large part of their wages to their families, thereby supplementing the family's cash income. At the same time, their absence reduces consumption. Figure 6 illustrates migration from Chan Kom broken down into four categories; it can be seen that of the total Maya migration, migration by males dominates. Within the female migration pattern, permanent migration is predominant over temporary migration.

The reconfiguration of the family among those who migrate breaks the bonds of the original village family, which the *milpa* economic system demands. The breakup of families is one of the primary points in *los Antiguos'* propaganda of the maladies associated with the modernity and progress brought by the migrants. In the contemporary chaotic context, for some poor peasants, the great hope for family survival is that their younger members can learn English and get a good job in a restaurant or hotel in the city. The great hope for the rich is that their sons or daughters become teachers, because this position implies a secure salary, fringe benefits, medical attention, and a pension. Some sons of wealthy villagers have very solid economic support and manage to become teachers; some even go to the university.

In sum, the preceding overview provides a general explanation of the articulation of the *milpa*, cattle, and migration economic processes in community life. *Milpa* work is still the most viable alternative for the poor Maya villagers; however, it is increasingly articulated with other economic alternatives such as migration or rural wages. To examine the contemporary socioeconomic categories of Chan Kom, I turn to a more detailed study based on a simple statistical analysis of the socioeconomic information I collected in my 1989 census. For a more detailed economic and statistical analysis of Chan Kom in the 1970s, with particular emphasis on the village socioeconomic transformations and their implications in the community and family life, I refer to the study that Elemdorf and Merrill (1977) conducted.

The Pieces of Chan Kom Within the Social Halves

Goldkind noticed a vertical social differentiation between "poor" and "rich," which he attributed to a social class formation process. This was more explicit in the social conflict spurred in the 1950s by the confrontation between the cattle owners-*cacique* family-Catholic coalition and the new Protestant forces. For the 1970s and early 1980s, Mary Elmendorf's and Merrill's statistical information also shows evidence of increasing social differentiation within the village. These earlier studies point out the increase of migration to Cancún and the gradual shift from a *milpa* subsistence system to a more capitalized system that combines *milpa* and beekeeping. With this combination of *milpa* production and beekeeping commercialization, the household maximizes its net cash income, and the range of diversified production systems is enlarged. Based on patterns in beekeeping production, Merrill's analysis (1985:383) shows four socioeconomic groups in the community, ranked from richest to poorest. Thus, there is an obvious increase in social complexity since the earlier stages of Chan Kom development.

The socioeconomic census I conducted during my 1989–90 field work season shows that two decades of migration to Cancún (1970s and 1980s) have altered the socioeconomic realm and the distribution of jobs among the Maya. To trace the community's socioeconomic development, I use the Goldkind (1965, 1966), Elmendorf (1979), Elmendorf and Merrill (1977, 1978), and Merrill (1985) data. For the most recent data, I use my own work.

In defining the differentiation of social groups, I could use neither *milpa* nor bees as criteria, given the arbitrariness of their actual distribution due to the destructive effects of Hurricane Gilbert. Cattle and private

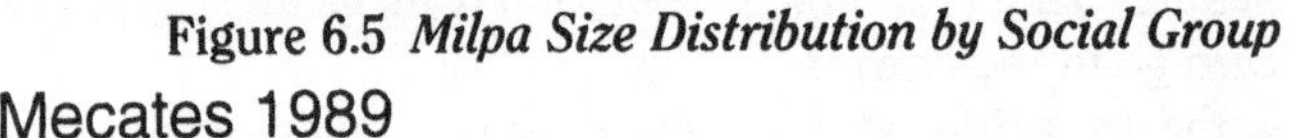

Figure 6.5 *Milpa Size Distribution by Social Group*

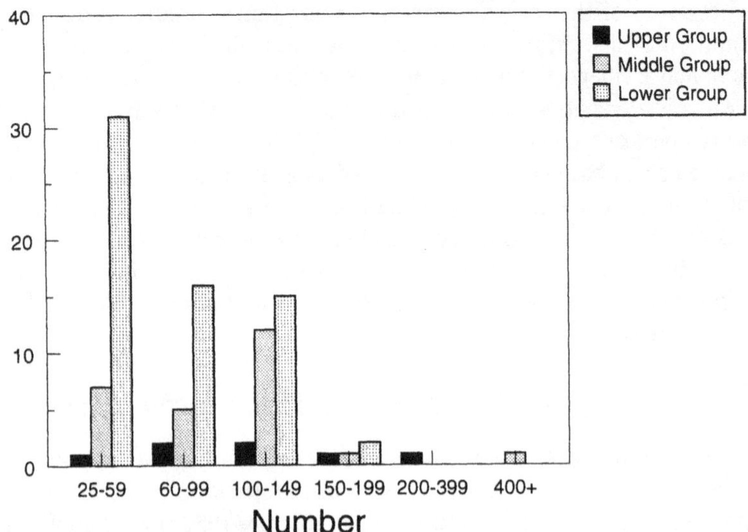

ownership (land, houses, and stores), however, remained stable after the hurricane; these are the criteria I use to mark the social boundaries in defining the different social groups in Chan Kom. I continue using the native perception of wealth, associated with cattle ownership, to develop my criteria for social grouping. Goldkind (1965, 1966) also mentions the native notion of wealth based on ownership of cattle, especially expressed in the "rich" and "poor" social categories.

Through my own observation and knowledge of Maya economic activity and behavior, I decided to incorporate a new social category to the already established rich-poor social division stated by Goldkind. This new social category comprises those whose economic power follows the patterns of the rich in terms of cattle and private property, but on a smaller scale. Table 6.1 outlines the criteria I use for social groups.

William Roseberry (1976:51) undertakes a similar method to analyze

Table 6.1 Social Groups in Chan Kom

	LAND PROPERTY	HEAD OF CATTLE	STORE	HOUSES
Group A	>600 mec.	>8	>0	≥4
Group B	≥250 mec. ≤600	>1, ≤8	>0	>1, <4
Group C	<250 mec.	0	0	1

peasant social differentiation based on rent (taxes, interest on loans, forced presale of produce at less than market price, and so forth). Roseberry's analysis incorporates social and cultural categories. For Roseberry, the cultural categories are implied in the social typology, but only as adaptations and responses to the rent system, which is the main variable defining the social groups in his analysis. Sheldon Annis applies Roseberry's typology in a less deterministic way, "to show how wealth differentiation within a changing economy undercuts traditional religious-cultural stability" (1988:64). Using private ownership as a criterion for social differentiation, I follow a similar methodology. Table 6.2 shows the distribution of the social groups in Chan Kom, by household, according to the variables in Table 6.1. Figure 6.6 shows this distribution by individuals. The average of the three major assets in Chan Kom, those of *milpa*, private land, and large animals, is skewed. As indicated in Table 6.2, eight households manage to have from 600 mecates to 1,500 mecates

Figure 6.6 *Population by Social Group*

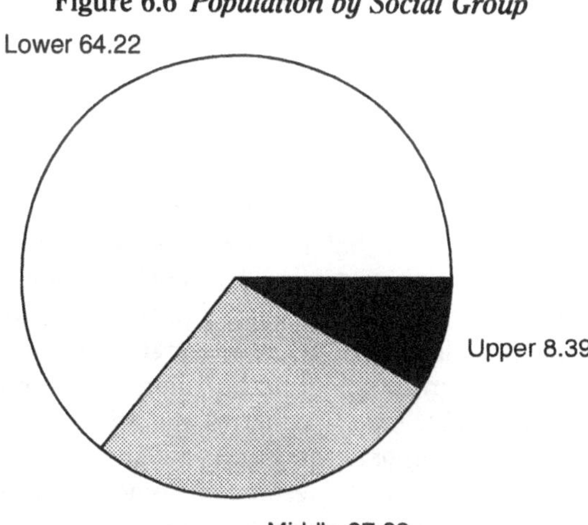

Table 6.2 Distribution of Social Groups in Chan Kom by Household

	NUMBER	PERCENT
Group A	8	7.62
Group B	26	24.76
Group C	71	67.72
Total	105	100

of private land. The average is also unequal regarding large animals. Thus, group A (eight households) controls on average 77.3 percent of cattle and work animals, group B (26 households), controls on average 22.6 percent, and group C (71 households) own or manage none (there are two families that managed to have a donkey for the *milpa* as well as a head of cattle). As noted in the tables, group A, 7.6 percent of the 105 households control most of the cattle in the community, they own great extensions of private land, and they have the largest *milpas*. Another 24.7 percent (Table 6.2), group B, follows the economic trends of group A, but on a smaller scale. And 67.7 percent (Table 6.2) of the households, group C, have no cattle, cultivate smaller sizes of *milpa*, and own an insignificant amount of private land. Members of group C frequently have to sell their labor locally or migrate seasonally to Cancún to survive. In Marxist terms, these economic categories correspond to the upper class, the middle or petty bourgeoisie, and the lower class. I call group A "upper social group" or "rural capitalists," group B, "middle social group" or "new traditionalists," and group C, "lower social group" or "rural peasants."

This economic analysis of community social differentiation does not quite agree with the self-imagery that Chan Kom presents in its division into *los Antiguos* and *los de Cancún*. My analysis reveals the social inequality that the elites avoid in their message of social differentiation based on the we/they dichotomy. How do we reach an agreement between the ideological dichotomy *we/they* and the socioeconomic triad? We need a multi-dimensional analysis that can reveal not only contradictions and conflicts in the social milieu, but also the set of life circumstances associated with the aggregation of groups. This analysis demands a strategy that considers, first, the social makeup of constituent groups, and secondly, the rhetorical dimension of the interpretation that people give to their own and other's involvement in the community transformations.

I argue that with the intensification of migration during the last two decades, and the creation of new occupational and economic roles, new groups are comprising the socioeconomic composition of Chan Kom. These new social components try to stabilize their positions within the social system and, consequently, they come into conflict with the traditional stratified order. Within this process, the old and new social groups face a reciprocal challenge: the old order must develop strategies to reinforce the set of values, symbols of status, and control over economic resources that form the traditional basis of political and economic power in the community, all of which are threatened by the competing newcomers. The new group must come up with a value code that enhances their positions, while at the same time it undermines the stability of the prior order. The defense of the traditional order and the creation of a new one are not separate social phenomena; rather, they are constantly interact-

Figure 6.7 *Total Migration out of Chan Kom by*
Gender and Permanence

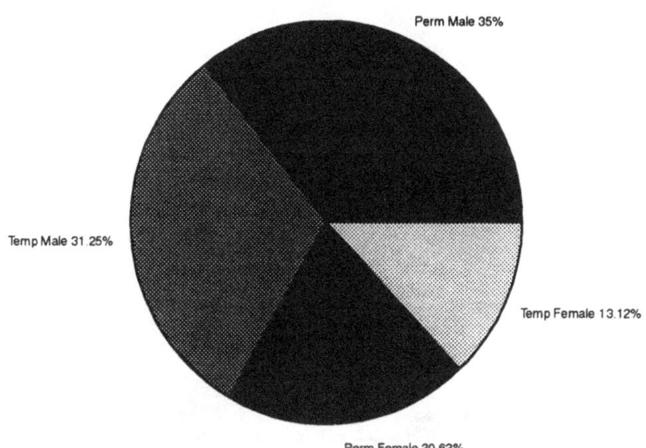

ing aspects of a larger community system. The related interplay between the old and the new ideological views also permeates this intimate relationship. The perception of social crisis is derived from this clash between the two socioeconomic and value codes in the community.

The Poor: Rural Subsistence and Survival in the City

The economic universe of the poor rural peasants is characterized by a noticeably low average of private ownership in the forms of real estate (28.82) (Figures 6.8 and 6.9) and cattle (0.07) (Figures 6.10 and 6.11).

These peasants are fully integrated into the *milpa* mode of production, as they depend on the *milpa* for their subsistence. *Milpa* work is the common productive denominator among the Chan Kom peasantry. These rural peasants, on average, had smaller *milpas* than group A and B during the agricultural cycle of 1989 (Figure 6.5). Because of the cash investment in agricultural implements needed for successful harvests in the poor, overused soils of Yucatan, along with the fear of natural disasters exacerbated by Hurricane Gilbert, the peasant is reluctant to run more risks.

There are a few exceptions of peasants who did not work their *milpas* at the time the census was collected. One case is Don Cata, the herbalist and *curandero* (curer), whose age, rheumatism, and asthma prevent him from working in the forest and fields; he supports himself and his wife, at a low level of subsistence, on the cash he receives from his *curas* (healings) and the labor services provided by his sons. There are two

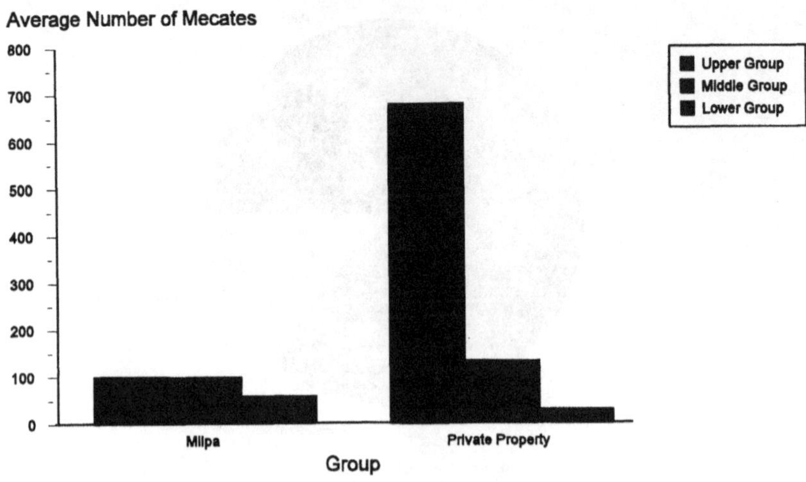

Figure 6.8 *Group Distribution of Land Holdings by Property Types (1989)*

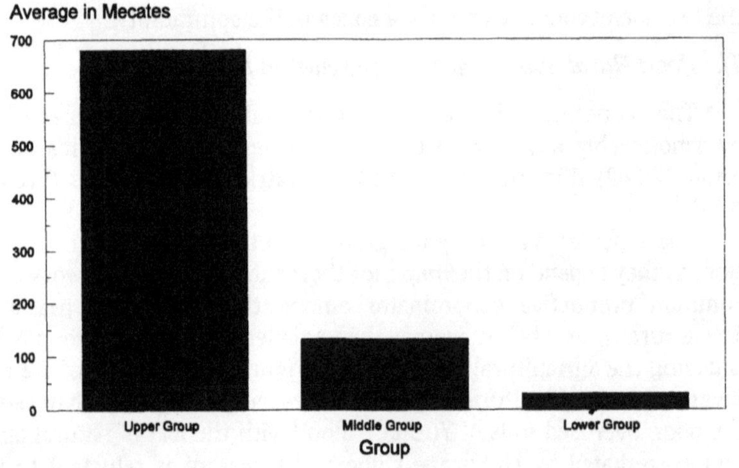

Figure 6.9 *Group Distribution of Private Property (1989)*

cases of *milperos* who were disabled and could no longer make *milpa*. Both were injured while felling trees to clear a field. They did not pursue medical care beyond the assistance of Don Cata, the healer. Any accident that disables the peasant so that he must abandon *milpa* work puts the household's level of subsistence at high risk. If there are sons, the *milpa* laborer can rely on them to continue to work the *milpa* to support the

Figure 6.10 *Group Distribution of Cattle Ownership (1989)*

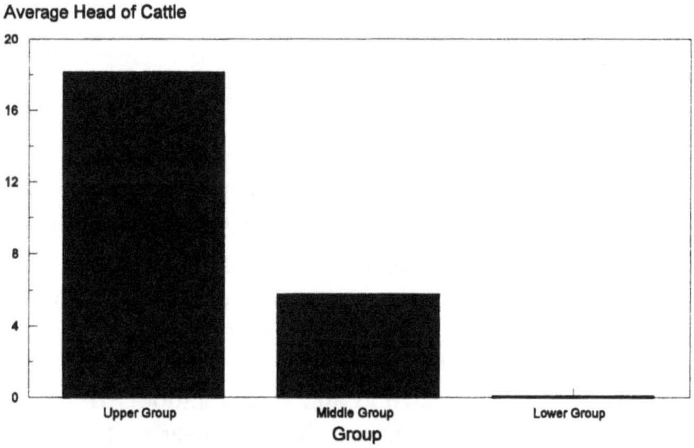

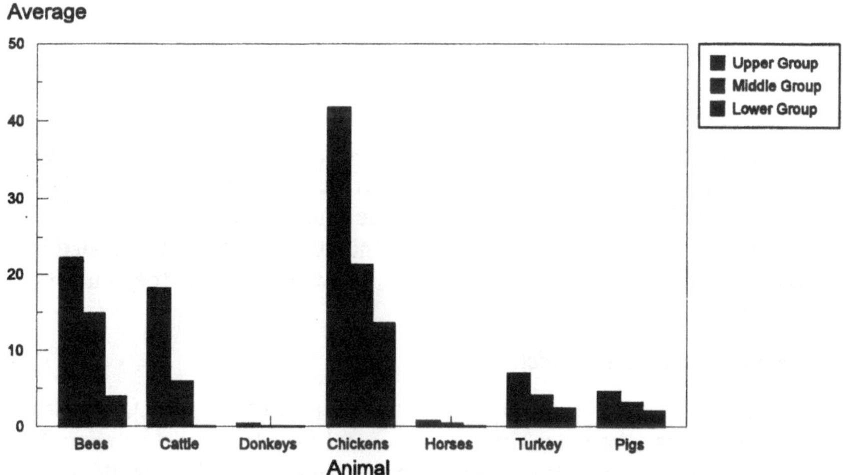

Figure 6.11 *Group Distribution of Farm Property by Animal type*

family; as a last resort, a son may be sent to work in Cancún and the wages spent on maize and other household expenses. In another case, a peasant suffered from a painful bone disease that totally disabled him and prevented him from working in the fields. As in the previous cases, lack of economic resources left this poor *milpero* in a state of economic inactivity that reinforced the already impoverished household situation.

The temporal migrants are called *mucuy. Mucuy* is a Maya bird that, no matter how far it flies, always returns to its original place. Mayas associate this term with those who migrate to Cancún in times of scarcity, but who always return to the village. As the larger economy progressively demands more cash expenditures from the villagers, the peasants are forced to sell most of the harvest, at which point they fall below a subsistence level. The family is then forced to find a mechanism to restore the economic equilibrium. There are two options: migrating to Cancún, or seeking wage labor in the village. The we and they categories of social discourse correspond to the peasants' choice between these two options, and establish the borders between *los Antiguos* and *los de Cancún*. That is, the ideological discourse in connection with the social structure manifests other aspects of the social reality: a horizontal distinction between migrants and non-migrants, within a broad lower social group in the process of expansion and segmentation. The *we* and *they* sociocultural categories become, within the universe of the Maya poor, the *milpero* and "temporal migrant" economic categories.

Figure 6.12 reveals that, on average, the young generation of Maya in Chan Kom tends to seek economic alternatives in Cancún. The lower social group follows this trend. Figure 6.13 shows the percentage of temporal and permanent migration in the village.

The *mucuy*, among the poor Maya, migrate the most. The alternative of migration pushes the peasants out of the village, and in the process changes the approach to *milpa* work. This is exemplified in the noticeable decrease of the size of *milpas* (see Figure 6.5). The principles involving the ritual and productive aspects of *milpa* work are altered due to a lack of full-time labor devoted to *milpa*, as the tradition requires.

What follows is a more detailed examination of what was revealed in the above figures from the point of view of the we and they cultural categories.

Peasants, the Rural Proletarians

I use the term "rural proletarians" to refer to those who work their own and others' *milpas*. They become rural proletarians in an effort to cover the cash demands necessary for subsistence in today's world. Government agricultural programs teach them how to cope with the increasing impoverishment of the soil by the use of fertilizer, herbicides and particular varieties of maize seeds.[40] These programs also promote a more efficient use of the *milpero*'s time for certain activities such as weeding; the use of herbicides can substitute for two or three days of intensive labor in the *milpa*. However, these technological advances demand cash expenditure, which requires the *milpero* to seek paid work from others.

When a peasant is in desperate need of cash, he borrows money. The cash loan can be used to finance production of maize or to meet the demands of consumption (clothing, festivals, medical care, education). The loan is made by people with whom the peasant has a permanent relation. Usually, the moneylenders are the labor providers, the wealthy Maya who demand peasant labor to work their lands. These patrons are likely to become *compadres* of the peasants who work for them. This set of social relations entails a client-patron bond that is clearly exemplified in the labor dynamic of the ritual context. These poor peasants are the *prestados* (the borrowed people) in charge of the laborious preparations of the ritual festivities that the rich *Antiguos* undertake to enhance their social prestige.

The economic realm of these poor peasants exemplifies the articulation of the *milpa* system with the extension of wage labor in village economic activities. This economic articulation pervades both the set of social relations and the *milpa* ideology. The following vivid description, taken from my field experience, exemplifies this articulation. The anomalous agricultural cycle of 1989 pressed the peasants, driven by their anxieties for rain to nurture the prematurely planted fields, to perform the *ch'a chaac*, the ceremony to ask for rain. It is performed in response to the crucial need for water during the driest months of the wet season (July and August, although it can also be performed in May or June,

The anomalous agricultural cycle pressed the peasants,
driven by their anxieties for rain to perform the ch'a
chaac, the ceremony to ask for rain. The
h-men has to preside over the ceremony.

according to the changes in weather). The *ch'a chaac*, which last for three days, is the most elaborate ceremony. Redfield describes the ceremony as a community activity in which the entire adult male population is gathered at the place of the ceremony (1934:138). The *h-men* presides over the ceremony, and it is required that men winthdraw fron contact with women during the ritual performance. While men are devoted to the preparation on the main ritual elements (building the altar, digging the *pib*, gathering wood and leaves from the forest to build and embelish the altar, sacrificing the fowls, and so forth), their spouses are gathered at the house of the *dueño*, the person in charge of inviting the rest of the participants in the ceremony. The Maya women are in charge of cooking the offerings.[41]

The Mucuy: The Rural-Urban Proletarians

The first *ch'a chaac* performed in 1989 was not a collective enterprise, as in Redfield's times, but was organized by *los Antiguos*. Today, these poor peasants make a great effort in following "the steps of our ancestors," meaning the ritual agricultural tasks related to *milpa* work. By close adherence to prescribed ritual behavior, they attempt to differentiate themselves from the *mucuy*. Before the *ch'a chaac* ceremony took

While men are devoted to the preparation of the main
ritual elements, their spouses are gathered at the house
of the dueño. The Maya women are in charge of cooking
the offerings.

place, they demanded some conditions from the ceremony director: he must not drink too much, to the point of becoming unconscious at the climax of the ritual, when the *chaaco'ob* descend from the skies to bless the Maya with the *santa lluvia* (rainwater); he must be present for three days, as the tradition requires; and all peasants must remain at the ritual site, away from their families, day and night, praying to *Nuestro Señor Jesucristo* (Jesus Christ) and the *yuntzilo'ob* (the owners of the forest).

Among the rural-urban proletarians, it is the head of the household who migrates, leaving the family in the community. The rural-urban connection of Chan Kom is best exemplified through the usual pattern that a migrant peasant follows: relatives and friends already established in the city search for potential jobs after the peasant communicates his need for wages. Knowing nothing about the urban context, the migrant peasant stays at the home of relatives or friends until he can pay the high rent for his own room. Figure 6.14 shows the relationship between social classes and job categories. The lower class is involved in unskilled construction and service jobs. That part of the lower class employed in the service sector mostly comprises young Maya janitors, dishwashers, and waiters. Figure 6.15 indicates that the male Maya among the poor villagers migrate the most, on a temporary basis, in contrast to young female Maya, who migrate on a more permanent basis. Figure 6.16 shows per-

Figure 6.12 *Average Age of Milpero versus Migrants by Social Group*

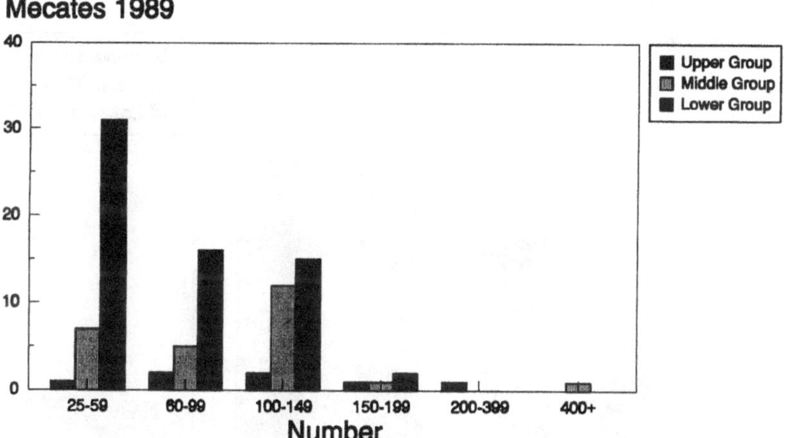

centages of Maya migrants as they are distributed among the three main occupation sectors in Cancún. Figure 6.17 shows the age distribution by job type within each class. Members of the lower class employed in the service sector tend to be younger than their counterpart in the blue-collar category.

Some of these migrants prefer to pay other Maya back in the village to work the land, which is still required to provide the family's subsistence. If the harvest is good and bears a surplus, some of the peasants decide to stay in the village and work for the *milpas* that other absent migrants pay to be worked.

The articulation of the *milpa* mode of production with the process of migration to Cancún is creating a new set of social relationships that is transforming both the economic and cultural approaches to *milpa*. The *mucuy* migrant cannot offer the *saca'* every day in order to procure the divine blessing. The traditional two or three days demanded for the *ch'a chaac* may be cut to one day or even to hours, or may be rescheduled for the weekend to accommodate urban labor constraints. Some poor families are so destitute that they are driven to break tradition and make some adjustments. For example, the son of a poor *milpero* may be driven off the land, for many of the above reasons, to go to Cancún and find a

Figure 6.13 *Percentage of Temporary and Permanent Migrants by Social Group*

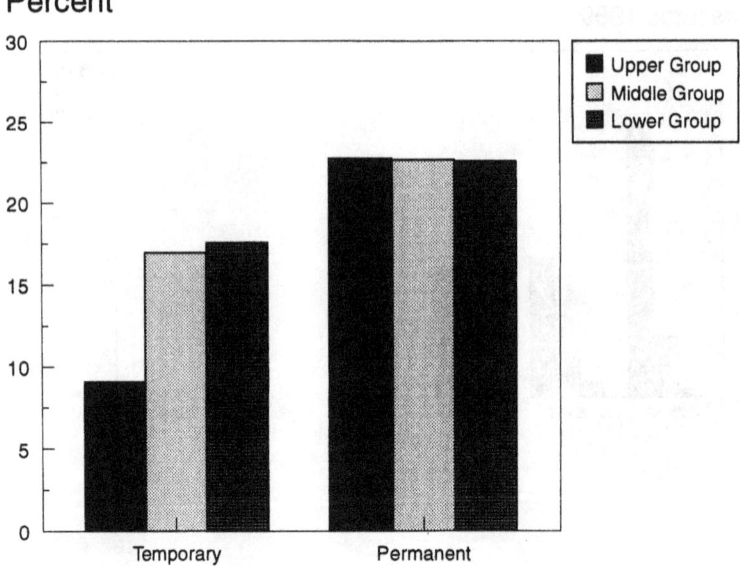

position where he can earn more than he would from the *milpa*-based livelihood prescribed by tradition. These alterations in the traditional practices are severely criticized by *los Antiguos*, and form the core of the arguments and admonitions against the migrants. In their discourse, *los Antiguos* cite these breaks with tradition as justification for the de-ethnification of the migrants' Maya identity. This charge of deviation is accompanied by a torrent of satiric images that portrays the migrants as lazy drunkards and thieves of cattle and corn.

The anomalous 1989 agricultural cycle also affected these peasants' *milpas*. Some of them were working in the city when the March weather suddenly turned dry, hot, and a little bit windy—just right to burn the fields. Some were not prepared to plant in May, when the group back in the village performed the *ch'a chaac*. Nevertheless, they were gradually catching up with the burning and planting, and by the middle of July *los de Cancún* group performed the annual *ch'a chaac*. It had to be scheduled during the weekend to allow the migrants in Cancún to participate in the ritual; instead of investing the traditional three days, they devoted only a day and a half to the performance of the entire ceremony. Sneakers, T-shirts with colorful drawings and English letters, and baseball caps with the PRI emblem (green-white-red in color) were worn by this group. When the time came to open the *pib*, most of the elders in the group were getting anxious. The *h-men* was not at the site and he was the only person, as the ritual mediator between the earth and the skies, allowed to open the *pib*. The *h-men* was drunk; he had gone to the village, but

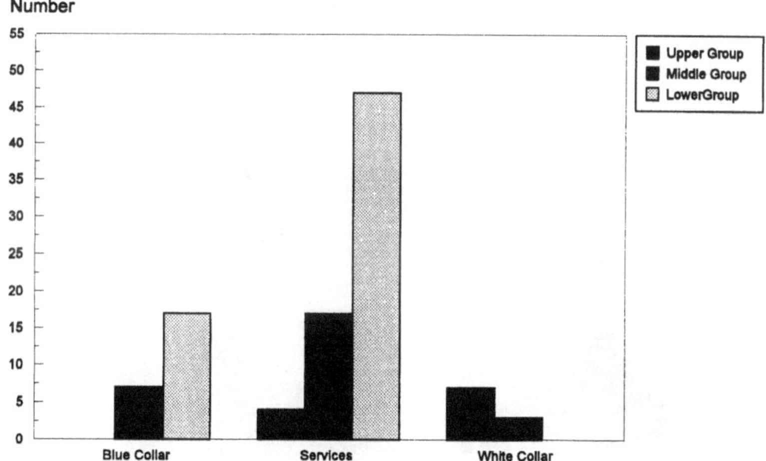

Figure 6.14 *Distribution of Occupations by Group*

no one knew exactly where he was. When he finally arrived to open the *pib*, the cornbreads were burned. At the climax of the ceremony, when the offerings are presented to the *chaaco'ob* to petition the rain from them, as a reciprocity, the *h-men* looks through the *zastún*, a small crystal ball, through which he can see if the gods are pleased with the Mayas' ritual-work and will bless them with the *santa lluvia* (holy water). That year, the rains did not come right away; the Maya had to wait for a few days. *Los Antiguos* interpreted this semi-failure of the ritual as a punishment for not following the traditional patterns of the ritual performance: *los de Cancún* group did not observe the traditional date and length of the ceremony, and they did not make the *Rosario* prayer at night. Instead, most of them fell asleep or got drunk. This was another episode in the long history of deviations from the traditional patterns that *los Antiguos* associate with *los de Cancún* group.

Los Ricos: the Old Caciques *and the New Bourgeoisie.*

Figure 6.18 graphically depicts Don Chano's and Don Lillo's worlds, which constitute the wealthy group in Chan Kom. Don Chano and Don Lillo represent the economic universe of the "rural capitalists," characterized by private ownership of land, houses, and cattle (group A; see Table 6.2). However, the upper group does not represent all the social divisions continued within it. Again, it is the *we* and *they* cultural categories that help to point out the social diversity enmeshed in this dominant social group. As such, Don Chano, the epitome of *los Antiguos*, repre-

Figure 6.15 *Social Group Distribution of Temporary Migration by Gender*

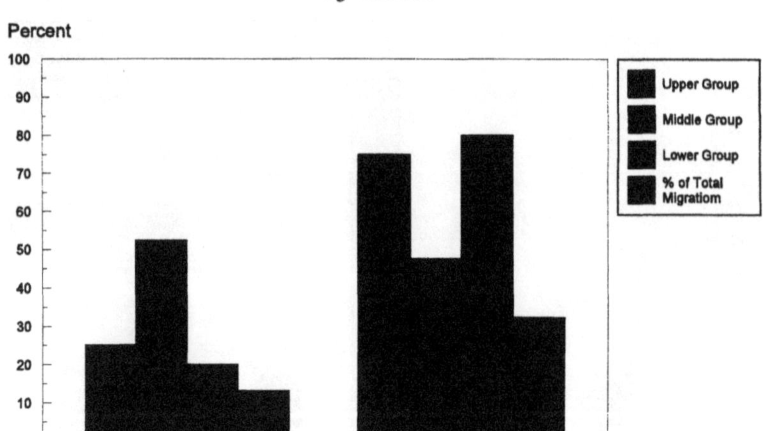

sents a rural wealth based on cattle and land ownership. Don Lillo, however, the model-portrait for *los de Cancún*, represents a different kind of rural wealth: no cattle, only a small amount of land, but a great deal of wealth invested in houses; in addition, all his children are pioneer migrants who demonstrate the success of migration, as they occupy high-status positions in business and in the administration in Cancún.

In sum, the socioeconomic universe of the upper group in Chan Kom is represented by Maya who are price-conscious, enterpreneurial producers of surplus, which they invest to earn more capital; that is, they are capitalists. This socioeconomic group is not homogeneous.

Old *Caciques*, Rural Capitalists

The old *caciques*, rural capitalists, are the main promoters of the *we/ they* ideological discourse. For them, "we" means hard workers of the *milpa*, good Catholics, and members of Chan Kom, because they have their houses and families in the village. Among this group, all these features are synonyms for "legitimate Mayas." This conception of the "we" as a group is flavored by a strong attachment to the land via ownership of cattle ranches (Figure 6.10), *milpa*, and other private land (Figures 6.8 and 6.9). At the same time, this group invokes a close connection to the ancestors via the performance of rituals associated with *milpa*.

This group makes up the *los Antiguos* elite, who grow corn both to meet household needs and to obtain surplus. They have the largest *milpas* in the community (Figure 6.5). They produce some surplus and create some profit, but hang on to the security that land ownership provides. The members of this elite can borrow from the bank to intensify their production and to purchase labor as needed. These elite peasants diversify production by investing money and labor in cattle, beekeeping, and *milpa* work. The diversification of production leads to a need to employ wage laborers, particularly for the *milpa* work (clearing the forest, planting, harvesting.) As a result of the purchase of peasant labor through wages and the appropriation of the economic surpluses, these rural capitalists reinvest their profits to create more capital. They can use the profit to intensify their production by, for instance, buying trucks; they can accumulate their capital in the bank; they can continue with the old economic source of their frugal wealth, moneylending; and they can invest their income in communal life mainly through orchestrating community ceremonies that reinforce their social prestige.

The diversification in production and enrichment of the old *caciques* accelerates the expansion of wage labor among the poor peasants. The social relationship between the rural capitalists and the wage laborers entails a vertical, unequal relation within the entire socioeconomic universe of *los Antiguos*. This social relationship is based in particular on a patron-client pattern seen mostly in *milpa* work. The wealthy of *los Antiguos* appear as benefactors of the poor by opening up the rural job market in times of crisis; in turn, the poor peasants offer their loyalty to those who help them to maintain a subsistence level of existence through provision of cash. Another strategy to increase the income of the rural capitalists is land rental in exchange for labor obligations; the owners of great tracts of forest may allow the peasants to cultivate *milpa* in exchange for labor obligations, such as clearing the forest to cultivate *sacate* (grazing grass) for the cattle or extracting of firewood.

In the same way that these poor peasants are *los prestados* (the borrowed people) for the labor chores of the rituals, they become *los prestados* labor in the *milpa* production for the wealthy *los Antiguos*. *La milpa* is appropriated in the ideological discourse by the wealthy of *los Antiguos* to symbolize Maya identity. Nevertheless, this primary economic activity, and identifying symbol of "Mayaness," *milpa* work, is not practiced by the wealthy *Antiguos*. Thus, these rural capitalists appropriate both their labor force and their signs of identity from the poor Maya *milpero*.

There is another outstanding contradiction in the identity program propagated by *los Antiguos* elite. They represent themselves as nonmigrants. Figure 6.13 demonstrates convincingly that there are no significant differences among the various social groups in Chan Kom regarding migratory movement to Cancún. This finding contradicts *los Antiguos* propaganda, in which they deny any connection with migration. Figures 6.15 and 6.19 show another important ideological mask: although *los Antiguos* elite publicize their opposition to female migration, their daughters in fact migrate, although at a slower rate than other groups. Othon Baños Ramirez also notices this deliberate omission of the fact of female migration among Maya peasant families in the henequen area in Yucatán (1989:240). He attributes this nonrecognition of female migrants as a deliberate effort to assert poverty among the Maya peasants. According to him, the peasants hang on to the myth of poverty by denying the existence of outside income in the household. In Chan Kom's case, I am more inclined to think that it is an ideological strategy to legitimize *los Antiguos*' position as Maya. Certainly, the peasants' everyday lives and customs bind female Maya to the domestic context as mothers and wives. Women are conceived as the conservative, transmitting bearers of tradition in the community. So, the links between traditional, conservative, peasant life and Maya community are ideologically joined in *los Antiguos*' opposition to female migration.

A general trend among these rural capitalists is that they invest their capital in the education of their children. They encourage their children to pursue careers in teaching, which they say is more attuned with the promotion of Maya culture and language.

New Bourgeoisie

The new bourgeoisie comprise the young migrant generation that were willing to run the risk of leaving the rural *monte* (*milpa*) for the urban *monte* (city wilderness). They are the permanent migrants of the upper class (Figure 6.19), and the white-collar Maya, with high status occupations in Cancún (see Figures 6.14, 6.16, and 6.17).

Under new conditions of economic change, *los Antiguos* elite (the rural capitalists) have continued to pursue traditional economic activities. As Maya began to look for new alternatives to diversify their activities, the elite did not follow them in the adventure; they had economic security in their cattle and land investments. At the beginning, *los Antiguos* elite were secure enough in their political power and economic wealth that they did not pay too much attention to politics. They did not realize the direction so-called "modernization" had taken in the community. For this reason, their loss in the 1987 political election was very shocking for them, particularly when they realized the power acquired by this new group of young migrants was strongly connected to the PRI.

These new bourgeoisie, who currently hold the political offices in the village, are poor in cattle and land (that is, rural wealth), but rich in capital invested in the city. When referring to their rural possessions, they always allude to their father's possessions, already established in the village, which mainly consist of a few heads of cattle, *milpa*, and a

Figure 6.16 *Occupation and Group Distribution in Cancún*

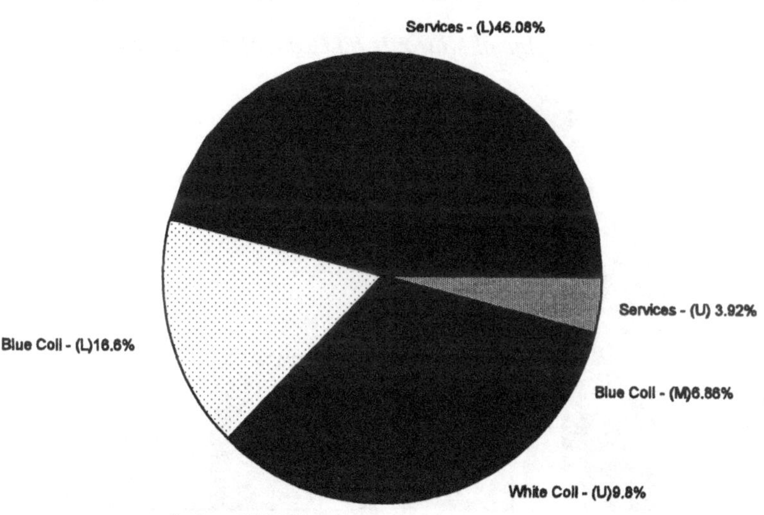

considerable amount of capital invested in stores and village houses. These new capitalists are businessmen in the city; they own, for example, bakeries, fruit stores, and grocery stores, or they hold high status occupations such as administrative offices and skilled positions in the service sector (for example, managers, or head-chef in a hotel restaurant). These new bourgeoisie do not reproduce their capital in the traditional activities controlled by the old *caciques*; instead, their capital circulates more rapidly and is more flexible. It is money, not livestock or land, and it can be used to buy cars, houses in the city, VCRs and other commodities, or to make loans; money also can be used to buy peasant labor for rural activities or poor, migrant labor for business in the city. These new speculators, with imagination, also perpetuate a patron-client social relationship with the poor peasants who migrate to the city.

Since their political success in the last two municipal elections, the new bourgeoisie, installed at the political center of community life, represent an important axis of articulation with Cancún and the nation. A good part of their power derives from their wealth in capital and their external contacts, which operate at a regional and national level.

The bourgeoisie of the upper social group also promotes the we/ they ideological discourse but with different arguments. For them, "we" represents democracy, progress, modernity, and civilization. "They" is synonymous with old fashioned, stubborn stagnation in the past, and with political elements reactionary to the government that need to be subdued.

By March 1991, the people living around the plaza started to say that

Figure 6.17 *Average Age of Migrants by Occupation and Social Group*

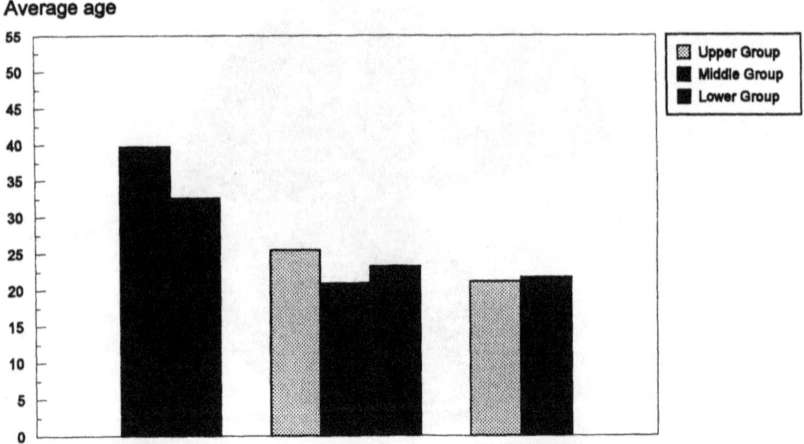

at night voices were coming out of the *cenote*; dogs were barking in an unusual manner, and sometimes the barks seemed like laments; birds were not singing any more. The president, pressed by people's fears, called *h-men* to ask for the reason. It had been a long time since the last *loh kah*[42] was celebrated in the village to expel the evil winds that cause such maladies. The last *loh Kah* had been headed by the old *cacique*, Don Chano, almost forty years earlier, just after the Protestants left the village. Now, it was the new president's turn. The president paid for the two *h-mens'* salaries. The danger and difficulty involved in the performance of the ritual raised the price requested by each *h-meno'ob* to half a million pesos. The president was very eager to publicly admit that he himself paid such a fortune for the benefit of the entire community. His monetary investment in social incentives maximized his social prestige and was aimed at legitimizing the political position held by his group. Clearly, some of the wealth originated in this group's high status, urban occupations, and business is used to purchase or maintain their rural positions by displaying their wealth through ritual paraphernalia.

New Traditionalists

These are the petty bourgeoisie in the Marxist terminology. Sometimes they are labeled "new rich" by the villagers. I call them "new traditionalists." They share economic activities with the rural capitalists: private land and cattle (Figures 6.8, 6.9, and 6.10) but on a smaller scale. To differentiate these two groups, I established a numerical criteria (see Table 6.1). This social category comprises 26 households and 24.6 percent of the village population (see Table 6.2). They live above subsistence level; sometimes they even produce some surplus that they invest in the maintenance of and technological advancements in *milpa* and cattle production. These families control 22.6 percent of the cattle, they own 32.31 percent of the private property, and they tend to cultivate larger sized *milpas* than the lower peasant group (see Figure 6.5). They are not confined to the productive limits of *milpa*, like the poor milpero are, although they cultivate it both intensively and extensively. These new traditionalists may reinvest their profits in ritual expenditure, a form of wealth that confers upon them a reputation of stability and prestige within the local milieu. These nonnegotiable ritual tasks provide them with a legitimate social and economic position in *los Antiguos'* view. The economic and ritual collaboration between the rural capitalists and the new traditionalists group unifies their political forces against the political control held by *los de Cancún*.

In Chan Kom, the celebration of the patron feast saint (San Diego) on November 13 is preceded by *los gremios*. In Chan Kom, the *gremios* are those individuals who host the representation of the patron saint

The ramilletes of the gremios at the cargador's house,
one of the new traditionalists in Chan Kom.

during one year. The *cargador* (bearer) of the *gremio* is responsible for
the expenses (food offerings, material to elaborate the *ramillete* (flowers),
mass payment, and the like). For the patron saint celebration of 1990,
the 13 *cargadores* of the *gremios* were rural capitalists or new traditionalists, all members of the upper, rural, social group. And most interestingly, the following year they passed their own *cargo* (office) on to
individuals of the same family or else retained it for another year.[43]

These new traditionalists follow the we/they ideology as defined by
the rural capitalists. They favor a public discourse against migration to
Cancún. Figures 6.13, 6.15, and 6.19 demonstrate, however, that they do
migrate.

Cancún, the Other Milpa

On the outskirts of Cancún, many ethnic groups from all over the
Mexican nation try to adapt to this "civilized, modern, and progressive"
world. Today, Maya from many regions of México and Central America

shape an integral part of the multiethnic landscape that is Cancún. The drastic economic development of tourism in Cancún has provoked a rapid spatial expansion of the city to give shelter to the avalanche of migrants, the urban proletarians. Parts of the Cancún scrub forest and *ejido* lands have been invaded by migrant families who cannot afford the extremely high cost of living in the city. With the invasion of *ejido* lands, new *barrios* of improvised huts, thatch-walled houses with cardboard roofs, have appeared. Electricity, running water, or any sanitary services are seldom seen in these urban migrant settlements called *colonias populares*. These services are urban luxuries that these migrants cannot afford. Those migrants who are more acquainted with urban life, who have longer experience as urban proletarians, live in more developed areas with water systems, electricity, and public transportation. They have televisions and VCRs in their homes. Still another group consists of the proletarian pioneers of Cancún, those who left their rural communities in the 1970s and believe themselves to be the creators of this international tourist emporium. They are, in fact, the infrastructural founders of Cancún, and are proud of it. They spread the propaganda of Cancún as *the Mecca* for those seeking progress and economic opportunity. These are the urban capitalists, the new bourgeoisie.

Migrants' actions in the city illustrate the maintenance and recreation of peasant images prompted by their current socioeconomic and cultural urban circumstances. The image of *milpa*, so central in the community identity debate, is carried into the urban context and endowed with new meanings. The migrants reinterpret *milpa*, not only to counterargue their de-ethnification by *los Antiguos*, but also to achieve a psychological equilibrium in the shift in their world view. By creating an urban *milpa*, they provide themselves with a recognizable identity through which they can make sense of the drastic move from the village to the city.

Within the migrants' social world, the internal class distinctions are quite meaningful. Certainly, those who are the fortunate migrants started at low-wage, low-prestige work; however, the political connections of their relatives back in the village, founded upon the close relationship between Don Eustaquio and the PRI, and their long urban experience as workers helped them to move out. Differences in the types of urban occupations lead to concrete class distinctions in migrant lifestyles.

Upper Class: The Pioneer Urban Milperos

The succesful migrants, the urban capitalist enterpreneurs, look at Cancún metaphorically, as a fruitful, splendorous, magnificent *milpa* that rewards them with capital accumulation obtained through their businesses and wages.

Through the political offices that they currently hold in Chan Kom, and via their direct access to public discourse, the urban upper class publicize Cancún as the *Mecca* of economic success. In this way, they help the government to permeate the peasant community in an attempt to obtain cheap wage labor for the development of the tourism industry.

This urban upper class is not a homogeneous economic category. The *we/they* discourse helps to illuminate the divisions embedded in this social class. As already mentioned, the rural capitalists also migrate. Who are these rural capitalists in the urban context?

Los de Cancún urban upper class are today involved in their own businesses, mostly related to the skilled occupations they learned when they first worked as migrants: cooking and baking. Today, they complement the incomes from their businesses (bakeries, food stores, fruit-stores) with high status positions in the service sector (chief pastry chef; chief chef in restaurants). The rural capitalists' sons, migrants in Cancún, have a preference for occupations dealing with bureaucracy (office and administration) and education (teachers). Both groups comprise young individuals (see Figure 6.17), who, although members of the same socio-economic cluster of the urban upper class, represent the two cultural categories of the upper class in the village. Education and literacy is the primary factor in this social differentiation; a high percentage of the migrant upper and middle class of *los Antiguos* completed a secondary school education (ninth grade), while *los de Cancún* upper class usually only attained a primary (sixth grade) education, and some of them have not even finished that.

The Lower Class. The Mucuy *and Permanent Migrants*

Figure 6.15 (temporary migration), and Figure 6.19 (permanent migration) show the different migration patterns among the lower class. Their commitment to working their own *milpas* and those of other migrants, which remains the basis for their family's survival, demands an urban occupation flexible enough to allow them to work seasonally (Figures 6.14 and 6.16); construction jobs are most in demand. The average age of the migrant lower class (Figure 6.17) also indicates that most of these people are male heads of households who need to supplement *milpa* production with their migration wages. The high cost of living in the city, coupled with low wages, make their dream of prosperity an unattainable episode in their continuing story of poverty. However, back in Chan Kom they advertise the success of their urban experience; they affect the urban lifestyle in their dress, and proudly display televisions, radiocassette players, and other commodities purchased in the city. The high cost of living in Cancún and the social lessons of consumption effectively shrink their wages so that the actual capital with which they return

Figure 6.18 *Percentage of Migrants by Cattle Ownership and Gender in the Upper Group*

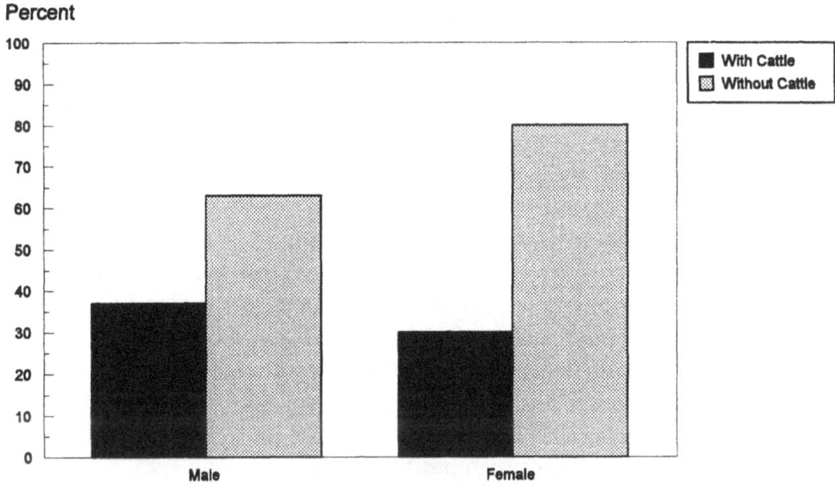

Figure 6.19 *Percentage of Permanent Migration by Social Group and Gender*

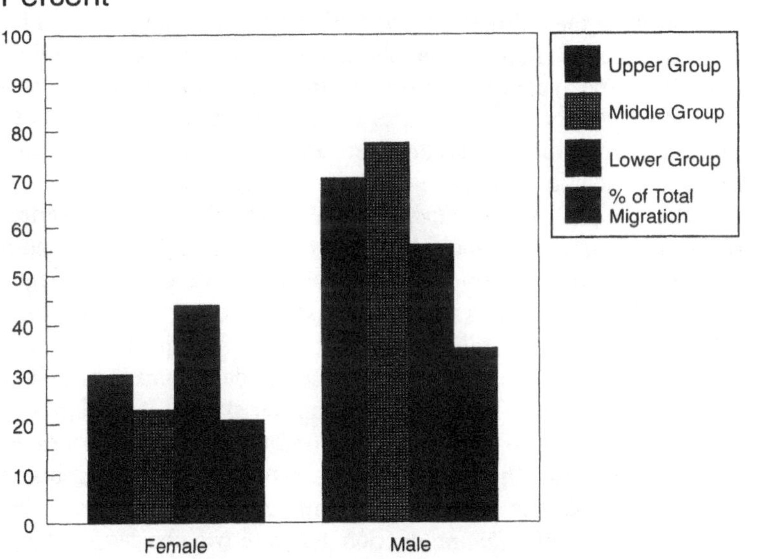

to the village is significantly reduced. Thus, the articulation of capitalism and the peasant subsistence system through migration among the lower class strongly promotes the stagnation and immobility of the poor.

As the figures indicate, most of the lower-class migrants who decided to live in the city permanently are younger than the shuttle migrants; generally they work low-wage jobs in the service sector (Figure 17). Those who decide to stay in the city eventually go on to acquire a small lot of land on which to build a house; the most affordable areas in which to live are the *colonias populares*. To establish themselves in the *colonias populares*, the migrants must clear the forest and weed the piece of land. The Maya is well-acquainted with these kinds of activities. In times of intense agricultural work at the *milpa*, the peasant has to clear a piece of forest and improvise a little hutch in which he can spend the night. Danger in the forest, lack of electricity and water, and other conditions at the *milpa* resemble the danger, the lack of water, electricity, and other basic necessities that the Maya has to face in Cancún. Envisioning their urban workplace and settlement as a *milpa* is more than an ideological trick to legitimize their urban position for *los Antiguos'* eyes.

A Concluding Note

Despite the apparent bisocial partition implicit in the *we/they* cultural categories, the simplest of quantitative methods reveals, first, a much more complex social structure within the village and the larger Chan Kom community, and second, a sizable discrepancy between the assets of the richest and the poorest families. The economic analysis does not invalidate the cultural categories that present Chan Kom as a bifurcated community. Rather, it emphasizes the relevance of integrating interpretive and economic analyses in order to achieve a better understanding of the complexities of social relations. And, at the same time, this economic analysis discovers and interprets the reasons for the social contradictions masked in the community's ideology.

The analysis of the *milpa* mode of production shows a variety of social relations and ideological legitimations among the various components of the contemporary Chan Kom social landscape. In the village, the *milpa* system perpetuates the lower-class position of the poor peasants. *Milpa* work is a form of self-employment that ties the peasant to the land. The rural capitalists' demands for economic development benefit from this self-perpetuation of economic impoverishment of the *milperos*, whose labor force and signs of identity (*milpa* work) are appropriated by the rural capitalists, the "we" cultural category. The new bourgeoisie also benefit from this. The strenuous economic conditions represented by the subsistence level of *milpa* production generate two choices for the poor:

they can work for wages in the village, or they can migrate. The migrant peasants form the source of a cheap labor force for the Maya bourgeoisie, the "they" cultural category that has been established in the urban context. Thus, the *milpa* system guarantees the disposability of cheap labor among the *we* and *they* poor, as well as for the *we* and *they* Maya upper class (rural capitalists and urban bourgeoisie). The *milpa* system subsidizes not only the economic development of the community's upper class, but also the nation that benefits from the disposability of peasant labor (for example, in the development of the tourist industry).

The urban upper class still needs the rural Chan Kom. They are subsidized by the poor migrants' labor; the upper class also take advantage of connections with the state government to achieve political control in the village. With this political power, they can acquire higher social positions and prestige in the urban setting. Thus, the struggle for political control becomes critical for both *we* and *they* categories of the upper class in Chan Kom today; for both sides, political power is a commodity, manipulated in different ways.

Chapter 7

Images of a Maya Community in the Postmodern World.

> *Los* Yuntziles, *los* aluxes *de Cancún no quieren que viva allí nadie porque es de ellos. Dicen que todo Cancún se va a hundir, que ni vehículo se puede escapar. Todos se van a hundir hasta que no quede nadie aquí, hasta los hoteles, todo va a desaparecer. (Narrador: Don Alito, Cancún)*
>
> *The* Yuntziles, aluxes *of Cancún, don't want anyone to live there because it [Cancún] is theirs. It is said that all Cancún is going to be flooded, not even cars will be able to escape. Everyone is going to drown, until no one is left there, even the hotels, everything is going to disappear. (Narrator: Don Alito, Cancún)*

The Maya from Chan Kom elaborate their own identity through a continual, conversational interaction. The task of describing and explaining Maya identity requires the emotional involvement of the participants in the performance of everyday life as much as my own involvement to convey this identity elaboration process to the anthropological audience. Certainly, I am analyzing the performance, but I also experience it, contribute to it, and create a way to express it in my own culture.

During the time I lived in Chan Kom, I provided my Maya family with the maize and other produce that I grew in my *milpa*. After coming from the fields and taking the ritual cleansing bath, one of my favorite pastimes was to walk around the *plaza* (public square) with one of Charo's children. I particularly enjoyed discussing agricultural matters

140

with the group of men gathered at the corners of the *plaza*: types of seed, the use of fertilizers, the best time to plant, and the prediction of weather were common issues in our exchanges of agricultural knowledge and experience. I believe that the men enjoyed our customary evening encounters as much as I did.

My pride was easily susceptible to male Maya remarks about me as *española abusada* (meaning hard worker of the land). Some of the men thought that I was just a bizarre *xunan* (white woman) doing bizarre things; others used my role as *milpera* in their diatribe against *los de Cancún*: "incluso una mujer viene de fuera y trabaja la tierra más que ellos" (even a woman comes from the outside and works the land more than they do). Certainly, comments about my *milpa* became a staple of Maya conversation, particularly among *los Antiguos*, who took it as my tacit recognition of their "true Mayaness."

As a student of the Maya culture, I was analyzing *milpa* work, the emblem of what *los Antiguos* considered the core of "Mayaness." For some of them, however, my bizarre role as worker of the fields was hard to accept; I was transgressing a cultural pattern. Acknowledging this transgression, I relied on my ambiguous role as an outsider to validate my anomalous position as a woman working in the fields. Invoking my status of outsider clashed, however, with *los Antiguos'* demands to fit eventuality, circumstance, and fact within their traditional fabric. The following anecdote illustrates this conflict.

I spent most of my fieldwork without menstruating. According to the doctor in the city, the problem was a combination of strenuous physical activity, a radical change in diet and living conditions, and stress. For the Maya *h-men* (curer), the problem had a very simple explanation: "es normal; usted esta haciendo trabajo de hombres" (it is normal; you are doing men's work).

Born in a working class suburb of Madrid, of a family with modest economic resources, I am considered by Spanish reckoning to be an "asphalt girl." My first contact with nature was at age eighteen when I worked for a friend collecting grapes. I always thought of myself as handicapped in agricultural matters. Chan Kom offered the chance to fulfill what I considered a significant void in my makeup.

While in Chan Kom, my schedule revolved around the daily and seasonal work in the *milpa*. In that environment, Cancún had become for me less a reality than a notion created by the stories about *el peligro* (the danger) of the city—the very image that I elicited from my informants[44]. Nevertheless, the issues I was studying—the perception of crisis; the division of a community in which political offices were in the hands of migrants who work in the city; the articulation of the *milpa* mode of production with the urban proletarianization—required that I move to the urban setting, Cancún.

Cancún, located about 225 kilometers from Chan Kom, is the city with the highest annual rate of population growth in México, 25 percent. The permanent population in Cancún was 105,733 in 1985; 200,776 by 1988; and 301,511 inhabitants by 1990 (Cardiel and Villalobos 1989:23). Of the total population, 29.3 percent is of Maya origin (Cardiel and Villalobos 1989:34).

On my first day in Cancún, I was overwhelmed by noises and fumes from automobiles; there seemed to be multitudes of people in the streets, tourists exhibiting their bodies almost naked—it was a contrast difficult to digest. Wearing my *huipil* and *rebozo* (shawl), with a scared Maya girl grabbing my hand (I had brought Charo's youngest girl, *la nené*, with me), I felt that I was crossing a boundary, entering an urban wilderness not so very removed from my memories of Madrid. The following is an extract of my diary that refers to my initial impressions of Cancún:

> This is really different: tourists in shorts, almost naked. A lot of people in the streets, too much traffic. I understand why Charo was so concerned about letting me bring *la nené* to Cancún, especially because of the *avenidas* (referring to the large roads with dense traffic). I have to recognize that it is quite shocking to see Mayas dressed in shorts, wearing golden necklaces, handing out restaurants, bars, hotel publicity in the streets, cooking and serving for the tourists. . . .
>
> I went with *la nené* to the beach. My Maya dress, *nené*'s Maya features, and my burnt but "white" skin puzzled the Mayan guard at the hotel entrance. It is really difficult to get to the beach without going through a hotel; the coast is hotel-packed! The guard asked me if we were clients in the hotel; I replied that we were going just to *gustar* (enjoy) the beach for a short while.
>
> Joy to see *la nené* playful with the waves. She discovered an entire new world: the sea and the sand. Her first words to express this encounter with the never-before-seen sea: "Do you think there is any *fondo* (bottom)? Is this rainwater? It is like *cenote*. . . ." (Diary, Thursday, March 29, 1990)[45]

The culture shock continued for quite a few days. Sharing my urban experience with Consuelo's (Charo's sister) family brought me the living knowledge of the way Maya construct their existence in Cancún. Quite often Consuelo did not have money to make lunch or dinner; she had to wait until the end of the day, when Miguel, her husband, came with some money in order to buy bread, eggs, and *refresco* (refreshment, mainly Coca Cola). Every morning started around 6:00 A.M., with the TV on to listen to *el noticiero* (the news). The early-morning ritual was performed every day:

> Luisa (dirigiendose a la hija mayor que se tiene que levantar para ir a la escuela), no entiendes lo que te digo?, parate ya!. Ya se *wixó* tu hermana!

Mira, esta todo mojado. Que se paren, digo, *chingaos* chamacos. (Consuelo, from my diary on Cancún, April 1990)

Luisa (addressing the eldest daughter who had to get up to go to school), don't you understand what I am saying?, get up! Your sister peed in the bed again! Look at it, I say, everything is wet. Get up you little bastards. (Consuelo, from my diary on Cancún, April 1990)

Daily customs, ways of addressing each other, habits and manners were strikingly different from those of the Maya in Chan Kom. Was I falling into believing the village myth of "the Cancún Maya without tradition"? Was I promoting the propaganda of the urban Maya as cultural losers?[46]

Through daily interactions, I increasingly recognized the migrants' use of Maya tradition and symbolism in the urban setting. How is this Maya imagery transferred to the urban environment to articulate the Maya experience with the invisible, urban boundaries of class and ethnicity? This quandrary is pointing out a very complex interplay between the Maya cultural and socioeconomic rural basis and the urban migrant experience. We can begin analyzing this process of creation and rural-urban transference of Maya imagery by examining how a Maya migrant conceptualizes Cancún:

Los *yuntziles*, los *aluxes* de Cancún no quieren que vive allí nadie porque es de ellos. Dicen que todo Cancún se va a hundir, que ni vehículo se puede escapar. Todos se van a hundir, hasta que no quede nadie aquí, hasta los hoteles, todo va a desaparecer. Dicen que los *yuntziles* van a cerrar los cuatro puntos de Cancún y lo van a inundar. "Kan" en Maya es serpiente, y "Kun" significa que es como cántaro grande, así es el nombre de Cancún . . . Pues si, así dicen que en Cancún hay una serpiente con alas, la *X-Kukikan*, que vive en el mar, que se va a voltear y va a mandar una lluvia muy grande, y todos van a morir. Pues mi mujer tiene un gran susto y quiere volver a Chan Kom. (narrator: don Alito, Cancún)

The *yuntziles*, *aluxes* of Cancún, don't want anyone to live there because it [Cancún] is theirs. It is said that all Cancún is going to be flooded, not even cars will be able to escape. Everyone is going to drown, until no one is left there, even the hotels, everything is going to disappear. It is said that the *yuntziles* are going to close the four corners of Cancún and they are going to sink it , . . "Kan" in Maya means serpent, and "Kun" means that it is like a big jar so that is the name of Cancún . . . So, it is said that there is a snake with wings in Cancún, the *X-Kukikan*, that dwells in the sea, that it is going to turn over and it is going to send a great rain, and everyone is going to die. So my wife is very scared, and she wants to go back to Chan Kom. (narrator: Don Alito, Cancún).

This Maya narration on the coming of the *X-kukikan*, with which I begin this chapter, expresses the urban experience in the light of Maya tradition. The narrator, Don Alito, after working for almost twenty years in Cancún, is preparing to return to Chan Kom. He sees Chan Kom as a retirement place, a place "para terminar mis días" (to end my days). He uses an ancient character from Maya oral tradition to validate the destruction of Cancún, and to justify his return to the village. This story exemplifies the reinvention of Maya culture, vacillating between assimilation and resistance, within a complex web of social, political, and ideological relations.

Cancún: The Transnationalization of Money and Culture

Cancún represents the success of the development of tourism at a national level. The original plans for Cancún were part of a national program to develop vacation resorts throughout México that would appeal to an international clientele. The purpose of this program was to attract hard foreign currency that could be used to pay off México's international debt (Cardiel and Villalobos 1989:5). The Cancún tourist industry provides two main types of employment: low-skilled jobs in the service sector (for instance, waiters and maids), and unskilled work in construction. Other tourist-related industries have been developed as well, such as handicrafts. Finally, Cancún represents a sociocultural environment where the indigenous folk and the tourist world are in a continuous exchage (Lee 1977:10).

More than one million tourists visited Cancún in 1987. Because Yucatán is easily accessible from the eastern half of the United States (Atlanta and Houston are about two hours away, and Washington, New York, and Chicago, three hours by airplane), the region is the main attraction to North American tourists. In 1988, an average of $4 million dollars was spent each day in Cancún; this represents 12% over the foreign capital invested in México (Cardiel and Villalobos 1989:5). This economic boom has another facet: the accelerated increase of an economically marginal population of rural migrants to Cancún is of Maya cultural origin (Cardiel and Villalobos 1985:34).

As part of the exotic adventure, the tourists expect to breathe an atmosphere of "Mayaness" in Cancún, and the Mexican government has responded with pyramid-shaped hotels, colorful murals that imitate pre-Hispanic Maya icons, and an abundance of stores that sell arts and crafts. For the tourist, the Cancún adventure is an escape from the routine of everyday life, and an entrance into the natural and cultural reservoir of an "other." The tourist seeks a stereotype of the "other," which comprises attributes such as carelessness, negligence, timelessness, and passion—traits that when they are found are a source of exasperation for most North American tourists. However, Cancún offers more than this psychological escape; it opens to the tourist an original cultural landscape, the land of the Maya.

As part of the international marketing campaign, most large hotels provide a tour of the hotel property showing the facilities, innovations, and future plans to improve the clients' comfort. In my explorations of the Maya experience as urban workers, I decided to work at a hotel where five Maya from Chan Kom were already employed. I worked in the hotel's time-sharing program, which consists of pursuing and convincing tourist couples to buy a hotel room for a period of two to three years. The following information on marketing in the tourist industry comes from my own experiences of working for this hotel in Cancún. I describe here some of the marketing paraphernalia used to persuade the tourists to sign the contract.

Some hotels use the "Aztec", "Toltec," and "Maya" categories to differentiate the types of rooms available; the guided tour may be flavored by some traditional Maya stories, in order to excite the tourists' imagination of living in, and with, the exotic. Thus, when showing the swimming pools or fountains, the guide may drop the parallelism with the Maya *cenotes*; sometimes, the guide chooses to touch on the ancient Maya sacrifices in the *cenotes* to remind the clients of their closeness to a "primitive other." The entire tour is punctuated by details that bring the Maya culture into the tourist discourse. Within this discourse, the present Mayas have a distinctive place. Most of the tourist packages include trips to Chichen Itza and other ancient Maya archaeological sites. Then, through these archaeological trips, the tourists will experience the living Maya culture that they were already exposed to via the discourse elaborated by the guide.

These local Mayas are perceived by the tourists as living museum pieces, part of the exotic environment. This perception is quite exploited by the tourist culture in the restaurants and hotels of Cancún: a traditional Maya woman making tortillas, or a young dark-brown petite Maya waiting tables, fulfill the tourists' demands for the exotic. In other words, the imagery used by the tourism industry transforms the Maya culture into a valuable commodity to be exploited for the capitalist market. It also promotes the folklorization of cultural strategies into commodities. "This leads to an alienated world in which cultural elements are received outside of the communities and traditions that initially gave them shape and meaning" (Lipsitz 1986:158–59). To meet market demands, the capitalist world produces what I call a "Magical World" that takes the remnants of historical cultures and converts them into a marketable ideological product.

This creation of an ancient, mythical, exotic world is adapted to the demands of a developed industrial world in need of the construction of a "primitive other." This "other" can provide the developed industrial world with reassurance about its own development, efficiency and perfection. At the same time, the exotic "other" feeds belief in the existence of cultural and natural reservoirs to which people can escape.

The plans to develop tourism in Cancún were first outlined in 1969; by 1974 the first hotel (Playa Blanca) was opened, and by 1987, Cancún was hosting more than 1,000,000 tourists per year. The initial plans included both the hotel and a residential area for the middle class; there were no specific plans for a migrant settlement. Today, some of the Chan Kom Maya recall those first days as similar to living in a *milperío*[47]:

> Nos pusieron en una casa de guano, muy grande, en medio del monte; allí dormíamos todos juntos. Allí, cerca de la obra, para tener la chamba cerca. (Narrator: Eduardo, Cancún)

> They placed us in a palm house, very large, in the middle of the forest; there we slept all together. There, near to the construction, to be near the work. (Narrator: Don Eduardo, Cancún)

Today, tourists never venture to those areas of Cancún where the living bearers of the present Maya culture live. The *colonias populares* (poor neighborhoods) are scenes hidden from the tourist; this could put at risk the beautiful construction of the magical Maya facade created out of the ancient past. For the metropolitan tourist culture, the Maya urban proletarians seem not to exist, except as cultural icons from an ancient past that are part of today's tourist decor.

The grandeur of the *zona hotelera* (hotel area)—the malls, the explosion of neon advertisements in English, and the tourist paraphernalia priced in dollars—contrasts with the *colonias populares*—cardboard-roof and stick-wall houses, the lack of running water and electricity, and no sanitation facilities—a world of chronic poverty. This is what R. Rosaldo calls "the implosion of the Third World into the First" (Rosaldo 1988, 1989).

The Implosion of Chan Kom into Cancún

> Ven negrito, trabaja bien y puedes tomar tu refresco (Come now, little nigger, work well and you can have a little soda to drink) (the manager of a restaurant speaking to a Maya waiter).

From their Cancún base, most of the permanent Maya migrants have found jobs in the service sector, as maids, gardeners, babysitters, waiters, and hotel staff. This employment requires a dramatic jump by the Maya into the urban class structure. The Maya, carrying a rural cultural tradition, must cope on a daily basis with a new urban environment. If we are to understand the process by which peasants articulate their rural heritage with their urban experience, we must consider, within peasant and proletarian forms, the ideological and socioeconomic background of the rural Maya. If we are to understand the terms and processes within this shift, we must take the peasant Chan Kom representation and socioeconomic components into account.

In the village, the *milpa* mode of production dictates that the patriarchal household is the main socioeconomic unit. Symbolically, the house encapsulates both the life and work of the peasant family. For *los Antiguos*, the principal indicator of community membership is possession of a house in the village. Thus, the household, the domestic domain, and the dependence on cooperative labor become indispensable terms to define village life. For the rural Maya, Cancún, which lies outside the security of the village domain, is a realm of chaos and danger.

Gender roles, so ingrained in the village cultural pattern, are the contrasting images of the idealistic Chan Kom for Cancún, and the hostile Cancún for Chan Kom. In the Maya cultural tradition in Chan Kom, women are identified with the ordered, safe, domestic realm, while men are identified with the world outside the limits of the house—the streets and plaza of the village, the *milpa* outside the village, and the world represented by Cancún. The village plaza, bound to the main institutions of community life (church, municipal offices, stores) is the male spatial domain *par excellence*. Women do not have such a customarily public domain where they can interact; the ritual context eventually provides occasions for female gatherings, because women are needed to prepare the food offerings. At one time, the *cenote*, at the very center of the plaza, was a female space where gossip was created and exchanged. Maya women went each morning to get the water necessary for their domestic chores. Chan Kom's *cenote* is no longer in use; today, the primary female public space is the mill-store where the Maya women bring their *nixtamal* (soaked maize) to be ground into *masa* (corn dough). Although *milpa* work is a male task, it requires the productive complement of female chores; the domestic and the *milpa* realms conform with a productive system which depends on their symbiotic relation. The merging of migration into the community's systems of production mechanisms alters the male/female symbiotic relationship, required for *milpa* work. When a peasant migrates temporarily, his wife and children usually remain in the village. The wife, in the absence of any son who may substitute for the father in the household decision-making, becomes the temporary head of the household. She performs the father's role in disciplining the children; in case of sickness or any problem in the *milpa* that demands the *h-men*'s assistance, she has to arrange for his service, although the final contract with him has to be undertaken by either the husband, or another male relative. Living expenses in Cancún (for instance, the high cost of rent, alcohol consumption), in conjunction with the low migrant wages, is the main threat in assuring part of the husband's earnings for the maintenance of the family. To overcome the uncertainty of the financial support coming from Cancún, women recur to other sources of income such as artisan production (*huipiles*) or small commercial transactions (selling vegetables and fruits and other products grown at the *solar*). Women may also offer their services as domestics for other Maya families, particularly the wealthy. If the husband is unemployed or delinquent in sending money home, which threatens the family's subsistence, the rural kinship-social network protects the family.[48] In any case, migration promotes the changes in male/female roles. Migration gives women in the village not only more autonomy and control, but also more responsibilities. Although Mary Elmendorf (1977) stated that men and women are the complements of the family unit in the 1970s, two decades of migration to Cancún have transformed this family pattern. Advertised by *los Antiguos*, particularly in their defense of *milpa* work as the source of "true Mayaness", family and house are the strongest links to community life, and serve also as the assurance of community membership. For this reason, *los Antiguos* stress the Maya woman's social value as the core continuity of Maya tradition. They put so much emphasis in this female contribution to the perseverance of Maya identity that they even deny the existence of female migration among their families.

In Cancún, Maya men have moved from the peasant *milpa* to the urban proletarian workplace. They are no longer anchored by *milpa* ideology and the ideals of equality and cooperation that it promotes—an ideal that *los Antiguos* elite make great effort to preserve. On the contrary, the urban workplace orders the migrants into a class structure within their own ethnic group and within the broader national class structure. Despite these drastic changes in lifestyle, Maya migrants continue to employ images and assumptions of their rural cultural baggage in the construction of a new world view. The migrant Maya create new representations to rearrange their known and comfortable views of the world into the unknown, threatening, and chaotic urban landscape. Thus, in Cancún, the spatial community arrangements are challenged. The clear division of labor according to gender that is evident in Chan

Kom is blurred in the faces of the national culture and international setting.

Among the urban challenges that the migrant faces, the factor that stands at the core of the changeable representation is the basic relation between home and workplace. All the imagery encapsulated in *milpa* production, the quintessence of socioeconomic and symbolic Maya identity, is based on the unit of production and consumption, the household. Migration breaks this connection between a household that is no longer the unit of production, and the workplace, the city. The urban workplace is no longer the legitimate site to cultivate social value and economic subsistence; now the workplace is organized around a hierarchical system of control, in which the migrant is rewarded by wages.

The Maya representation of community space, based on the opposition of domestic and public spheres, is challenged as well. Back in the village, *los Antiguos* elite refuse to let their daughters migrate either through marriage (permanent migration), or as single women; in this way they reinforce their representation as the guardians of Maya tradition and identification. Female migration occurs frequently, however, among the rural capitalist and new traditionalist groups in the village. In order to cope with inflation in Cancún, both husband and wife must work; women shuttle back and forth between the domestic and the public workplaces. Their social interactive space, the mill-store and ritual gatherings, are challenged in the wider urban world.

Food habits among the Maya are transformed in Cancún. The simple Maya diet, based on beans and tortillas, is replaced by a much wider selection of food products. Shopping for food and other consumer goods becomes a necessity. Women go to the *tortillería* (store where *tortillas* are produced and sold) for the manufactured tortillas consumed daily. For women in the urban setting, the *tortillería* and the small neighborhood stores have replaced the mill-store of the village as meeting places; however, the arena of social interaction is enlarged to include diverse ethnic groups. As wives and mothers, women continue to form the core of domestic activity, but they may also participate in the search for wage labor. Indeed, when the man loses his job, the financial contribution of the wife becomes critical to the household's survival.

In sum, the concepts of home and workplace meet new challenges when brought into the urban, proletarian context. Probably the part of the urban realm that causes the most anxiety for Maya migrants is the public space of the *avenidas*—a term Maya use to encompass busy city streets, malls, supermarkets, bars, discos, and the like. The familiar core of public life, seen in the village, the mill-store, and the plaza, is transformed into a nightmare of larger spaces where representatives of different ethnic groups interact. Via their move to Cancún, the migrant Maya create a human geography with the rudiments of their symbolic and cultural baggage. For instance, the urban homes and work places are conceptualized under the same Maya socio-economic and ideological construct, the *milpa*. New geographies constructed with familiar cultural notions imply the redefinition of the genderized home and workplace space, and consequently, the resulting hypergenderized relations; development of machismo, supersubservient attitudes among women, and increase of domestic violence towards women are included among the social effects of the blurred gender roles of the urban Maya performance.

Once back in the village, the migrants, full of the impressions of their urban experience, enjoy enormously the retelling of urban anecdotes, news, or events, which ignite the imaginations of their peasant peers. To enhance the prestige that they receive through their ability to cope with adventure in the outside world, they do not hesitate to flavor these urban tales with exaggerated descriptions of the obstacles and the violence of city life. In turn, *los Antiguos* use these images of danger and adventure to fuel their rejection of the urban lifestyle.

> Allí hay mucho peligro, no es tranquilo . . . Suceden muchas cosas, son personas que tienen vicios, hay mujeres que se llevan con otros hombres . . . Allí uno no puede tener sus sembrados, sus animales, sus gallinas . . . Uno tiene que comprar todo, sin en cambio, en el pueblo, con poco dinero te da. En Cancún no hay donde jueguen los chamacos, . . . es mucho peligro. (Narrator: Doña Emilia, Chan Kom)

> There is much danger, it is not tranquil there [Cancún)] . . . Many things happen; they are immoral people [those who live in Cancún]; there are women who go with other men . . . There one cannot have his garden, his animals, his chickens, one has to buy everything. In contrast, in the village, with little money you can survive. In Cancún there is no place for the children to play, . . . it is much danger. (Narrator: Doña Emilia, Chan Kom)

The quotation above underscores the social and economic dangers to the community represented by Cancún, and ideologically legitimizes a social reality of community division—a reality in which *los Antiguos* defend their position as the legitimate Maya, opposed to the dangers and threats of Cancún. There is an expression that has become popular among the people in Chan Kom: *dzu sut sac* (he/she has returned white), referring to the whitening of the skin due to working indoors in Cancún. The term *Dzul* can also be used in Maya to refer to humans who do not cultivate *milpa*. In addition, the expression *dzu sut sac* may also refer to the adoption by Maya of the external trappings of the *dzulo'ob* (white) socio-economic and cultural world. As this expression implies, in addition to the physical dangers of city life, the migrants risk the loss of their Maya identity: the dark Maya skin leathered by the sun during countless hours of work at the *milpa* is whitened by the indoor urban jobs. So the Maya migrants seem to lose their identity in two ways: they change their workplace (*milpa*), and the color of their skin lightens.

Migrant construction workers, more exposed to the burning tropical sun, do not lose their dark coloring; in fact, they become darker. The access to construction jobs represents the best option for those temporary migrants who still depend upon *milpa* production. The temporary contracts in Cancún during the resting periods of the *milpa* allow them to articulate migration with the agricultural cycle. These temporary migrants keep home, family, and *milpa* in Chan Kom. That is, with the help of some extra cash from low wages, these Maya keep their economic and sociocultural umbilical connection to village life. This is why *los Antiguos* are not using them as the target of their corrosive insults. For them, these construction workers maintain the core Maya values (*milpa*, house, and family), and their dark skin, which still identify them as Maya. Furthermore, their low construction wages do not represent a threat of increasing wealth that could compete with the peasant wealth of *los Antiguos*'s elite. Therefore, these Mayas bridge the identity gap between Chan Kom and Cancún. In other words, the competing representations for Maya identity in this current phase of community life are built on the transformations of home, workplace, places for social interaction, and the ethnic-racial notion. While for the Maya in Chan Kom, the migrants lose the external signs of their Maya identity through the whitening of their skin, for the *dzulo'ob* (white) society of Cancún, the Maya are recognizable because of their dark skin, as the term *negrito* (little nigger) at the beginning of this section indicates.

Within the urban framework, men and women are pressed to face extreme social contrasts in their daily activities. In the workplace, the laborer lives in a world that exists to satisfy the tourist's dream of a relaxing vacation in one of the world reservoirs of ancient civilization. Some of them can enjoy the tourist beach paraphernalia (men and women almost naked, windsurfing exhibitions, and the like) while working in construction. Others, mainly women, alternate between the bourgeois, domestic environment of their employers and the hardships of daily survival in the *colonias populares*. After being actors at their workplace stage, migrants return to their already familiar stage, which encompasses a high risk of parasitic diseases, extremely high cost of living, lack of government services, and other such problems.

Cancún is also a place for entertainment: movie theaters, discos, cantinas:

En Cancún hay más para diversión; el baile . . . De todo hay allí, allí estan mis amigos. Aquí, cuando llego, mi familia veo no más. Aquí sales a la plaza y no hay nadie; los domingos sales y platicas con los amigos. En cambio allá todo el tiempo tienes amigos; cuando agarras tu quincena, compras unas chivas y te reunes con los amigos . . . Cancún es más fácil para buscar la vida, allí me quedo a ganar un poco. En Cancún uno come más, hay carne, hay más cosas, uno se conserva mejor . . . Sin en cambio vienes al pueblo y esta muerto, no hay donde ir, . . . sólo la familia y ya. (Narrator: don Miguel, Chan Kom)

There are more ways to have a good time in Cancún; the disco . . . There is everything there; my friends are there. When I come here [Chan Kom] I only see my family. You go out to the plaza and you don't see anyone; Sundays you go out and talk to your friends. However, there you have friends all the time; when you get your paycheck every two weeks (quincena), you buy some beer and you get together with your friends. Cancún is an easier place for survival (buscar la vida); I stay there to make a little money. In Cancún one can eat more, there is meat, there are more things, you can take better care of yourself . . . On the other hand, you come to the village and it is dead, there is no place to go, . . . only the family. (Narrator: Don Miguel, Chan Kom)

The leisure domain is greatly advertised back in the village; it also exemplifies the capitalism's successful role in the migrant experience. These urban places for entertainment are the equivalents to the plaza, the rural place for social interaction, but the ethos they generate is quite different. Legally, some of these places are not public; they are private property. For instance, although hotels cannot own the beaches, which are public, they can restrict access to any individual who is not a client. Just like the workplace, the pleasure palaces of corporate capitalism are regulated spaces. Most Maya migrants find their recreational access to the tourist domain restricted. The migrant of the upper social group, however, which has more economic resources, participates in a wider social, political, and employment network, and has much easier access to these urban, private spaces (for example, fancy restaurants and hotel beaches).

In the *colonias populares*, the capitalist network is manifested in the proliferation of food, clothing, and sometimes video stores. To a large degree, the mass media inculcates the migrant with the values and expectations of the urban middle class. For instance, one of the weekend leisure activities for a peasant family is to rent three or four videos that are passed around a broad circuit of relatives, neighbors, and friends.

On the weekend, the street corners in the *colonias populares* are filled with men and cases of beer. The street corners are the most common social-gathering places for lower-class males. These male groupings comprise people from different parts of the national landscape; what unifies them is the migrant condition and lifestyle. Migrants seek a psychological outlet for their frustations as exiles and proletarians, and they mostly find it in alcohol consumption. Frequently, these drunken gatherings result in fights, which, unfortunately, may involve the use of knives or other weapons. Certainly this potential for violence reinforces a perception, primarily strengthened by the urban bourgeoisie, that Cancún is a dangerous place.

The urban bourgeoisie disapproves of the way in which the lower class uses its disposable income. The middle and upper classes profess to value the accumulation and investment of capital as the means to a better way of life. In their stereotyping of the lower class, they criticize the poor for spending their income frivolously. This is ironic, given that the purpose of the national government in establishing Cancún was to encourage the consumption of luxury goods and services to support the national economy. The urban Maya are therefore confronted with contradictory messages from the national culture. Further, by promoting the reputation of danger in the *colonias populares*, the bourgeoisie justifies restriction of both the spatial movements of the migrant lower class within the city, and the potential of the lower class for mobility within the class structure. The bourgeoisie make a great effort to maintain the physical and social separation that marks the invisible borders between the three Cancúns: the tourist zone, the middle class residences, and the migrant ghetto.

The Implosion of Cancún into Chan Kom

In Chan Kom, there is ample expression of public hostility against *los de Cancún*. Migration is what clearly differentiates the economic systems and the world views of the two Chan Kom Maya groups. In general, migration represents disunity, the collapse of tradition, the abandonment of community, family ties, and social obligations. *Los Antiguos* respond to this stereotyped representation of migration by reinforcing a community image of unity, mutual aid, and residential propinquity. They stress the idea of collective labor, insisting that it is most fully realized by parents and children exerting physical effort in a collective project. The *milpa* mode of production inherently evokes this idea of community egalitarianism and unity, which is deeply rooted in the solidity of family.

The following voices present two different Maya versions of the life of a peasant farmer. The first voice comes from the rural capitalists' realm, that is, from *los Antiguos'* elite. The second voice comes from the rural Maya proletariat, the *milperos*, whose *milpas* are their economic sustenance and their symbolic existence.

> Yo veo la vida del campesino más tranquila que los que van a Cancún y dicen que ganan millones y millones, pero están más fregaos que el campe-

sino que esta aquí en su milpa porque cada que agarra su dinero, lo derrocha. Allí en Cancún lo ganan, pero lo gastan. En cambio, un pobre milpero, cuando amanece anda y agarra su costalito, tiene su calabacita, su maicito . . . Ellos mueren de un ataque cardíaco porque cuanta memoria hacen con las cuentas. En cambio, el campesino, cuando llega el día hasta empieza a roncar, come y al rato se va a acostar, ¡cuánto descanso tiene su cuerpo! (Narrator: Don Antonio, Chan Kom)

I see the peasant's life as more tranquil than those who go to Cancún and say that they earn millions and millions, but they are in a much worse condition than the peasant that is here, in his *milpa*, because when he [the migrant] gets his pay, he wastes it. They earn money in Cancún, but they spend it all there. However, a poor *milpero*, when the sun rises, goes and grabs his bag, he has his little plot of squash, his little bit of corn . . . They [the migrants] die from a heart attack because what memory they must spend to keep account of their money. On the other hand, the peasant can lie abed snoring well after dawn. He eats, and in a little while, he goes to lie down. How much rest his body gets! (Narrator: Don Antonio, Chan Kom)

La milpa, nuestro trabajo, es la vida. Cuando amanece, primero la vida. Hay que pensar primero lo que hay que hacer, trabajar, y si tenemos cosecha, pues quedamos muy conformes, estamos contentos que amanece pues podemos ir a trabajar de nuevo . . . El trabajo del campesino es duro, te tienes que romper el cuerpo. (Narrator: Don Juanjo, Chan Kom)

The *milpa*, our work, is our life. When the sun rises, life comes first. We must think first, what needs to be done, to work, and if we have a harvest, well, we are very happy, we are glad that the sun rises, so that we can go to work again . . . The work of the peasant is hard, you have to break your body. (Narrator: Don Juanjo, Chan Kom)

Once again, in contrast to the efforts of *los Antiguos* elite to create an ideological frame that homogenizes the peasant farmers under the symbolic umbrella of *milpa* production, these two voices manifest a rather disjunctive picture of what a Maya *milpero* is meant to be. The first voice describes the *milpero* within an unified and coherent design. The negative references to the city and the threat of the migrant economic enrichment are clearly articulated in this rural, capitalist model of a romanticized peasant lifestyle. Such a model preserves the economic power of the rural capitalist by reinforcing the stagnation and immobility of the rural peasant tied to *milpa* and rural proletarianization. The second voice describes life and work in the *milpa* from his own experience. In contrast to the rural capitalist's celebration of uniformity and idyllic peasant life, this second voice offers muted considerations of the actual conditions in which the contemporary peasant works.

Another dimension to the multiplicity of Chan Kom representations is the image that national politicians have of the community and the peasant lifestyle. For this discussion, I shall draw on one of my experiences during fieldwork in Chan Kom.

It is Saturday afternoon, time to celebrate the weekly Mass. Throughout the morning, the visit of a political representative of the PRI has been announced repeatedly from loudspeakers in front of the municipal building; the announcements are interspersed with popular salsa and cumbia music. The municipal president and the other political officials are very busy shunting between the village and the *comisarías* in an effort to drum up a crowd of peasants to receive *el Gobierno*.[49]

Los Antiguos, as always, congregate on the steps of the Catholic Church to await the arrival of the priest. Facing the plaza, they watch the growing crowd of Maya from the *comisarías*. At 5:00 P.M., the priest begins the religious service with the majority of *los Antiguos* in the church. Meanwhile, *el Gobierno* has arrived at the plaza and begins his address to the large crowd of *los de Cancún* supporters. This incident, with its polemic spatial configuration, exemplifies not only the competition between the two sociopolitical factions, but also the distinct arena within which each group seeks to legitimize its own political and social positions.

The purpose of the visit by *el Gobierno* is to obtain peasant cooperation and assistance for some construction work in the *comisarías*. After a brief allusion to the dignity of the Maya peasants' work as *milpero*, *el Gobierno* goes on to refer paternalistically to the people of Chan Kom as *mayitas* (a diminutive form of the word Maya). *El Gobierno* extensively develops the symbol of *fagina* (the Maya institution of free, communal labor in the service of the community) as a metaphor for peasant cooperation with the government. He attempts to transfer the institution of *fagina* from the peasant community to the larger arena of the nation-state and implores the *mayitas*, as national citizens, children of the government, to perform *fagina* for the welfare of the nation. This appropriation of local symbols into a broader, national context, via political discourse, demonstrates that the state government is acquainted with Maya cultural symbols. Through efforts to comprehend Maya cultural logic, the government is prepared to launch into more persuasive and effective strategies to get Mayan cooperation.

Below is part of an interview with a political deputy in charge of the administration and control of the eastern region of Yucatan, where Chan Kom is located:

Chan Kom es un lugar misterioso, es un lugar romántico, es un lugar que fascina a propios y extraños. Por lo profundo de su raiz maya, por lo pro-

> fundo de sus convicciones tradicionalistas y por lo grande que es su gente
> . . . Chan Kom es uno de los municipios más grandes de la entidad. Los
> asientos vienen realmente de la época de los antiguos mayas . . . Ahí pode-
> mos encontrar nosotros una etnia, una etnia de mucho porcentaje autén-
> tico, autóctono, ahí está la gente maya auténtica. (Diputado Pacheco, Chan
> Kom)

> Chan Kom is a mysterious place, it is a romantic place, it is a place that
> fascinates both people from this area and foreigners. Because of its deep,
> Maya roots, because of its deep, traditionalist convinctions, and because of
> the grandeur of its people, . . . Chan Kom is one of the most important
> townships in this area. These settlements are from the times of the ancient
> Maya . . . There we can still find an unique, ethnic character, an ethnicity
> that retains a high percentage of authentic, indigenous, Maya culture,
> there are the authentic, Maya people. (Narrator: Diputado Pacheco, Chan
> Kom)

For both the rural capitalist and the political representative of the
nation, the Maya peasant is endowed with an idyllic, romanticized aura.
For the property owners, the notion of an idealized peasantry, protected
from the constraints of urban proletarian life, hides the social inequalities in the village's economic life. This representation of the peasantry,
which centers Maya identity in the *milpa*, forms the very core of the
homogeneous community world envisaged by the ideological propaganda
of *los Antiguos* elite. In the national political discourse, the peasantry not
only stand as the reservoir of a idyllic life in harmony with nature, but
also as the last remnants of the glorious ancient Maya civilization, a
source of national pride and a main attraction for tourists.

Conclusion

As seen from Cancún, the neat, social bisection of Chan Kom into
two groups, *los Antiguos* and *los de Cancún*, gets blurred. As Don Benas,
the owner of a bakery in Cancún, puts it:

> Porque ya ve que en el pueblo hay, como en la ciudad, diferentes clases.
> Claro que en el pueblo no te das cuenta de eso; uno lo nota cuando ya estás
> fuera. (Don Benas, Cancún)

> Because as you see, there are in the village, as in the city, different classes.
> Of course, when you are in the village you are not aware of this; one notices
> it when you are on the outside. (Don Benas, Cancún)

As seen from Chan Kom, Cancún is a homogeneous, unified, dangerous entity that strips Maya of their identity. The urban Maya are thought
to be members of another kind of society where they fall prey to the
dangers of money, stress, and physical violence. Certainly, for the mi-

grants, Cancún represents an inexorable transition to a new form of soci-ocultural order. For *los Antiguos*, however, Cancún is a threat to the traditional order. The values that *los Antiguos* articulate in their conversations to describe this threat are twofold: the consideration of money as evil, and the view of Protestantism as a dangerous encroachment on their Catholic ethos.

> Dicen que el dinero no es una cosa muy bonita, dicen que es como diablo, asi lo dicen. Por eso se va, desaparece . . . Dicen que en Cancún muchos ya se volvieron Protestantes, que dicen que ya no existe Dios, porque muchos tienen dinero y adoran al dinero . . . Ni piensan si existe Dios, no más el dinero. Ni las gracias le dan a Dios por ser ricos . . . nunca van a la iglesia; por eso Dios, para que les quite un poco de su dinero que tienen, creo que mando eso, el castigo, el Gilberto. Porque eso no dañó a los pobres, sino a todos, pobres y ricos. Aquí hay muchos que se están virando de Protestantes, pero en la ciudad, todos son así. (Narrator: Don Juanjo, Chan Kom)

> It is said the money is not a very nice thing, it is said that it is like the devil, so they say. Because of that it leaves, it disappears . . . It is said that many in Cancún turn into Protestants, that they say that God doesn't exist anymore, because many have money and they worship the money . . . They do not think that God exists, just only the money. They don't even thank God for their being rich, . . . they never go to Church; for that reason, God, in order to take some of their money, I believe he sent that, the punishment, *el Gilberto* [the hurricane], because it did not damage only the poor, but everyone, poor and rich. Here, there are many people that are turning into Protestants, but in the city, everyone is that way. (Narrator: Don Juanjo, Chan Kom)

As both a witness and, to a small degree, an actor in the performance of Chan Kom in crisis, I had to move from the comfortable and personally satisfying arena of peasant life and logic to venture into the urban wilderness. The blind spots of the norms established by the ideological portrait of Cancún from Chan Kom became clear to me as I shared in the urban experience of life in the *colonias populares* with the migrant Maya. My exploration into the lives of these "asphalt Mayas" added a new perspective to my understanding of the community in transformation. It also brought me closer to the issue of urban poverty so ingrained in my own past, and became, therefore, disturbing to me, as I was forced to reenact my past experiences in another place, at another time, with other people.

The salience of the social analysis of Chan Kom in Cancún, and the implosion of Cancún into Chan Kom, leads to a social and ideological picture of a community that transcends the empty space between the rural and urban realms as those realms were set forth by Redfield in his studies of community change. The peasant homogeneous milieu as conceptualized in Redfield's folk-urban continuum, along with Wolf's closed corporate community, has given way to a hybrid of international, national, and class-related issues. If Chan Kom was the ideal, experimental laboratory to study cultural change in the 1930s and 1940s, certainly it continues as such today; it is one example of many worldwide indigenous communities increasingly driven to active participation in the postmodern world.

Chapter 8

Conclusion: No Hay Novedad

SATAHOL: *Good night* my friend!

CHEQUEREQUE: ¿Qué dice señor?, no le entiendo.

SATAHOL: Dije "buenas noches", huiro. ¿Ya no te acuerdas de mi?, tu gran amigo Satahol . . .

SATAHOL: *Good evening, my friend.*

CHEQUEREQUE: What do you say, sir? I don't understand you.

SATAHOL: I said "Good evening." Don't you remember me? I am your great friend Satahol . . .

On the night of June 27th, the everyday life social scenario of Chan Kom is transformed into an evening theater. Chan Kom's people are the audience and I am among them. The young graduating Maya, apprentices of adulthood, are going through the ritualistic liminality that will bring them to the mature world; a world full of expectations and new responsibilities. This transient stage carries them from the familiar adolescent world nurtured in Chan Kom's social and cultural womb into the adults' world, a world in which they will discover the multifaceted arenas connected to Chan Kom's umbilical cord. This ritualistic liminality is stamped this evening with the short performance of *No Hay Novedad*, in which the just-graduated students transform themselves into social actors, living participants of the social schism in their community's adult world. The performance of *No Hay Novedad* is the contextualized social stamp in the life cycle of these students, the children of a community in which the adult social actors perform their everyday lives as marked by Chan Kom's social crises. Then, the enactment of *No Hay Novedad* is not only a symbolic pause in the student's life cycle, as social products of

159

Chan Kom, but is also a pause in the social cycle of the community that openly shows the audience the current sources of Chan Kom's social maladies.

A play, *No Hay Novedad*; a plot, the confrontation between the migrant and the traditionalist worlds; an audience, the Maya from Chan Kom, and me among them, were the main elements used to construct my own ethnographic theater on Chan Kom, a community that represents itself as one in crisis. As any product of the human creative endeavor, which becomes a living entity, struggling for independence from the creator's heart, mind and hand, this account of Chan Kom has been a process of constantly sculpting the actors with flesh and bone words. It is precisely their everyday activity, the atmosphere that travels along this ethnographic production, that endows them with a living, human identity as people, as Maya, and as social actors. Thus, this final ethnographic product is designed and created in a theatrical shape and mood to bring you, the reader, into the liminal trance of traveling simultaneously throughout Chan Kom's different social living scenarios, as *No Hay Novedad* did for Chan Kom's audience.

The social groups within the Maya community, which extends towards its urban version, Cancún, and the ethnographer, as narrator, actor, and critic, are the main characters of the play. The plot of the ethnographic account has the arduous task of rendering understandable the convoluted and complex Chan Kom social theater, particularly when scenarios transform according to the urban-rural, the social-economic, the local-national, the male-female, and the Protestant-Catholic roles of the actors. In the first act of the ethnography the audience is provided with the background necessary to follow the performance; this background sets out my research problem and the theoretical-methodological framework that I designed to present and analyze my data. This is the seminal setting of the theoretical-methodological character in the ethnographic performance, the interactive approach. This ethnographic character hangs on to the strand of anthropological understanding while juggling with so many different, sometimes parallel, sometimes juxtaposed, sometimes overlapped scenarios. The actors, socio-economic and ideological elements, and the setting to which they currently conform announce the hardships of the battles the interactive approach will have to face in bringing to fruition its main endeavor, which is to facilitate the conversation among political economy and symbolic interpretations, in the intertwined local, regional and national contexts, all of it filtered through the prism of fieldwork experiences. The insertion of Chan Kom's social scenario into the postmodern realm facilitates the pursuit of the intricate task entrusted to the interactive approach. If we accept the analysis of David Harvey (1989), among many others, the social conflicts of

Chan Kom exhibit a logic that reaches well beyond the community, the region, México, or Latin America. As such, the social scenario is presented as integrated into, and part of the global political and economic transformations, which have given rise to new forms of cultural production, from ethnic identity reformulations to new forms of consciousness that can animate social movements. Introducing Chan Kom as a product of postmodernity raises intriguing possibilities to suggest that both the case study and the ethnographic analysis, are the epitome of this new multi-diverse postmodernity; a world that is influenced by a world-scale growth in importance and legitimacy of "identities" embroidered in a complex fabric of social, cultural, economic, and political features.

The first ethnographic act is the preface; it provides the audience with the theoretical-methodological means to follow and understand the social plot, the crisis of Chan Kom, and to get into the intriguing motivations of the different actors in their particular socio-economic, cultural, ideological and political roles. In parallel, the first scenario presented in *No Hay Novedad* introduces the main characters, Satahol and Chequereque, who have the transcendental role of conveying the meanings of the social schism in Chan Kom. They meet in the village. The migrant, Satahol, does not come from Cancún, where Chan Kom's Mayas migrate to work, but from the United States. Maya not only convey their perception of Cancún as part of a realm that goes beyond the national border, but also, with this geographical perception, make themselves participants of a global world with a plural cultural personality. After working in the United States, Satahol returns to the village overtly displaying his new monetary wealth, and affecting the rationale of the urban world.

The second act in *No Hay Novedad* is a contest of riddles between the migrant and his peasant friend; in this duel of symbolic weapons, the two cultural value systems (the peasant and the migrant) are contrasted. This dialectical confrontation of the two worlds broadly displays the images each has of the other's world. The second act ends with the defeat of the urban rationale, symbolized by the migrant, under Maya knowledge and wisdom, symbolized by the peasant. The humor embedded in this Maya play with words softens the clash between the two worlds. As these contemporary Maya riddles poke fun at the arrogance of the "civilized" world, through the riddles of the Chilam Balam of Chumayel, "the Maya enjoy poking fun at the arrogance and demands of the upper classes, whether native or foreign" (Burns 1991).

Satahol and Chequereque are the epitomes (my ethnography) of *los Antiguos* and *los de Cancún* in the ethnography. The second act, chapters 3 through 7, comprise the ethnographic field for the interactive approach to fully display the process-oriented essence that impregnates the ethnographic analysis. When the theater curtain is opened, the scenario is controlled by *los Antiguos* and *los de Cancún*, the social warriors whose competing forces have the transcending role of composing the atmosphere of social chaos. To enhance this community's crisis environment, each collective actor gets involved in the performance of short scripts, the process metaphors of this book, in order to convey their social messages in their struggle for legitimation. Let me go beyond the ethnographic analysis of the metaphors with which *los de Cancún* and *los Antiguos* so colorfully document this account, to reflect upon how we can apply their perception of crisis and chaos as lessons for anthropological knowledge. The social crises that erupted through the competition between the two socioeconomic worlds in Chan Kom have shown that such phenomena as passions, spontaneity, corrosive gossip and rumors, and other improvised activities cannot be dropped out of sight in the process of understanding culture. The chaos provoked by the clashing between the traditional and the new cultural orders drive us to focus on the realm that falls outside the normative order. Chan Kom's case is teaching us how people's actions alter the conditions of their existence, and without any planning ahead, they can respond to unforeseen contingencies by improvisations which can result in joyous or catastrophic experiences. If we, as anthropologists, are to understand human actions, no such analysis can be deprived of people's own notions of what they are doing, and the legitimation of their acts. *Los Antiguos*'s and *los de Cancún*'s notions, perceptions, and interpretations of political elections, along with the effects of Hurricane Gilbert and ritual performances, teach us how thoughts and feelings are culturally shaped and influenced by biographies, socio-economic context, ideological legitimation, and historical compositions. These social actors also prodigiously enact the role of change as the society's enduring stage. Propelling the second part is the chronological twist of the plot, protagonized by the historical account of Chan Kom told through a Maya's voice. This story facilitates the comprehension of Chan Kom's present through the retelling of its own past. The story, narrated according to a contextualized present, unravels the village past by discovering a historical legacy of social schisms and ostracism anchored in Chan Kom since its origins. Changes, conflicts, clashes, halves, splits, ostracism, and migration are the main topics discussed in the long conversation between the village and its past; a conversation on social dichotomy in which I appeared at a specific stage: the migrant/non-migrant socioeconomic, political, and ideological confrontation, generally perceived as the dichotomic social split between *los Antiguos* and *los de Cancún*. The historical account contributes a significant lesson to the ethnographic plot, in that it discovers the recurrence of a dichotomic social pattern that embodies conflict and change. The reappearance of this schism is another episode in the long and cyclical Maya conversation with the past, deeply rooted in the ancient pre-Hispanic world. After several unsuccessful attempts, the most perfect world, the Fifth world of the corn people, humans who can speak and move, is created through the adventurous life of the dichotimic mythical power of the *Popol Vuh* cultural heroes *Hunahpu* and *X-balanque.* Through their battles with their enemies they promote the change needed to create the Fifth world; through the conflict always faced in the encounter with the competing forces in the battles, they prepared the Fifth world to be strong enough to surmount any kind of danger and threat. This preHispanic mythological understanding of the world also uses a conversational argument that validates the dual creative force, assisted by the metaphors for change and conflict.

In sum, the episode of this Maya community representing itself in crisis, at the preamble of the second millennium, illustrates another version of challenge and response to an eternal debate that structures and shapes any particular historical phase. The socioeconomic, political, and ideological contextualization of these historical phases constitute the circumstantial source through which people construct their own histories. The arbitrariness of this circumstantial historical argument, intertwined with the feelings and the tempo of everyday life, comprise the main source of the actor's spontaneity and change, which, for instance, may turn today's *los Antiguos,* Don Chanos and Chequereques, into *los de Cancún,* Don Lillos and Sataholes of tomorrow; today's *uayes* into the *aluxo'ob* and 'holy men' of tomorrow.

In the same way that Satahol and Chequereque are involved in a long contest of riddles, the two worlds of Chan Kom, the *we* and *they,* in their *los Antiguos/los de Cancún,* or Don Chano/Don Lillo versions are absorbed in the arduous quest for metaphors of identity. The stage monopolized by the *we* and *they* gradually is taken over by other social characters, who are in turn uncovered by the intervention of the interactive approach. This explosion of multi-social group presence and action on the stage facilitates the audience to discover the new forms of power and subordination that had given rise to the formation and self-representations of *los Antiguos* and *los de Cancún.* This plural social composition of the community is represented in juxtaposed scenarios, framed by the rural and the urban settings of Chan Kom. The neat and clear borderline between *los Antiguos*'s and *los de Cancún*'s worlds, which designed a bifurcated ethnographic scenario, is transformed and swallowed up by a promiscuity of sign images and simulations, all of which claim a way to reach a meaning among such a schizophrenic social panorama. The interactive approach becomes the purge expelling any threat of scenographic chaos. With this, the ethnographic venture of understanding filters the theater atmosphere and turns it into a symbiotic juxtaposition of social scenarios. This is the apotheosis of the postmodern endeavor in presenting Chan Kom's postmodernity as a community of plural personality, juggling with different cultures, and dealing with a pluralistic social composition. The interactive approach also contextualizes me, as the author of the ethnographic script, into the postmodern realm. I start in the ethnographic performance as the actor who participates in the everyday Maya social performance and negotiates within the anthropological analysis. The interactive approach, demanding my participation in the development of the ethnographic performance, gradually brings me an awareness that shifts from being "the other" among "them" (the Maya people), to a recognition of the intricacies of my "self" being placed among "them." *The Two Milpas of Chan Kom* is the celebration of the cultural plasticity of Chan Kom, mediated by the sign of *milpa* as the ethnic identifier, in the midst of a polyglot scenery with traditional elites, new traditionalists, poor milperos, *mucuys*, new bourgeoisie, international tourists, national politicians; that is, a scenario in which Maya, Mexicans, *Gringos*, and Spanish are dancing together. *The Two Milpas of Chan Kom* is also a jubilee of my own personal and cultural plasticity. Chan Kom's ethnographic performance as a figure criss-crossed by an intriguing web of socioeconomic and cultural borders represents a lesson that opens new ways to understand not only itself, but also myself. Through the process of conceiving and designing this ethnographic performance, I learned to celebrate my own crossroad identity of being born and raised in Spain, educated professionally in the United States, and further educated as a field worker among the Maya of Yucatán. It is my writing in English that is the medium to guide you through my crossed cultural identity which impregnates the scenario milieu. I have discovered that, as Chan Kom, I had to learn how to juggle cultures, how to cope with ambiguities and contradictions in order to develop a pluralistic personality through which I can make sense of my contextualized 'postmodern condition.' This ethnographic writing, emanating as it does from such a smoldering identity stew, may provide you with an unusual taste, particularly when the spices of my Spanish grammar and syntax are mixed with those of the English language. As such, this writing stew is part of the ethnographic plot.

Refusing the authenticity of its cultural purity, represented as a dichotomic entity, Chan Kom is ethnographically scrutinized as a complex persona; a complex persona with many stranded possibilities. Filtering, organizing, weaving together my overlapping cultural strands, the threat of a confused identity gets blurred and becomes ever stronger. The apotheosis of the second ethnographic act ends with the apex of the interactive intervention that exposes the entire theatrical crew: the *we's, they's,* myself as the ethnographic mediator between the juxtaposed scenarios and the audience.

The third and final scene in *No Hay Novedad* is a new confrontation between the migrant and a new character, Pichirila, a young Maya woman. This act pokes fun at the migrant image of the peasant village as static, unchanging, and dull. When the migrant inquires about his village home and family, the woman responds to each question with a detailed description of tragedy and woe. She ends each response, however, with the expression *"No hay novedad,"* meaning that there is no news. The Maya woman is a moralizing voice, charged with presenting the migrant as a traitor, as a transgressor of the community norms. Pichirila, a modern version of *la X-tabay*, leads the migrant through an ordeal of discovery in which he learns of tragic personal losses during his absence from the community; this ordeal is the penitence he has to endure to ameliorate his transgression. The play reaches its climax when it appears that the migrant can endure no more; he has nothing more to lose. The performance ends in an ironic finale that encapsulates a reordering of the social composition of Chan Kom:

SATAHOL: Se murió mi mamá, se murió mi papá, y se murieron mis hijos; me quedé solito y con tanto dinero que gané en Estados Unidos.

PICHIRILA: Y cuánto ganaste? A lo mejor me caso contigo y te ayudo a gastarlo.

SATAHOL: De veras!, y de puro gusto vamos a bailar una *jarana*.

SATAHOL: My mother died, my father died and my children died. I am left alone, and with all this money that I earned in the United States.

PICHIRILA: And how much did you make? Maybe I'll marry you and I will help you spend it.

SATAHOL: Do you mean it? And now, to celebrate, let's dance a *jarana* (traditional Yucatec dance.)

Pichirila is the mediator between the two worlds, Satahol's and Chequereque's. She becomes the cultural vehicle through which Sataholes and Chequereques can start communicating each other. Levi-Strauss already taught us the symbolical importance of females as tokens to be exchanged for the sake of social and cultural development. *Los Antiguos's* efforts to strengthen their legitimacy by using their group's women as irreplaceable forces to perpetuate tradition is a version of the female role as mediator between the social group and the cultural performance. The two equally powerful, patriarchal forces embedded in the representation of *los Antiguos* and *los de Cancún* are involved in an eternal confrontation process, appropriating any event as a possibility to win the social battle. Pichirila's role is to open the terrain for change within the chain of continuous conflict.

Let me illustrate how this part of the script runs in the *The Two Milpas of Chan Kom* by telling the readers about an event during a short visit to Chan Kom in summer of 1993. It was June, the village was involved in the preliminaries of the next political election for Chan Kom's officers. The leaders of *los Antiguos* belonged to PAN, the opponent political party to the PRI. This political group had a female candidate for the next election. For the first time in Chan Kom's history, the political path to reach the village leadership had opened for women. This change in the patriarchal social and political village pattern was brought to the social scenario by those who had tradition as the emblem of their Maya identity, *los Antiguos*. The word "crisis" was not as predominant among the people as it was during my previous field work in Chan Kom. Now, "change" was the leading word in the description of Chan Kom's social landscape:

> Todo esta cambiando, comadre. Supió lo de Bush?, ya no es el presidente. Parece que lo mataron. Saben cómo lo mataron?. Si, hay muchos Ahorita creo que algún que lo llaman Clinton, muy joven, y su esposa. Ella habla muy bonito, y cuida de la gente." (Narrator: Doña Sole, Chan Kom)

> Everything is changing, *comadre*. Did you know that Bush is not the president anymore? I heard that he was killed. Do they know how he was killed? There are lots of changes going on up there. Now, I think there is someone called Clinton, a very young guy, and his wife. She speaks very well, and she takes care of people. (Narrator: Doña Sole, Chan Kom)

Once again, Chan Kom's realm goes beyond national borders, seeking local legitimation in the global contextualization. Certainly, quite a few changes had occurred since I left in 1990. The NAFTA agreement, called TLC (Tratado de Libre Comercio) in México, started appearing in people's conversations, although I do not recall any mention of it among the conversations with the Maya during my 1989–90 field work. It was after I left as well that a change in article 27 of the Mexican constitution allowed for private sale of *ejido* lands. During a brief visit in 1993, I gathered Chan Kom's responses to this agrarian reform. *Los Antiguos* opposed the privatization of the *ejido*. The poorer *milperos* were used to working the lands that traditionally had been worked in the past. The poor quality of the soil is an important factor in the nonexistence of competition for fertile lands. The rural capitalists controlled the *ejido* lands that traditionally had been monopolized by their families; there was no need to invest capital in the privatization of their lands, if they had free access anyway. By their opposition, these rural capitalists were also expressing concerns about the possibility that the private *ejido* lands, in *los de Cancún*'s hands, would become an extra source of economic power. In the case of privatization, *los de Cancún* were expressing their plans of selling their lands to multinational corporations like Coca-Cola. There was a community vote; the *milperos*, the majority of Chan Kom's Mayas, won. The *milpas* in Chan Kom still are *ejido* lands.

Through the social analysis presented in the scenario of *No Hay Novedad*, the figure-symbol of woman comes into sharp focus, adding a new light to the study of cultural practices by encapsulating the process of cultural mediation. Pichirila somehow refreshes the vicious dichotomic social atmosphere by bringing the pragmatical meaning of mediation. Pichirila's appearance on the scene in the third act delays the ethnographic focus in *The Two Milpas of Chan Kom* on Maya women, their mundane practices in everyday life, their overlooked socioeconomic and cultural roles in the *los Antiguos* and *los de Cancún* struggle for power. Maya women had been at the wings of the focal stage in the *The Two Milpas of Chan Kom*'s scenario; a theatrical stage mostly dominated by the socioeconomic and ideological spells of *milpa* work which predominantly reach the men's world. *No Hay Novedad* provides, then, the cultural solution for the social conflict by bringing Pichirila from the wings into the center of the stage. The process metaphor that Pichirila encapsulates, the transition and mediation from "crisis" to "change", is called to protagonize the final act. However, this final act is not a final period; it is an open end that announces new episodes like the Chan Kom social scenario created during the election in 1993. Certainly Pichirila is shouting for another ethnographic representation; she is the umbilical metaphor for the analysis of another of Chan Kom's episodes that infuse the scenario with the fumes of "change." We need to add another scenario to *The Two Milpas of Chan Kom*. When the curtain opens, Tina, the PAN candidate in the 1993's election, will be at the center of the scenario. Pichirila, the symbolical encapsulation of the process metaphor for changes, will be backing up. NAFTA, PRI/PAN political and ideological intricacies will be contextualized in the everyday social scenario of Chan Kom. Other scenarios will gradually assault the stage: scenes portraying the multiple productive strategies taken traditionally by women in the past, interwoven with the current penetration of capitalism and wage labor; the Maya female landscape, the world of the *X-tabai*, the moon, the gardens, the caves. . . . A new ethnographic scenario is needed to continue with the new episodes in *The Two Milpas of Chan Kom*.

Appendix

No Hay Novedad

Personajes: Satahol
Pichirila
Chequereque

SATAHOL: *Good night my friend*!

CHEQUEREQUE: ¿Qué dice señor, no le entiendo?

SATAHOL: Dije "buenas noches", huiro. ¿Ya no te acuerdas de mí? Tu gran amigo Satahol, peón del monte, médico naturista, graduado en la Universidad de hechicería de Yobain, experto de pesca-pesca y busca-busca, cantante exclusivo de Tixcocob y puntos intermedios y probable picher de refuerzo de los Leones de Yucatán.

CHEQUEREQUE: Maare, Lotería y no borren. ¿Y que tanta cosa, eh?

SATAHOL: Pues ya lo viste, Chequereque, estoy llegando directamente de los Estados Unidos y con muchos dólares en la bolsa.

CHEQUEREQUE: Maare, cuando eras chico te creías un pan de peso, pero ahora te crees un pan de a dólar. ¿Masinó?

SATAHOL: Pues cuando era chico . . .

CHEQUEREQUE: Auuuu . . .

SATAHOL: *Sherap* (Cállate), cuando era chico era nada más que Satahol, pero ahora, ya me ves.

CHEQUEREQUE: Si, ya vi que te caiste de chico y te aporreaste tu cabezota, huac, sonó hueco, ¿que no?

SATAHOL: ¡Cállate!, cómo se ve que eres ignorante.

CHEQUEREQUE: Eso no es cierto, porque yo pasé por la escuela.

SATAHOL: Si pasaste, pero por la puerta de la escuela.

CHEQUEREQUE: Para que veas que si se, preguntame lo que quieras.

SATAHOL: A ver si es cierto, pero cada vez que falles, me tienes que pagar. A ver, ¿cuántas estaciones hay?

CHEQUEREQUE: Eso es muy fácil. La estación de camioneros, la de ferrocarriles . . .

SATAHOL: Pero qué tonto, las estaciones son cuatro: primavera, verano, otoño e invierno. Ahora, págame.

CHEQUEREQUE: Y esas, ¿dónde quedan?, porque en Valladolid no hay.

SATAHOL: ¡Qué barbaridad!, cómo se ve que no sabes nada. A ver, ¿en qué si eres bueno?

CHEQUEREQUE: En Historia. Allá si, para que veas.

SATAHOL: A ver si es cierto, ¿quién descubrió América?

CHEQUEREQUE: Eso es muy fácil, Cristóbal Cortez.

SATAHOL: ¿Pero si no te digo que eres un tonto? Fue Cristóbal Colón. ¡Págame!

CHEQUEREQUE: Bueno, bueno, dime la 'hach' y si no puedo, pues mato mi pavo.

SATAHOL: Aquí te va de matemáticas. ¿Cuánto es uno y uno?

CHEQUEREQUE: Eso sí lo se, eso sí lo se; son dos.

SATAHOL: Muy mal, uno junto a otro son once.

CHEQUEREQUE: Ah, con que así vamos. Pues ya que te crees el papá de Tahua, ahora te voy a decir unas adivinanzas, y si no las adivinas, pues tú me vas a pagar.

SATAHOL: Vengan las adivinanzas, que para eso me pinto sólo.

CHEQUEREQUE: A ver, ¿qué animal tiene cuatro patas, tiene cola, plumas, y dice guau-guau?

SATAHOL: (pensando y diciendo) cuatro patas, cola, plumas y dice guau-guau. Pues no conosco a ningún animal así.

CHEQUEREQUE: Pero si tienes uno en tu casa. Matas tu pavo? Si, pero primero me pagas.

SATAHOL: Está bien, aquí esta.

CHEQUEREQUE: Pues el perro.

SATAHOL: ¿Cómo que el perro, si no tiene plumas?

CHEQUEREQUE: Pero las plumas son para despistar.

SATAHOL: Ajá, muy bien (molesto), a ver, dime otra.

CHEQUEREQUE: A ver, dime ¿qué planta es la que no tiene raíz, ni tallo, ni hojas . . .

SATAHOL: Sin raíz, sin tallo, sin hojas. No sé . . .

CHEQUEREQUE: ¿No que eres muy salsa?, a ver, ¡demuéstramelo!

SATAHOL: Eso no existe, no seas mentiroso.

CHEQUEREQUE: Que te mueras si mientes.

SATAHOL: Pues que te mueras tú mejor.

CHEQUEREQUE: Y si me muero, ¿quién te lo cuenta?

SATAHOL: Ah, pues si es verdad. A ver, ¡cuéntamelo!

CHEQUEREQUE: Hombre, pues la planta del pie. Pero, ¡págame!

SATAHOL: Grrr, ya no soporto más tus impertinencias. Eres un baboso; toma tu dinero y aléjate de mi vista. Ojalá que todo lo que vayas a comer te haga daño, te de pirixta con chivanac y que ho huishes en una semana hasta que revientes, condenado. ¡Vete, vete de aquí! Ahí viene Pichirila. *Hello, pretty girl.*

PICHIRILA: ¿Qué dice, señor?

SATAHOL: Dije "hola, preciosa." ¿A dónde vas?, ¿ya no te acuerdas de mí, Satahol?

PICHIRILA: Ah, pues si es verdad, pero como hace tanto que no te veía, pues no me acordaba de tí. ¿Y dónde estabas ido?

SATAHOL: Pues en los Estados Unidos. Oye, ¿y qué me cuentas de las novedades que han habido en el pueblo durante mi ausencia?

PICHIRILA: Pues aquí, nada, solo tu caballo que se murió, pero fuera de so, no hay novedad.

SATAHOL: ¿Cuál caballo?, ¿aquel bonito, de raza, que me costó mucho?. ¿Y de qué se murió?

PICHIRILA: Pues como lo pusieron a sacar agua de la noria y como creo que no estaba acostumbrado a trabajar tanto, pues agarró y se murió. Pero fuera de eso, no hay novedad.

SATAHOL: Pero, ¿para qué querían tanta agua?

PICHIRILA: Pues para apagar el incendio de tu casa.

SATAHOL: ¡Ay!, y ¿por qué se quemó mi casa?

PICHIRILA: ¿Y cómo más?, es que dejaron prendidas unas velas.

SATAHOL: Y ¿para qué querían unas velas habiendo energía eléctrica?

PICHIRILA: Pues, ¿cuándo habías visto un velorio con luz eléctrica?

SATAHOL: ¿Un velorio?, pues ¿quién se murió?

PICHIRILA: Pues tu mamá; pero fuera de eso, no hay novedad.

SATAHOL: ¡Ay, Dios mío!, ¡algo me va a dar! ¡Ay, ay! (le dan temblores). Creo que me va a dar. Y ¿de qué se murió mi mamá?

PICHIRILA: Pues de un susto, ¿de qué más?

SATAHOL: ¿Y quién la asustó? (molesto)

PICHIRILA: Pues tus hijos, los gemelos.

SATAHOL: Ahora que llegue a ver a esos condenados van a ver lo que les pasará.

PICHIRILA: Pues eso si que no se va a poder, por eso se murió tu mamá, porque tus hijos se pusieron a brincar alrededor del pozo y se cayeron y se murieron. Pero fuera de eso, no hay novedad.

SATAHOL: ¡Ay, mis hijitos! ¡Ay mi mamá! ¡Y mi papá se quedó tan solito!

PICHIRILA: Si, tan solito que está a cuatro metros bajo tierra. Si, se murió, pero fuera de eso, no hay novedad.

SATAHOL: ¿Y cómo se murió mi mamá?

PICHIRILA: Pues al querer apagar el incendio de tu casa, en lugar de echar agua en un bote, echó un bote de gasolina y se quemó todito. Pero fuera de eso, no hay novedad.

SATAHOL: Se murió mi mamá, se murió mi papá, y se murieron mis hijos; me quedé solito y con tanto dinero que gané en Estados Unidos.

PICHIRILA: ¿Y cuánto ganaste? A lo mejor me caso contigo, y te ayudo a gastarlo.

SATAHOL: De veras!, y de puro gusto, vamos a bailar una jarana!

(Chan Kom, Junio 1989)

There Is No News

Characters: Satahol
              Pichirila
              Chequereque

SATAHOL: *Good evening, my friend!*

CHEQUEREQUE: What did you say, sir? I did not understand you!

SATAHOL: I said "Good evening." Don't you remember me? I am your good friend Satahol, peon from the forest, naturalist doctor, graduate of the school of witchcraft at Yobain, and expert in fishing-fishing and seeking-seeking (meaning looking for survival), the chic and popular singer from Tixcocob and probably pitcher for *Los Leones de Yucatan* (the principal baseball team in the region).

CHEQUEREQUE: My God, you are really something, aren't you?

SATAHOL: You see, Chequereque, I just came from the USA with a lot of money in my pocket.

CHEQUEREQUE: My God, when you were little you were content to be a one-peso (national currency) piece of bread, but now you believe that you are a one-dollar loaf of bread. Isn't that right?

SATAHOL: Shut up! You are obviously ignorant!

CHEQUEREQUE: That is not true because I've been to school and I passed.

SATAHOL: Sure, sure. You've been to school, alright, but you've just passed by the front door.

CHEQUEREQUE: To demonstrate to you that I know, ask me any anything you want!

SATAHOL: We'll see if you are right but, each time you are wrong, you have to pay me! Let's see, how many seasons are there?

CHEQUEREQUE: That's easy! The bus station, the train station (In Spanish, "estacion" stands for both "season" and "station").

SATAHOL: You are really stupid; the seasons are four: spring, summer, fall, and winter. Now, give me the money!

CHEQUEREQUE: And, where are those? There aren't any in the Valladolid.

SATAHOL: My God, you do not know anything! Let's see, what are you good at?

CHEQUEREQUE: I am good in History.

SATAHOL: Let's see if you are right. Who discovered America?

CHEQUEREQUE: That is so easy: Cristobal Cortez!

SATAHOL: You are really stupid. It was Cristobal Colon! Give me the money!

CHEQUEREQUE: Alright, alright, ask me the last one and if I cannot answer, I will give up!

SATAHOL: Now, in mathematics. How much is one and one?

CHEQUEREQUE: I know that! I know that! It is two.

SATAHOL: Very bad, one next to one is eleven!

CHEQUEREQUE: Well, since you think that you are so great, I am going to ask you some riddles, and if you cannot answer, you will pay me!

SATAHOL: I am very good at these!

CHEQUEREQUE: Let's see. Which is the animal that has four legs, a tail, feathers, and says *guau-guau*?

SATAHOL: (Thinking and saying) four legs, a tail and feathers, and says *guau-guau* . . . I do not know.

CHEQUEREQUE: You have one in your house! Do you give up? But first, you will pay me!

SATAHOL: Alright! Here it is!

CHEQUEREQUE: It is the dog.

SATAHOL: The dog? It does not have any feathers!

CHEQUEREQUE: The feathers are just to confuse you.

SATAHOL: Alright (very upset). Ask me another one!

CHEQUEREQUE: Tell me what plant is the one that does not have any root, nor stalk, nor leaves!

SATAHOL: No root, no stalk, no leaves . . . I do not know!

CHEQUEREQUE: I thought you were clever!

SATAHOL: That does not exist, you are a liar!

CHEQUEREQUE: I hope you will die if you lie!

SATAHOL: Better if you die.

CHEQUEREQUE: If I die, who will tell you!

SATAHOL: That is true! Let's see, tell me!

CHEQUEREQUE: The plant of the feet!

SATAHOL: *Grrr!* I cannot stand your insolence anymore! You are a driveling; take your money and get out of my sight! I hope everything you eat hurts your stomach and you cannot pee in one week until you explode, bastard! Go, go away from here! Here Pichirila comes. *Hello, pretty girl.*

PICHIRILA: What do you say, sir?

SATAHOL: I said "hello, pretty woman." Where are you going?, Don't you remember me, Satahol?

PICHIRILA: That's right! It has been such a long time since I have seen you that I did not recognize you. Where were you?

SATAHOL: I was in the United States. Listen, what can you tell me on the news in town since I was away?

PICHIRILA: Nothing, except that your horse died; other than that, there is no news.

SATAHOL: What horse? The nice one, the one that was so expensive? What did he die from?

PICHIRILA: They used him to pull out water from the well, and since, I think, he was not used to working so hard, he died. But other than that, there is no news.

SATAHOL: What did they want so much water for?

PICHIRILA: To extinguish the fire at your house.

SATAHOL: Ay! and why did my house burn?

PICHIRILA: Because they left some candles burning.

SATAHOL: Why did they want candles if there is electricity?

PICHIRILA: Have you ever seen a wake without candles?

SATAHOL: Who died?

PICHIRILA: Your mother; but other than that, there is no news.

SATAHOL: Oh, my God! I am going to have a heart attack! (He starts trembling) What did she die from?

PICHIRILA: She was scared!

SATAHOL: Who scared her? (He is getting upset)

PICHIRILA: Your sons, the twins.

SATAHOL: As soon as I see those bastards, they will see . . .

PICHIRILA: That won't be possible; this is why your mother died, because your sons started to jump around the well and they fell down it and died. But, other than that, there is no news.

SATAHOL: Ay, my little sons! Ay, my mother! And my father is left so lonely!

PICHIRILA: Yes, so lonely that he is four meters below the earth. Yes, he died, but other than that, there is no news.

SATAHOL: And, how did my mother die?

PICHIRILA: Since she wanted to extinguish the fire at your house, instead of throwing a can with water, she used a can with gasoline and everything burned. But other than that, there is no news.

SATAHOL: My mother died, my father died, and my sons died; I am left so lonely and with so much money that I made in United States.

PICHIRILA: How much did you make? Perhaps I will marry you and I will help you spend it all.

SATAHOL: You are right! and to celebrate, we are going to dance the jarana!

Notes

1. I use the term Maya to refer to the indigenous population of the Yucatán. This is the category that the people of Chan Kom used to call themselves. It also coincides with the language that they speak, "the Maya" (Maya Yucatec). The term *mazehual* is also used, mainly by the elderly, to imply poor people, peasants, Indian or Maya (see Reed 1964:35). I use "Maya" for the singular and plural sustantive, and for the adjective.

2. The *huipil* is the female Maya dress, impossed by the Spaniards to cover the naked breast of the Indians. During the colonial times, the use of the *huipil* marked the distinction between *mestizas* (non-Indian women) and Maya women. The Maya's *huipil* had a more simple embroidery, and the *pik* or *justán* (the underskirt) fell to the feet. As a complement of the dress, *mestizas* also wore a type of embroidered shawl which became the *rebozo* at the end of the nineteenth century. The impact of the *mestizo*/Maya confrontation in the *Caste War* provoked a strong rejection among the nonMaya population against those symbols representing Indian tradition. As such, the use of the *huipil* retreated from the urban areas and became the signal for female Maya identity. Maya women use the *huipil* in a similar fashion to the way the *mestizas* used it in the past. Today, "any woman that wears *huipil* is called *mestiza*" (Rejón 1992:28.) When the *huipil* is embelished with vibrant and multicolor flowers is called *matizado*.

3. For a better understanding of the play as the main guide of this ethnographic argument, please read the Appendix with the full transcription and translation into English of the play.

4. The term *milpa* comes from the Aztec word for the place to cultivate maize (Morley 1972).

5. The history of the Maya as it extends back in time into the Preclassic and forward to the Classic and Postclassic (Coe 1965, 1966; León Portilla 1968; Morley 1972; Rivera 1982, 1985; Thompson 1954, 1960, 1970), and through the Colonial period (Bartolomé 1988; Farris 1984) preserves the cultural symbolism associated to *milpa*, the source of their survival.

6. While I am rereading, reflecting and making the last corrections to this manuscript at the starting year of 1994, the mass media is bombarded by the Chiapas Revolt, as México restructures according to the North American Free Trade Agreement. The first day of 1994 moved the hearts of those who have shared and cared for the lives of the peasant Mayas. The Chiapas Revolt, led by the Zapatista National Liberation Army (EZLN), raised the Indian voices against the Mexican government, calling for access to land and just wages in the face of growing wealth discrepency (Nash 1994). I mention this transcendental historic event as a contemporay example of Maya response, reaction to and action upon the contextualized socioeconomic reality. I consider both, the Chiapas revolt and the events embedded in Chan Kom's perception of social crisis as cultural and economic reactions against the government pressures. In both cases, ethnic identity becomes the core of the peasant appeal for the recognition of Maya cultural and economic rights.

7. *Solar* is the piece of land, part of the Maya dwelling, where Maya women perform part of their productive domestic roles; they raise domestic animals, the main protein source for the food-offerings in the ceremonial contexts. Small gardens with short season maize, silantro, squash, chaya, fruit tress and other agricultural products are also part of the *solar.* They also may have raised garden platforms or *kanches* for delicate seedlings (silantro, chilis and other spices and herbs). See Kintz (1990) for a more detailed description of "kitchen gardens" and their role in the economic system among the Maya.

8. Because of the lack of natural superficial sources of water in Yucatán, most of the communities are settled around the *cenote.* Mayas believe that the inhabitant of these *cenotes* is this beautiful young woman, that sometimes turns into a *ceiba.* This is why this tree is to be avoided after nightfall, when the *X-tabai* turns into a woman. Even today, the curiosity of the visitor of any Maya village in Yucatan, when asking about the customs of the villagers, may be satisfied with different versions on the *X-tabai.* She is a very ambiguous female symbol that encapsulates strength and power (she can kill), but at the same time she is pitiful (she is alone, living at night). This ambivalence of the female symbol in the oral tradition can also be recognized in the representation of the Mexican *La Malinche*, and two Mexican archetypical patterns of feminine behavior, *La Chingada* and *La Llorona.* As the nobel Prize winner Octavio Paz summarized in his *Labyrinth of Solitude* (1964), *la Malinche* is identified as both the Mexican Eve and the betrayer of the nation. *La Chingada* represents the invasion by the Europeans and their violent rape of virgin land, which is symbolized by the "deflowering" of *la Malinche. La Malinche* is also conflated with *la Llorona*, the legendary woman who weeps

for her lost children, which equates the lots of the Indian culture after the rape, the Spanish conquest.

9. The *hetzmek* is the Maya ceremonial baptism that celebrates the first time a baby is seated on the mother's hip. See Redfield and Villa Rojas (1934:188–90) for a description of the ritual.

10. *Dzul* is the Maya term for white male. *-o'ob* is the Maya plural morpheme. The social categorization of the Mayas of Yucatán is very complex. The Mayas of Chan Kom use the term "Maya" to identify themselves in reference to the nonMaya population of *dzulo'ob* (whites). In some other communities, the term *mestizo* is more commonly assigned to people with Indian background (see Hervik, 1994). In the discussion on terminology used for social categorizations, based on my experience in Chan Kom, the term *mestizo* is most commonly used in the costume context, that is, when the focus is on the way the person is dressed. As such, the Maya woman dressed with the traditional *huipil* is mostly referred to as a *mestiza*. Sometimes, the term *catrines* is used among non-Mayas to distinguish themselves from people of Maya background. Here, I use *dzulo'ob* to encompass the population of nonMaya background, what will be the parallel of *ladinos* as the social categorization in Guatemala, or *mestizos* as it is conventionally used in México and Latin America.

11. Personification of a variety of phenomena and events is very common throughout México. These phenomena include political institutions (*el Gobierno*), more abstract concepts (*la Democracia*), and events or circumstances (*el Gilberto*, and *la Política*).

12. According to different accounts about Chan Kom's origins, the founders of the village are two: Don Eustaquio and Don Epifanio Cimé. Depending on the social faction of the native voice speaking, the emphasis is placed on one or the other as the "authentic" founder and leader of the village. The autobiography of Don Eustaquio Cimé recorded by Villa Rojas (1934:214–29) recognizes Don Epifanio as Don Eustaquio's uncle. Be that as it may, both are Cimés.

13. The Yucatec Maya oral tradition provides a broad corpus of "evil" representations that are accommodated today to the process of economic transformations. I will extensively develop this relationship in the following chapters. See Taussig's extensive analysis of the image of the devil among peasants in Colombia involved in capitalist transformations. See also Sarah Blaffer's (1972) analysis of the "blackman" and other related images of the devil in the oral traditions of Zinacantan, Chiapas.

14. *Arrancamonte* refers to the ferocious wind that unroots the trees of the forest (*monte*).

15. The godfather/godson relationship referred to in this narration can be understood on two levels. The municipal president was in fact the godson to an individual in the state government. But more importantly, the speaker uses the godfather-godson linkages as a metaphor to convey the close, kinlike relationship between the group in political control of the village and the state/national government. For further analysis on the social networking implications of the kinship system, see Hunt (1969). Lomnitz's (1977) study on the social implication of the kinship system, as an important factor in the urban social network among migrants, is of great relevance for this discussion. Also, see note 34 below, for a further explanation of the godfather-godson linkages which fall within the institution of *compadrazgo*.

16. See note 10.

17. The link between fiesta sponsorship and community leadership has been one of the favorite research topics of Mesoamerican ethnographers. This type of cult sponsorship reaches its most elaborate form in the Maya Highland (Guatemala, and particularly Chiapas) where it is known as *cargo* (Bunzel 1952; Cancian 1965; Vogt 1970; Wagley 1949). Through the *cargo* system a man is in charge of organizing and subsidizing the religious fiesta and other annual devotions dedicated to the saint. The *cargo* system is channeled through *cofradías* or a civil-religious hierarchy. The religious expenditure involved in this saint sponsorship has promoted different ethnographic explanations. First, it was interpreted as a prevention mechanism for the formation of an elite. It translates accumulated wealth into social status and prestige, and with this, it keeps the reciprocity and redistribute exchange system in the community (Wolf, 1957). Cancian's (1965) objection to this position points out the fact that there exists an economic stratification in Zinacantan besides the operationalization of the *cargo* system. According to Cancian's analysis, the fiesta sponsorship may promote ways to amass capital rather than to redistribute the wealth.

18. *Dueño* is the parallel of 'holder of the *cargo*' in the Maya Highlands. Sometimes the term *dueño cargador* is also used, which implies the dual meaning, borrowed from Spanish, of burden and office.

19. *Maestro Cantor* is the specialist in the recitation of memorized prayers from the Catholic liturgy.

20. *El Baile de la Cabeza del Cochino* (the dance of the pig's head). This dance is performed at the end of a major festivity. A decorated head of a pig is carried by men and women dancers. The head of the pig is given to the person in charge of the ceremony (*the owner*) for next year.

The current *owner* has to pay for the musicians and dancers. Farris (1984:346) suggests that this dance has preHispanic origins, the head of the pig being "the transmogrified deer head of preColumbian offerings."

21. *Rezadoras* are a group of young women who assist the *maestro cantor* to officiate in the Christian rituals in Chan Kom. They comprise a group of 13 *rezadoras*; all of them are the daughters of Mayas affiliated with *los Antiguos* group. Note the close relations between *los Antiguos* and participation in the Catholic liturgy via female ties.

22. *Las cabañuelas* and *tzolkin* are terms that the Maya use interchangeably to refer to a system to predict the weather for a new annual agricultural cycle. The Maya term, *tzolkin*, or "count of the days" refers to the ancient Maya calendar which determined for everyone the pattern of ceremonial life. *Las cabañuelas*, as a prediction of the weather system, is a Spanish custom that still is in practice in some peasant villages and towns in Spain. Taking as a temporal reference the days of January, with some formula, the peasants record the weather characteristics for the next months to come in the following fashion: twelve *jícaras* (gourds) with salt are placed hanging from the ceiling and based on changes in the displacement and the dry/wet quality of the salt in the *jícara*, the Maya "reads" the weather for every month. The first of January represents January, the second of January represents February, the third of January is March, and so on, until the 12th, which is December; then, the count starts but inversevely: the 13th, is December until reaching the 24th, which represents January in this second round. From here, there is a third round by half of the day, being January the 25th of January, until noon, and February the 25th of January until midnight. Finally, the 31st of January encapsulates every month of the years in two turns, one until noon, and the other until midnight. The quality and characteristics of the dryness or humidity of the *jícaras* throughout these consecutive six cycles tell the Maya what to expect for the the seasons of that year.

23. *Primicia* is any ceremony dedicated to the *yuntzilo'ob* or Maya gods of the field and wood.

24. The Maya man I call here Raimundo was the source of my agricultural knowledge on the *milpa*. He taught me the simplicity, transcendence, and complexity of the work in the fields. Raimundo was, and still is my inspiration to think and write about corn as if it has life by itself.

25. According to the Maya, the *aluxo'ob* are spirits that dwell in the pottery idols and incense burners occasionally found in the bush.

Sometimes the *aluxo'ob* are considered the guardians of *the milpa* as well; in most Maya ceremonies related to *milpa*, the peasant offers a corngruel to these spirits for their protection of his fields.

26. The Maya term *Uay* is associated with sorcery, witchcraft and shamanism, being the individual's spiritual alter-ego that is transformed into an animal. *Uay* or *Way* has been identified in ancient texts (see Freidel 1992.)

27. Mexican popular song mostly related to celebration contexts.

28. The Maya conception of time is embroidered in a cyclical continuum of history intertwined with prophecy. The Classic Maya stamped their time recording by the ocurrence of the *katun*, a 7,200 days cycle within the Maya calendrical round. This time span was used for seating Maya rulers. It was thought that at the end of each of their twenty-year *katun* periods, the historical cycle will repeat itself. This prophetical recurrence is consignated in the way the Maya recorded the Spanish and other preColumbian invasions (Roys 1967; Sanchez de Aguilar 1937; Tozzer 1941). As such, the historical Maya colonial version (Chilam Balames) assign the Spaniards the role of being the malady, among others that came in the past, and other evils expected to endure in the future. The nineteenth-century Indian rebellion in the Yucatán, against the *dzulo'ob*, known as *Guerra de Castas* (Caste War), was perceived by the Maya as the end of the time cycle ruled by the *dzulo'ob*, and the initiation of the emergence of the Indians from the margins of the society (see Reed 1964). Approaching the end of the second millenium, the contemporary Maya, as inheritors of the prophetic cyclical view of time, insert themselves in the liminal chaos of the end of this macro cycle.

29. See note 7 for a description of *solar*.

30. In 1847 the Maya of eastern Yucatan revolted against the *dzulo'ob* or whites. As their ancestral prophetic vision of the world taught them, the time arrived to rise up in arms against the oppressors (see Reed 1964; Bricker 1977; Burns 1977). The revolt sprouted in the areas where the social, economic, and political organization of the Maya survived the colonial pressures. One of these areas was the district of Valladolid where Chan Kom is located. One of the consequences of the revolt was the movement and reallocation of populations. Apparently, the area of Chan Kom was abandoned during the Caste War. After the war, some of the original inhabitants of Chan Kom were displaced Mayas who had been left without a village, home, or *milpa*.

31. Loret de Mola, an active Yucatec politician in the 1960s, devoted an extensive commentary to Don Eustaquio in his book, *Los caciques*

(1979:103–8). He narrates an encounter with the *cacique* agrario (as he denominates Don Eustaquio). He met Don Eustaquio during one of his political campaigns around the area. After that, then, Don Eustaquio would not hesitate to request improvements from the government in order to fulfill his dream: "the progress of Chan Kom." In turn, Loret de Mola had Maya support for his political advancement that brought him to the Senate, and later on, facilitated Chan Loret's (Loret's son) political career.

32. The communal labor or *fagina* is an institutional legacy of the colonial regime in Yucatán. Under the *encomienda*, Indians had to tribute the *encomendero* in labor; this access to human labor became a source of increasing wealth during the *estancia* and *hacienda* periods (see Wolf 1956; Patch 1976, 1979). After the Caste War and the Mexican Revolution, the *hacienda* regime, also known by the Indians as *the time of slavery*, was abolished. Certain institution pervailed, although accomodated to different socio-economic contexts. La *fagina* is one of these institutions, which goes through socioeconomic redefinitions, also acording to the development of the community. Later in the chapter, it will be indicated that the *fagina* becomes an important mechanism manipulated by the *caciques* to select political and economic allies. That is, it becomes a social and political regulator of the population.

33. In order to have a more general view of the *milpa* economic system in relation to the production of cattle, and in relation to other economic areas in the peninsula, see Varguez Pasos (1962); Labreque (1982).

34. The system of *compadrazgo* was introduced in Latin America by the Spanish. According to this Catholic concept, a man and a woman other than the natural parents are chosen to sponsor a child at baptism; they assume a certain responsibility along with the parents for the education and welfare of the child. This spiritual bond is supposed to be equivalent to the natural one. In Latin America, this system of co-parenthood has developed in a more elaborate system of fictive kinship that embraces different kinds of ritual occasions other than the Christian sacraments. The multitude of social links between adults is the focus of *compadrazgo*, more oriented toward the mutual economic and social assistance of those involved in the network of *compadres*. This different development of this institution in Latin America may be due to its usefulness in reconstituting networks that were being destroyed by the Spanish. There is an abundant bibliography on the examination of this "fictive" kinship institution. Eva Hunt's (1969) work on the genealogical terminology is a pioneer in demonstrating the social interactions embedeed in the kinship

terminology. Foster (1963) also used *compadrazgo* to exemplify his model of dyadic socioeconomic contract based on patron/client relationships.

35. For a more specific view of the emerging phenomena of migration to Cancún and its repercussions among the female Maya group, see Elmendorf (1979; Appendix D). Regarding the connection between migration and changing patterns in marriage, family planning, and economic activities, see Elmendorf and Merrill (1977:IV 8–26).

36. By "permanent basis," I point out here, those migrants in the early 1970s who, after experimenting in low-skill jobs (dishwasher), have a gradual access to more specialized and better-paid jobs (pastry-cook), until getting involved in small-business enterprises, like a store. This change in occupation performance, escalating wealth, and increase of social prestige is associated to the definitive establishment of the family in Cancún. With this, the network of social relations is expanded and strengthened to facilitate the incorporation of village *compadres* and relations to the migrant world in Cancún. This young generation of successful migrants were mostly descendants of Don Eustaquio.

37. Do not confuse with *X-Juan-Thul* of the Yucatec oral tradition; in that case, it is a rabbit. Here, it is a deity.

38. The general meaning of *loh* is to redeem from evil. When this ceremony is performed in the cattle-pens, it is refered to as *loh corral*.

39. Here *la balacera* refers to the conflict between cattle owners and milperos, or Protestants against Catholics during the 1950s.

40. Although the use of fertilizers and herbicides improves the yields of the harvest, it also promotes the escalating exhaustion of the soil, as well as the increase of allergies, pulmonary infections and other health-related problems.

41. For a more detailed description of the *ch'a chaac* see Redfield (1934:138–43).

42. The *loh kah* is a ceremony to redeem the village from the evil winds. The four corners of the village are spread with burning chili, and other objects are buried by the *h-men* to dispel the evil winds from the community.

43. *Gremios* in Yucatán is a kind of *cofradía*, a religious institution that developed during the colonial times. See Farris (1984) for a detailed description and explanation of this religious institution.

44. These stories on violence in Cancún originated with the first

years of migration to Cancún. Elmendorf and Merrill recorded the existence of this type of narrative during the first half of the 1970s (1977: III64.)

45. The language I used to write my field notes was English.

46. Here, I paraphrase Reinato Rosaldo (1989) in his discussion on "people without culture" in relation to his fieldwork among the Ilongots.

47. Remember that *milperío* was the first stage of the settlement of Chan Kom, according to the story analyzed in the previous chapter.

48. See Libby (1994), another ethnographic study dealing with the similar effects of migration among Maya women in Cuncunul, a peasant community in Yucatan.

49. The Maya use the term "el Gobierno," meaning any political representative of the government.

References

Anda, Francisco V (ed). 1984. *Capitalismo y Vida Rural en Yucatán*. Yucatán: Instituto de Estudios Económicos y Sociales. Centro de Investigaciones Regionales "Dr. Hideyo Noguchi."

Annis, Sheldon. 1987. *God and Production in a Guatemalan Town*. Austin: University of Texas Press.

Arizpe, Lourdes. 1972. *Parentesco y Economía en una Sociedad Nativa*. México: Instituto Nacional Indigenista.

———. 1978. *Migración, Etnicismo y Cambio Económico*. México: El Colegio de México.

Baños Ramírez, Othon. 1989. *Yucatán: Ejidos sin Campesinos*. Mérida: Universidad Autónoma de Yucatán.

Bartolomé, Alberto M. 1988. *La Dinámica Social de los Mayas de Yucatán. Pasado y Presente de la Situación Colonial*. Mexico: INI.

Bartra, R. 1974. *Estructuras Agrarias y Clases Sociales en México*. UNAM: Instituto de Investigaciones Sociales.

Batt, Laura. 1981. Capitalist Class Formation in Dependent Economies. The Case of Espita, Yucatan, Mexico. Ph.D. Dissertation. University of Kentucky, Lexington.

Blaffer, Sarah. 1972. *The Black-man of Zinacantán: A Central American Legend*. Austin: University of Texas Press.

Bloch, Maurice. 1989. *From Blessing to Violence*. Cambridge: Cambridge University Press.

Bourdieu, Pierre. 1977. *Outline of a Theory of Practice*. Cambridge: Cambridge University Press.

Bricker, Victoria. 1977. "The Caste War of Yucatán: The History of a Myth and the Myth of History." *Anthropology and History in Yucatán*, ed. Grant D. Jones. Austin: University of Texas Press: 251–58.

———. 1981. *The Indian Christ, The Indian King: The Historical Sub-*

strate of Maya Myth and Ritual, ed. Grant Jones. Austin: University of Texas Press.

Bunzel, Ruth. 1952. *Chichicastenango: A Guatemalan Village*. Publications of the American Ethnological Society, no.12. Seattle: University of Washington Press.

Burns, Allan. 1973. "Patterns in Yucatec Mayan Narrative Performance." Ph.D. dissertation, University of Washington.

————. 1977. "The Caste War in the 1970's: Present-Day Accounts from Village Quintana Roo." *Anthropology and History in Yucatán*, ed. Grant Jones. Austin: University of Texas Press.

————. 1980. "Interactive Features in Yucatec Maya Narratives." *Language in Society* 9: 307–319.

————. 1983. *An Epoch of Miracles: Oral Literature of the Yucatec Maya*. Austin: University of Texas Press.

————. 1991. "The Language of Zuyua: Yucatec Maya Riddles and Their Interpretation." In *Past, Present, and Future: Selected Papers on Latin American Indian Literatures*, ed. Mary Pruess. Culver City, CA: Labyrinthos.

Cancian, Frank. 1965. *Economics and Prestige in a Maya Community: The Religious Cargo System in Zinacantán*. Standford: Satandford University Press.

————. 1989. "Economic Behavior in Peasant Communities." In *Economic Anthropology*, Stuart Plattner, ed. California: Stanford University Press.

Canclini, Néstor G. 1989. *Las Culturas Populares en el Capitalismo*. 2nd edition. México: Nueva Imagen.

Cardiel, Cuauhtemoc. 1989. "Cancún: Turismo, Subdesarrollo Social y Expansión Sectaria Religiosa." In *Religión y Sociedad en el Sureste de México*. Vol VI, eds. C. Cardiel and Villalobos and M. Villalobos. México: CIESAS.

Carmack, Robert. 1973. *Quichean Civilization: The Ethnohistoric, Ethnographic, and Archaeological Sources* Berkeley, California: University of California Press.

————. 1976. "Estratificación y Cambio Social de las Tierras Altas Occidentales de Guatemala: el caso de Tecpanaco." *América Indígena* 36: 253–301.

————. 1981. *The Quiché Mayas of Utatlán: The Evolution of a High-*

land Guatemalan Kingdom. Norman, Oklahoma: university of Oklahoma Press.

Coe, Michael. 1965. "A Model of Ancient Community Structure in the Maya Lowlands." *Southwestern Journal of Anthropology* 21:97–114.

———. 1966. *The Maya*. New York: Praeger.

Condominas, George. 1977. *We Have Eaten the Forest: The Story of a Montagnard Village in the Central Highlands of Vietnam*. New York: Hill and Wang.

Comaroff, Jean. 1985. *Body of Power, Spirit of Resistance*. Chicago: University of Chicago Press.

Contreras, Arias. 1959. "Bosquejo Climatológico." *Los Recursos Naturales del Sureste y su Aprovechamiento*, ed. E. Beltran. México: Instituto Mexicano de Recursos Naturales Renovables. Vol I: 93–158.

Dumond, Louis. 1970. "Competition, Cooperation and the Folk Society." *Southwestern Journal of Anthropology* 26: 261–86.

Earle, Duncan. 1990. "Appropriating the Energy: Highland Maya Religious Organization and Community Survival." In *Class, Politics and Popular Religion in Mexico and Central America*, ed. Lynn Stephen and James Dow. Society for Latin American Anthropology Publication Series, Vol 10.

Eber, Christine. 1991. "Before God's Flowering Face: Women and Drinking in a Tzotzil-Maya Community." Ph.D. dissertation, University of New York at Buffalo.

Elmendorf, Mary. 1970. *Nine Mayan Women: A Village Faces Change*. New York and London: Schenkman.

———. 1972. *The Mayan Woman and Change*. Mexico: CIDOC Cuaderno No. 81.

———. 1979. *Women and Technological Change in Developing Countries,* ed. Roslyn Dauber and Melinda L. Cain. Westview Press.

Elmendorf, M. and Merrill, D. 1977. Socioeconomic Impact of Development in Chan Kom 1971–1976: Rural Women Participate in Change. Unpublished manuscript prepared for the World Bank Population and Human Resources Division, Development Economics Department.

———. 1978. Socioeconomic Impact of Development in Chan Kom, Yucatán, 1971–1976—A Preliminary Study. Unpublished paper presented at the 1978 Society for Applied Anthropology Meetings. Mérida.

Fabian, Johannes. 1983. *Time and the Other: How Anthropology Makes its Object*. New York: Columbia University Press.

Farris, Nancy. 1984. *Maya Society Under Colonial Rule*. New York: Princeton University Press.

Foster, George. 1963. "The Dyadic Contract in Tzintzuntzan, II: Patron-Client Relationship." *American Anthropologist* LXV: 1280–94.

Foucault, Michael. 1983. *Power and Knowledge: Selected Essays*. New York: Pantheon Books.

Freidel, David. 1992. "The Trees of Life: Ahau as Idea and Artifact in Classic Lowland Maya Civilization." In *Ideology*, ed. Arthur A. Demarest and Geoffrey W. Conrad. School of American Research Press. Santa Fe, New Mexico.

Friedlander, Judith. 1975. *Being Indian in Hueyapan: A Study of Forced Identity in Contemporary Mexico*. New York: St. Martin's.

Geertz, Clifford. 1973. *The Interpretation of Cultures*. New York: Basic Books.

Godelier, Maurice. 1972. *Rationality and Irrationality in Economics*. New York: Monthly Review Press.

Goldkind, Victor. 1965. "Social Stratification in the Peasant Community: Redfield's Chan Kom Reinterpreted." In *American Anthropologist* Vol 67: 863–84.

———. 1966. "Class Conflict and Cacique in Chan Kom." In Southwestern Journal of Anthropology. Vol 22: 325–45.

Good, Catharine. 1988. *Haciendo la Lucha: Arte y Comercio Nativos de Guerrero*. México: Fondo de Cultura Económica.

Goodman, David and Michael Redclift. 1981. *From Peasant to Proletarian*. Oxford: Basil Blackwell.

Gossen, Gary. 1974. *Chamulas in the World of the Sun: Time and Space in Maya Oral Tradition*. Prospect Heights, Illinois: Weaveland Press.

———. 1986a. "The Chamula Festival of Games: Native Macroanalysis and Social Commentary in a Maya Carnival." *Symbol and Meaning Beyond the Closed Corp[orate Community: Essays in Mesoamerican Ideas*, ed. G. Gossen. Studies in Culture 1. Albany: Institute for Mesoaemrican Studies. SUNY/The University at Albany: 227–54.

————. 1986b. *Symbol and Meaning Beyond the Closed Community. Essays in Mesoamerican Ideas*. Albany: Institute for Mesoamerican Studies, University at Albany. n.d. To be Indian in a Euro-African Matrix: Personal Reflections on Chamula Tzotzil Identity.

————. 1989. "Life, Death, and Apotheosis of a Chamula Protestant Leader: Biography as Social History." In *Ethnographic Encounters in Southern Mesoamerica*. eds. V. Bricker and G. Gossen. Studies on Culture and Society 3. Albany, New York: Institute for Mesoamerican Studies. SUNY/The University at Albany.

————. 1993. "The Other in Chamula Tzotzil Cosmology and Hiustory: Reflections of a Kansas in Chiapas." *Cultural Anthropology* 8(4): 443–475.

Greenberg, James. 1981. *Santiago's Sword: Chatino Peasant Religion and Economics*. Berkeley: University of California Press.

————. 1987. *Religion y Economía de los Chatinos*. México: INI.

————. 1990. "Sanctity and Resistance in Closed Corporate Indigenous Communities: Coffee Money, Violence and Ritual Organization in Chatino Communities in Oaxaca." In *Class, Politics and Popular Religion in México and Central America*, ed. Lynn Stephen and James Dow. Society for Latin American Anthropology. Publication Series No 10.

Halperin, Rhoda. 1975. *Administración Agraria y Trabajo: Un caso de la Economía Política Mexicana*. Mexico: INI.

Hanks, William. 1990. *Referential Practice. Language and Lived Space among the Maya*. Chicago: University of Chicago Press.

Hervik, Peter. 1994. *Social Categories in Yucatán*. Durhan: Duke-UNC Programm in Latin American Studies.

Harvey, David. 1990. *The Condition of Postmodernity*. Cambridge, MA: Basil Blackwell.

Hawkins, John. 1983. "Robert Redfield's Culture Concept and Mesoamerican Anthropology." *Heritage of Conquest: Thirty Years Later*, ed. Carl Kendall, John Hawkins, and Laurel Bossen. Albuquerque: University of New Mexico Press: 299–336.

Hernández, X. E. and Padilla y Ortega R., eds. 1980. *Seminario sobre Producción Agrícola en Yucatán*. Mérida: Gobierno de Yucatán, Secretaría de Programación y Presupuesto, Secreatría de Agricultura y Recursos Hidraúlicos, Colegio de Postgraduados de Champingo.

Hunt, Eva. 1969. "The Meaning of Kinship in San Juan: Genealogical and Social Models." *Ethnology* VII: 37–53.

Jameson, Frederic. 1984. "Postmodernism, or The Cultural Logic of Late Capitalism." *New Left Review* 146: 53–92.

Kertzer, David. 1988. *Ritual, Politics and Power*. New Haven: Yale University Press.

Krotz, Esteban. 1991. "A Panoramic View of Recent Mexican Anthropology." *Current Anthropology* 32 (April): 183–88.

Knauft, Bruce. 1994 "Pushing Anthropology Past the Posts: Critical Notes on Cultural Anthropology and Cultural Studies as Influenced by Postmodernism and Existencialism." *Critique of Anthropology* 14: 100–117.

La Brecque, Marie France and Ivan Breton. 1982. *La Organización de la Producción de los Mayas de Yucatán*. Mexico: INI.

Lee, Rosemary Louise. 1977. The Tourist Identity in Yucatán: a Case Study in the Interaction Between Class Structure and Economic Development. Ph.D. Dissertation. University of California, Irvine.

León-Portilla, Miguel. 1968. *Tiempo y Realidad en el Pensamiento Maya*. Instituto de Investigaciones Historicas. UNAM, Mexico.

Lipsitz, George. 1986. "Postmodernism and Popular Music." *Cultural Critique* 5:157–77.

Littlefield, Alice. 1976. *La Industria de las Hamacas en Yucatán, México*. Mexico: Estudios de Antropología Económica, INI.

Lomnitz, Larissa. 1977. *Networks and Marginality: Life in a Mexican Shantytown*. New York: Academic Press.

Loret de Mola, Carlos. 1979. *Los Caciques*. México: Editorial Grijalba.

Libby, Elizabeth. 1994. The Women of Cuncunul, Yucatan: Stories of Migration and Change. Master's Thesis, Department of Anthropology. University of Florida at Gainesville.

Marcus, George and Michael Fischer. 1986. *Anthropology and Cultural Critique*. Chicago: University of Chicago Press.

Meillassoux, Claude. 1981. *Maidens, Meal and Money. Capitalism and the Domestic Community*. New York: Cambridge University Press.

Merrill, Devorah. 1984. The Mixed Subsistence-Commercial Production System in the Peasant Economy of Yucatán, México. Ph.D. Dissertation, Cornell University.

Morales, Carmen, ed. 1992. *Cinco Artesanías del Oriente de Yucatán.* Mérida, Yucatán: Cuadernos de Cultura Yucateca 1.

Morley, S. 1972. "Agricultura." In *La Milpa entre los Mayas de Yucatán.* Luis a Varguez Pasos, ed. México: Universidad de Yucatán.

Municipios de Yucatán. 1988. Gobierno del Estado de Yucatán. Delegación de Fomento y Desarrollo, Mérida, Yucatán.

Murphy, Robert. 1971. *Dialectics of Social Life.* New York: Columbia University Press.

Nash, June. 1970. *In the Eyes of the Ancestors: Belief and Behavior in a Maya Community.* New Haven: Yale University Press.

———. 1979. *We Eat the Mines and the Mines Eat us: Dependency and Exploitation in Bolivian Tin Mines.* New York: Columbia University Press.

———. 1994. n.d. The Revindication of Indigenous Identity: Mayan Responses to State Intervention in Mexico and Guatemala. Paper presented at the Applied Anthropology Meetings. Cancún, April.

Nash, Manning. 1957. "The Multiple Society in Economic Development: Mexico and Guatemala. *American Anthropologist* 58: 825–33.

———. 1958. "Political Relations in Guatemala." *Social and Economic Studies* 7:65–67.

Ortner, Sherry. 1984. "Theory in Anthropology since the Sixties." *Comparative Studies in Society and History* 26: 126–66.

Palerm, Angel. 1976. *Modos de Producción.* México: Edicol.

———. 1980. *Antropología y Turismo.* México: Editorial Nueva Imagen.

Patch, Robert. 1979. "A Colonial Regime: Maya and Spaniard in Yucatán." Ph.D. dissertation. Princeton University.

———. 1979. "La Formación de Estancias y Haciendas en Yucatán durante la Colonia." *Boletín de la Escuela de la Universidad de Yucatán* 4:21–61.

Paz, Octavio. 1964. *The Labyrinth of Solitude: Life and Thought in México.* New York: Grove Press.

Pelto, Pertti. 1970. *Anthropological Research. The Structure of Inquiry.* New York: Harper & Row.

Peraza, María Elena and Lourdes Rejón Patrón. 1989. *El Comercio de*

Artesanías en Chichén Itzá y algunos Efectos del Turismo en la Región. Yucatán: INAM, Centro Regional de Yucatán.

Pozas, Ricardo and Isabel M. de Pozas. 1971. *Los Indios en las Clases Sociales de México*. Mexico: Siglo Ventiuno.

Press, Irwin. 1968. Continuity in Transition: The Anatomy of a Yucatec peasant community. Ph.D. dissertation. Chicago: University of Chicago.

————. 1977. "Historical Dimensions of Orientation to Change in a Yucatec Peasant Community." *Anthropology and History*, ed. Grant D. Jones. Austin: University of Texas Press: 275–88.

————. 1975. *Tradition and Adaptation: Life in a Modern Yucatán Maya Village*. Westport: Greenwood Press.

Re Cruz, Alicia, n.d. "When the Canícula Comes. Effects and incidence of Diseases (intestinal infections)."

Redfield, Robert. 1941. *The Folk Culture of Yucatan*. Chicago: University of Chicago Press.

————. 1950. *A Village that Chose Progress*: Chan Kom Revisited. Chicago: University of Chicago Press.

————. 1960. *The Little Community and Peasant Society and Culture*. Chicago: University of Chicago Press.

Redfield, Robert and Villa Rojas, Alfonso. 1934. *Chan Kom: a Mayan Village*. Washington: Carnegie Institute Publication.

Reed, Nelson. 1964. *The Caste War of Yucatan*. Standford: Standford University Press.

Rejón, Lourdes. 1992. "Los Huipiles y Justanes Bordados." Pp. 27–36 in *Cinco Artesanías del Oriente*. Mérida: Cuadernos de Cultura Yucateca 1.

Rivera Dorado, Miguel. 1982. *Los Mayas, Una Sociedad Oriental*. Editorial de la Universidad Complutense, Madrid.

————. 1985. *Los Mayas de la Antiguedad*. Madrid: Editorial Alhambra.

Rosaldo, Renato. 1988. "Ideology, Place and People Without History." *Cultural Anthropology* Vol. 3 (1):77–78.

————. 1989. *Culture and Truth. The Remaking of Social Analysis*. Boston: Beacon Press.

Roseberry, William. 1976. "Rent, Differentiation and Development of Capitalism among Peasants." *American Anthropologist* 78:45–58.

———. 1989. "Peasants and the World." In *Economic Anthropology*, ed. S. Plattner. California: Stanford University Press.

———. 1991. *Anthropologies and Histories*. New Brunswick, NJ: Rutgers University Press.

Rosenbaum, Brenda. 1993. *With Our Heads Bowed: The Dynamics of Gender in a Maya Community*. Austin: University of Texas Press.

Roys, Ralph, ed. 1967. *The Book of Chilam Balam of Chumayel*. 2d ed. Norman: University of Oklahoma Press.

Sahlins, Marshall. 1976. *Culture and Practical Reason*. Chicago: University of Chicago Press.

Sánchez de Aguilar, Pedro. 1937. *Informe Contra Idolorum Cultores del Obispado de Yucatán*, 3rd. ed. Mérida: E.G Triay e Hijos Publisher.

Scott, James. 1985. *Weapons of the Weak. Everyday Forms of Peasant Resistance*. New Haven: Yale University Press.

Schwimmer, E. G. 1972. "Symbolic Competition." *Antropologica* XIV (2): 117–55.

Silverblatt, Irene. 1987. *Moon, Sun and Witches. Gender Ideology and Class in Inca and Colonial Peru*. Princeton: Princeton University Press.

Smith, M. G. 1969. "Social and Cultural Pluralism." *Annals of the New York Academy of Sciences* 83: 763–77.

Stavenhagen, Rodolfo. 1963. "Clases, Colonialismo y Aculturación." *América Indígena* 6: 63–104.

———. 1968. "Seven Fallacies about Latin America." *Latin America: Reform or Revolution?* ed. J. Petras and M. Zeitlin. Greenwich, CN: Fawcett: 14–31.

———. 1969. *Las Clases Sociales en las Sociedades Agrarias*. México: Siglo XXI.

———. 1976. "Capitalismo y Campesinado en México." *Capitalismo y Campesinado en México*, ed. R. Stavenhagen. México: SEP-INAH.

Steinberg, Stephen. 1981. *The Ethnic Myth*. Boston, Mass.: Beacon Press.

Strickon, Arnold. 1965. "Hacienda and Plantation in Yucatan: An Historical-Ecological Consideration of the Folk-Urban Continuum." *América Indígena* 25 (1): 35–63.

Sullivan, Paul Robert. 1985. "Contemporary Yucatec Maya Apocalyptic Prophecy: the Ethnographic and Historical Contexts. Ph.D. Dissertation. The Johns Hopkins University, Baltimore.

———. 1989. *Unfinished Conversations. Mayan and Foreigners between two Wars*. New York: Alfred Knoff.

Taussig, Michael. 1980. *The Devil and Commodity Fetishism in South America*. Chapel Hill: University of North Carolina Press.

Tedlock, Dennis. 1985. *Popol Vuh. The Definitive Edition of the Mayan Book of the Dawn of Life and the Glories of Gods and Kings*. ed. and trans. D. Tedlock. New York: Simon and Schuster.

Tedlock, Barbara. 1991. "From Participant Observation to The Observation of Participation: The Emergence of Narrative Ethnography." *Journal of Anthropological Research* 47 (Spring): 69–94.

Thompson, Eric. 1954. *The Rise and Fall of Maya Civilization*. Norman, Oklahoma: University of Oklahoma Press.

———. 1960. *Maya Hieroglyphic Writing*, new edition. Norman, Oklahoma: University of Oklahoma Press.

———. 1970. *Maya History and Religion*. Norman, Oklahoma: University of Oklahoma Press.

Thompson, Richard A. 1974. *Aires de Progreso. Cambio Social en un Pueblo Maya de Yucatán*. Mexico: INI.

Tozzer, Alfred. 1941. *Landa's Relación de las Cosas de Yucatán*. Peabody Museum of Archaeology and Ethnology. Papers 18. Cambridge, MA: Harvard University.

Turner, Victor. 1957. *Schism and Continuity in an African Society. A study of Ndembu Village Life*. Manchester University Press.

———. 1967. *The Forest of Symbols*. Ithaca: Cornell University Press.

———. 1968. *The Drums of Affliction: a Study of the Religious Precesses among the Ndembu of Sambia*. Oxford: Clarendon Press and the International African Institute.

Varguez Pasos, Luis A. 1972. *La Milpa entre los Mayas de Yucatán*. Varguez Pasos, ed. México: Universidad de Yucatán.

———. 1981. "Economía Campesina en el 'Oriente' de Yucatán. Un Informe Etnográfico." Ph.D. Dissertation. Universidad de Yucatán, Escuela de Ciencias Antropológicas.

Vogt, Evon. 1970. *Zinacantan: A Maya Community in the Highlands of Chiapas*. Cambridge, MA: Harvard University Press.

———. n.d. "Theoretical Paradigms and Field Methodologies for The Long-Range Study of Tzotzil-Mayan Cultural Continuity and Change." Presented at the Symposium Entre el Acontecimiento y la Significación: el Discurso Sobre la Cultura en el Nuevo Mundo (Dec. 1992) Trujillo, Spain.

Wagley, Charles. 1949. "The Social and Reliogious Life of a Guatemalan Village." *American Anthropological Association Memoir* 71. WI: Menasha.

Wallerstein, Emanuel. 1974a. *The Modern World System: Capitalist Agriculture and the Orgins of the European World Economy in the Sixteenth Century*. New York: Academic Press.

———. 1974b. "The rise and future demise of the World Capitalist System: concepts for comparative Analysis." *Comparative Studies in Society and History* Vol 16, 387–415.

Warman, Arturo. 1972. *Los Campesinos: Hijos Predilectos del Régimen*. México: Editorial Nueva Imagen.

———. 1976. *Y Venimos a Contradecir: Los Campesinos de Morelos y el Estado Nacional*. México: CIS-INAH.

———. 1980. *Ensayos Sobre el Camepesinado en México*. México: Editorial Nueva Imagen.

Warren, Kay B. 1989. *The Symbolism of Subordination*. Austin: University of Texas Press.

———. 1991. n.d. Transforming Memories and Histories. The Resurgence of Indian Identity. Paper presented at the Meetings of the American Anthropological Association, Chicago.

Wasserstrom, Robert. 1983. *Class and Society in Central Chiapas*. Berkeley: University of California Press.

Wolf, Eric. 1955. "Types of Latin American Peasantry: a Preliminary Discussion." *American Anthropologist* 57: 452–71.

———. 1956. "Aspects of Group Relations in a Complex Society: Mexico." *American Anthropologist* 58: 1056–78.

————. 1957. "Closed Corporate Peasant Communities in Mesoamerica and Central Java." *Soutwest Journal of Anthropology* 13: 1–98.

————. 1966. *Peasants*. Englewood Cliffs: Prentice Hall Publishers, Foundations of Modern Anthropology Series.

————. 1969. "On Peasant Rebellions." *International Social Science Journal* 21 (2): 286–93

————. 1982. *Europe and the People Without History*. Berkeley: University of California Press.

————. 1986. "The Vicissitudes of the Closed Corporate Peasant Community." *American Ethnologist* 13: 325–29.

Index

9 780791 428306